A Prologue to

ENGLISH
LITERATURE

A Prologue to
ENGLISH LITERATURE

W.W. Robson

Masson Professor of English Literature,
University of Edinburgh

B.T. Batsford Ltd, London

© W.W. Robson 1986

First published 1986

All rights reserved. No part of this publication
may be reproduced, in any form or by any means,
without permission from the Publisher

Printed in Great Britain by
Billings, Worcester

Published by B.T. Batsford Ltd
4 Fitzhardinge Street, London W1H OAH

British Library Cataloguing in Publication Data
Robson, W.W.
   A prologue to English literature.
   1. English literature—History and criticism
   I. Title
   820.9   PR83

ISBN 0-7134-1890-7
ISBN 0-7134-1891-5 Pbk

Contents

Preface

This book does not deal with the whole of literature in English, but only with that of the British Isles, and it is chiefly concerned with the literature of England.

A brief sketch of Anglo-Saxon literature is included, in the belief that it is the parent literature of English. The best defence of this view is still to be found in R.W. Chambers, *On the Continuity of English Prose from Alfred the Great to More and his School* (1932). The common notion that English arose out of the fusion of two languages, Anglo-Saxon and Norman-French, is incorrect. Anglo-Saxon is merely another name for early English, which would have developed in the same way if there had been no Norman Conquest. Norman-French is only one of the many foreign languages which have from time to time enriched the English vocabulary. For an authoritative account of the matter R.W. Burchfield's *The English Language* (1985) should be consulted.

An essay of this kind inevitably includes many personal judgments. My intention, where these are concerned, is described in the words of an expert witness in a famous criminal trial, when he was asked by counsel about some point: 'Will you swear that that is so?' He replied, 'No, I will not swear that that is so, but I will give an opinion, and I swear that this opinion shall be an honest one'.

I should like to express my gratitude to Mr A.W.R. Seward and Professor Graham Martin for their valuable help and advice.

W.W.R.

ONE

The first eight hundred years

England has been a unified state for more than a thousand years. No other great European state has so long a history. Most of its administrative geography has remained the same as it was in the tenth and eleventh centuries, even after the redrawing of county boundaries in 1974. The English have never made up their minds whether they are part of Europe or not, but it is reasonably certain that from the fourth century AD onwards Continental peoples – Angles (who gave their name to the country), Saxons, Frisians, Jutes – came to the island of Britannia and gradually wrested control from its Romano-British inhabitants.

The centuries before 1066 are known as the Anglo-Saxon period. This period saw the establishment of Christianity in England. That made little difference to entrenched moral values, but it changed the culture radically. The Anglo-Saxons introduced books and reading, and they built in stone. They were creative in government and law, art and literature. They were culturally far superior to the Normans who conquered them under Duke William. As the philosopher Wittgenstein said to M.C. O'Drury in 1940, 'William the Conqueror got himself a very good bargain'.

Much of what is known about pre-Conquest England is due to Bede (Baeda) (673–735), the greatest Anglo-Saxon historian. For 400 years no chronicler came near him for intelligence, literary style, or capacity for research. To Bede, father of English history, we owe nearly all of what is to be known about the England of the seventh century, which would otherwise be lost in the darkness that covers the fifth and sixth centuries. Bede's *Ecclesiastical History of the English Nation* – written in Latin, the international language of scholarship – is indispensable as history in both senses of the word. Similarly we see the ninth century and the Viking invasions very much as Alfred, king of Wessex, and the writers of his court would have us see them. Bede in 731 distinguished five nations in Britain: the English, the Britons, the Scots, the Picts, and the Latins. He makes it plain that the English for him were the A-stream people, favoured by God, and having a mission to establish political hegemony in the whole of the island. But this, because of inter-tribal rivalries and Danish invasions, they did not succeed in doing in the Anglo-Saxon epoch.

The last period of Anglo–Saxondom saw the unification of England, the achievement of the tenth-century kings of Wessex. It is the predominance of their dialect (West Saxon) that gave the West Country burr to the extant Anglo-Saxon texts. The English language originated in a humble dialect of Low German. In its Anglo-Saxon phase it is unintelligible to a modern English reader, as different from the present-day language as Latin is from Italian. And like Latin it was a highly inflected language. But the emptying into English, from time to time, of vast quantities of Latin and French words greatly changed its character. By the twelfth century Anglo-Saxon had turned into Middle English, the linguistic ancestor of Modern English. Still the tap-root of English is Anglo-Saxon, the language of the English people. Centuries of dominance by a French-speaking élite after 1066 could not root it out.

Anglo-Saxon England is thought to have been rich in poetry, but very little of it survives. Four manuscript books contain almost every known Anglo-Saxon poem. No poetry from pre-Christian times survives (though there may be 'fossils' of it embedded in versified maxims and in heroic poetry composed in Christian times). But Anglo-Saxon metre and poetic diction were survivals from the pagan past. Sometimes the poetry was sung to the harp by minstrels, and lowlier performers, like the Northumbrian peasant Caedmon (fl. 670). Bede says Caedmon was the first to use the traditional metre and diction for Christian religious poetry.

The survival of poetry was due to the Church: it was the result of the tenth-century monastic revival. The four manuscript collections which contain nearly the whole of Anglo-Saxon poetry were all written about 1000 AD. They are the Junius, Vercelli, Exeter and Beowulf manuscripts. The Junius manuscript consists of Biblical poems. *Genesis* shows us Satan in Hell.

Could I lift my hands and feel my strength, be free for an hour, with one winter hour, with this host, I would – but bands of iron bind me about . . . I am stripped of my kingdom . . . firmly hell's fetters are fastened upon me; the fires burn above and below.

This is taken from the part of *Genesis* known as *Genesis B* (lines 235–850), an interpolation closely translated from an Old Saxon original. The unknown poet was clearly a spiritual ancestor of Milton in *Paradise Lost*. The Vercelli manuscript includes a dramatic monologue, *The Dream of the Rood*, in which Christ's cross speaks. It is one of the treasures of early devotional poetry. The

Exeter Book poems are lyrical and elegiac. In *The Wanderer* the solitary exile dreams 'how he embraces and kisses his lord, lays his hand and head upon his knee, as he once gave pledge of loyalty in days long past. Then the friendless man awakens, sees before him the dark waves, seabirds bathing, spreading their plumes, falling sleet and snow, sifted through with hail'. *The Seafarer* is a similar figure:

. . . lonely and friendless and far from his home, in his ears no sound but the sound of the sea, the icy waves, the cry of the swan; in place of the mead-hall and the laughter of men his only song the seamew's call, the gannet's scream, the gull's shriek.

The Anglo-Saxons had many words connected with the sea. Once it was thought that that was because they were a seafaring people; but these words are chiefly poetical, not used in prose. The fact is that the nation had been a seafaring people, and had given up that life, but reminiscences of it lingered in their imagination. Down to our times, in the work of the last great English poet, John Betjeman, feelings about the sea give rise to poetry of great power. But it is associated with the past, with loss, with regret. From *Beowulf* to Betjeman, English poetry has been characteristically nostalgic, backward-looking.

Beowulf is the chief Anglo-Saxon poem. It is wholly mysterious. No one knows who wrote it, or when, or where, or why. (It is as if in a later period we had to discuss a poem not knowing whether it was composed in 1500 or in 1900.) *Beowulf* is a narrative poem of 3183 lines, transmitted in a manuscript written between the tenth and the twelfth centuries, but much older. To some (and emphatically not to others) it is the symbol of the antiquity and continuity of English poetry. But it is a challenge to cultural nationalism. It never mentions people who are known to have lived in Britain. All its allusions are Continental or Scandinavian. Did it come from the Baltic shore, brought to England by invading Northmen? Or was England the place of composition, and was the Yorkshire coast the real scene of the story? No one knows.

It is generally agreed that the genre of *Beowulf* is that of ancient epic poetry, belonging to the Germanic culture (as described by Tacitus in *Germania*). It is far and away the oldest known poem of 'Germania'. Perhaps it was fashioned from old lays. The raw material may have been heathen; the sentiment and reflections are Christian. (But the Biblical allusions are only to the Old Testament.) *Beowulf* opens with a memory of the pagan past, the ship burial of Scyld.

They . . . let the sea bear him, gave him to the ocean. Their soul was sad, their spirit sorrowful. Counsellors in hall, mighty men beneath the heavens, cannot say truly who received that cargo.

The modern discovery of the treasures of Sutton Hoo has brought this part of the poem suddenly into the light of real history. Other unforgettable moments include the song of the fight at Finnsburh (which appears in another fragment of heroic narrative poetry outside *Beowulf*), Beowulf's death and burial, the monster-haunted mere.

They dwell in a land unknown, wolf-haunted slopes, wind-swept headlands, perilous marsh-paths . . . Not far hence the lake stands over which hang groves covered with frost . . . There may be seen each night a fearful wonder – fire on the flood! Though pressed by hounds the ranger of the heath, the hart strong in its horns, may seek the forest, chased from far, he will give up his life, his being, on the brink, sooner than plunge in it to save his head. That is no pleasant spot!

The poet Hopkins might have found in *Beowulf* the background of 'distance and darkness and doom' which he could not find in the *Iliad*. The monsters are enemies of God. 'Then came Grendel, advancing from the moor under the misty slopes; God's anger rested on him'. Grendel hates feasts, lights, laughter, the communal life in the lord's hall. He comes to threaten it out of the dim impalpable unknown, the long nights of the northern winter. Yet to modern taste Grendel (and his mother) sustain some emotional regard. They anticipate a long line of sympathetic monsters – Caliban, Frankenstein's creation, the Hunchback of Notre Dame, King Kong.

What the poem meant to the poet himself is problematic. Its most influential critic, J.R.R. Tolkien, author of *The Lord of the Rings*, has defended its curious and much criticized structure ('two moments in a great life'.) The influence of *Beowulf* is clear in *The Lord of the Rings*, and in some of W.H. Auden's poems, but not elsewhere in English literature. There is nothing to help us find what the author meant. Indeed to speak of 'the author' seems strange, so impossible is it to imagine him (or her). What Roland Barthes calls 'the death of the author' is here total.

Something of the spirit of *Beowulf* is found in other Anglo-Saxon poems, the fatalism of *Deor* with its refrain 'That evil ended; so may this'; the fighting ethos of 'the Battle of Brunanburh'; the fragmentary *Battle of Maldon*, written soon after 991, and so one of the latest Anglo-Saxon poems. *Maldon* exalts loyalty and courage. 'Heart must be braver, courage the bolder, mood the stouter, as our strength grows less'. This strikes a chord in the national temperament from time to time. It can be paralleled in Malory's *Le Morte D'Arthur*, in Hemingway's story 'The Undefeated', in Douglas Haig's order of the day of 11 April 1918. 'There is no other course open to us but to fight it out. Every post must be held to the last man. There must be no retirement. With our backs to the wall, and believing in the justice of our cause, each one of us must fight to the end'.

Anglo-Saxon poetry has been attractive to later English poets, such as Auden, because it seems both familiar and alien. The best translation of a complete poem is Tennyson's 'Battle of Brunanburh'. The most influential is Ezra Pound's version of *The Seafarer*, the objection to which is not its omissions and inaccuracies but its occasional substitution of nonsense for sense. The Anglo-Saxon effect is hard to reproduce in modern verse. The poetry was not syllabic and did not use rhyme. Its basic elements are stress and alliteration. The classic line, as in *Beowulf*, consists of two half lines, each containing two stresses, bound together by alliteration. (In later poetry, like *The Dream of the Rood*, the lines can be expanded.) Auden in his *Age of Anxiety* gives a modern equivalent.

> And country curates in cold bedrooms
> Dreamed of deaneries till at daybreak
> The rector's rooks with relish described
> Their stinted station.

Eliot in *Murder in the Cathedral* and *Four Quartets* now and then uses a similar verse form. In these lines from 'The Dry Salvages' the subject could have been Anglo-Saxon poetry itself:

> And the ragged rock in the restless waters,
> Waves wash over it, fogs conceal it;
> On a halcyon day it is merely a monument,
> In navigable weather it is always a seamark
> To lay a course by; but in the sombre season
> Or the sudden fury, is what it always was.

Anglo-Saxon verse belongs solely to the history of poetry. The Anglo-Saxons preferred the nameless and timeless kind of poetry, free from personal associations. For intellectual history we have to turn to the central tradition of Anglo-Saxondom, the tradition of Bede, Aldhelm and Alcuin, and to the vernacular prose of Alfred, Aelfric and Wulfstan. The first great book in English prose is *The Anglo-Saxon Chronicle*, inspired (though not written) by King Alfred (849–901). It is a composite piece of work, with various revised versions. The original nucleus belongs to Winchester, capital of the West Saxon kingdom. The Alfredian version comes down to 892 only. This is the first continuous history of a Western nation in its own language. The account of the years 893–7, of the struggles with the Danes in southern England, provides moments of gripping historical narrative. Later, the time of Ethelred the Unready (979–1016) has a very modern feeling about it. ('Unready' = redeless, i.e. not knowing what to do.) Canute (king of England 1016–35) and other famous figures are presented unromantically: the *Chronicle* is quite free from effusion. Now and then the language of Anglo-Saxon poetry makes a pleasant appearance, when the sea is 'the gannet's bath'. Bits of verse here and there offer relief from the *Chronicle's* bald statements.

Asser's life of Alfred (in Latin) is the first extant biography of an English king. Asser (d. 909), a Welsh monk in the king's service who became a bishop, gives us the image of Alfred as the mighty warrior, the prudent statesman, the industrious jurist, the protector of the poor; the cosmopolitan, making journeys to Rome, corresponding with the courts of Europe; the man of letters behind the stockade at Athelney, writing prefaces, translating, while the rush-lights on his camp table flickered in their ox-horn shades. Even the sceptical twentieth century has found it hard to debunk Alfred the Great. 'While historical tradition has a way of distorting truth', say the sternly critical scholars S. Keynes and M. Lapidge, 'in this case there can be no doubt that justice was done'. (*Alfred the Great*, Penguin Classics, 1983).

The Anglo-Saxon Chronicle continued till 1154. The Norman Conquest had little effect on English writing. Changes in it came gradually, through influences from the culture of the Continent. Latin came to be used for all works other than entertainments, not because of the Conquest, but because of the twelfth-century revival of learning in the West. Latin was used for lives of saints; and it was used for one of the most influential European books, Geoffrey of Monmouth's *History of the Kings of Britain* (completed about 1139). Geoffrey (1100–54) was Bishop of St Asaph. His book describes the kings who lived in Britain before the Christian era. His *History* is allegedly derived from a 'most ancient book in the British tongue'. Modern historians have found it difficult to discover Geoffrey's sources (if any), but he established once and for all the traditions of the Celtic West: Brutus the Trojan, first king of Britain; Lear; Cymbeline; King Lud; Merlin; and Arthur. He was the real father of the Arthurian legend, which soon conquered literary Europe. Arthur is Geoffrey's hero. When Merlin appears, at the close of the sixth book, we are in the world of romance. Geoffrey knows nothing of Tristram or Lancelot or the Holy Grail, but in the Mordred and Guenevere episodes he first suggested the love-tragedy that became the imperishable possession of European romanticism. He also introduced the Celtic wonderland, the fables of the 'little people', linked by Chaucer in his 'Wife of Bath's Tale' with the Arthurian world. The *History* was a great bestseller. Even before Geoffrey's death Wace had begun to translate it into French. It was praised by Chaucer and Spenser and Wordsworth; it gave stories to Shakespeare. Hugh A. MacDougall in his *Racial Myth in English History* (Montreal 1982) has shown how this enduring romance of Celtic Britain served multiple political purposes, until the Renaissance and the Reformation brought its credibility and ideological usefulness under attack. Teutonism, or Anglo-Saxonism, supplanted it in the sixteenth century, strengthened in successive centuries by England's rise to national and imperial greatness. But for the medievals it was the British Myth that reigned supreme.

From the eleventh century to the fourteenth it is difficult to extricate a distinct 'English literature' to write a history of. Latin prose and French verse predominate. But it is impossible to believe in the once traditional account of English in these centuries as a despised dialect, relegated to the lower orders. No one could believe this who had read the *Ancren Riwle* (or *Ancrene Wisse*), which dates from about 1200. Its English style unmistakably comes from a world of ladies and gentlemen. But it is not a novel of manners, but a book of guidance to three anchoresses. Original, charming, humorous, it is one of the great quiet books that crop up now and then in literature. In poetry France still led Europe; but English prosody was being transformed. Layamon (fl. 1200), in his *Brut*, developed an interesting compromise between the Anglo-Saxon alliterative line and the Old French octosyllabic couplet, producing an irregular metre of which the resources could still be explored by poets. The *Ormulum* (from the first half of the thirteenth century), though very boring, at least shows a praiseworthy concern for establishing a regular metre. The much more interesting *Owl and the Nightingale* (late twelfth century) introduces the octosyllabic couplet, then the standard metre of French poetry, and soon to be the standard English metre for narrative and discursive verse. The *Brut* begins with Brutus, eponymous founder of Britain, leaving Troy, and ends with Cadwallader, the last British king with any real claim to dominion in England. Layamon's history comes from Geoffrey of Monmouth, through Wace's translation in French verse. He has a sense of the heroic, often traced back to Anglo-Saxon tradition. But Professor Derek Pearsall finds that his sources and models were available in Anglo-Norman and French. Whatever his debt to Anglo-Saxon verse, he is entirely pro-British. Layamon can be read with pleasure for his intrinsic merits as a writer. One sample is his description of dead knights in the river Avon. 'Steel fishes lie in the stream . . . their scales float like gold-painted shields, their fins float as if they were spears.' *The Owl and the Nightingale* has been dated by scholars, from internal evidence, between 1189–1216. The English is probably English of Dorset. This is the first English debate poem. It is a beast story. Forerunners of this genre are the Bestiaries, so popular in the Middle Ages, and, earlier, the fables of Aesop. The genre gained in impetus from the general vogue of allegory. Chaucer's *Parliament of Birds* and Clanvowe's *The Cuckoo and the Nightingale* are later examples, and in more modern times Dryden's *The Hind and the Panther*, Anatole France's *L'Île des Pingouins*, and Orwell's *Animal Farm*. What underlies beast-fables is the belief that an idea becomes more profound, and more likely to seize attention, if it is expressed in a roundabout manner. It is not known what the Owl and the Nightingale 'stand for'. Professor E.G. Stanley has suggested that they stand for 'the solemn and joyous ways of life'. The debate is not resolved; the contestants go off to ask 'Master Nicholas of Guildford' to arbitrate, but we are not told what his decision was. Was 'Nicholas' the poet, or an admirer complimenting him? This, too, is not known.

A new genre of those centuries was lyric. Anglo-Saxon had no lyric metres, no poetry of love and springtime. The verse lyric of Western Europe began about 1100, with the Provençal troubadours. To most readers (except Ezra Pound) they are boring, but they stimulated some good poetry in English, including some of Pound's own. Echoes of them had appeared in English by the early thirteenth century. The earliest extant English secular lyric belongs to about 1200. To this time also belongs 'Sumer is icumen in'. From the middle thirteenth century come the lyric anthologies, the most famous of which is the Harleian Miscellany, compiled about 1330.

Verse-romances in English were widely cultivated by the mid-thirteenth century, for example *King Horn* (?1225) and *Havelok the Dane*. These seem intended for a popular rather than an aristocratic audience. The hero of *Havelok* has decidedly 'working class' virtues. There is also evidence of the popularity of the Breton lay, a tale of love and marriage, often with a Celtic setting. The great French name here is Marie de France, so called because she lived in England in the twelfth century. Something of her quality can be seen in the English romance of *Sir Orfeo*, which retells the Orpheus legend in Celtic terms. The scribe of one manuscript sets the scene in 'Winchester', an absurd, yet charming, touch.

The English language was alive, and being put to literary use, in those centuries, but the linguistic situation was such that a national literature did not yet exist. Most educated people in England were bilingual, some trilingual (in English, French and Insular Latin). The situation is described by Robert of Gloucester, about 1300.

People of rank in this country who came of their [i.e. the Normans'] blood all stick to the same language. If a man knows no French people will think little of him. But the lower classes stick to English and their own language. It is well known that it is the best thing to know both languages, for the more a man knows the more he is worth.

The fourteenth century in Europe was the age of the great romances. These are anonymous, like medieval cathedrals. They show no consciousness of patriotism or nationalism; they are tales of universal Christendom at war with the powers of darkness. They reveal a passion for beauty and ceremony, colour and pageantry, marvels and magic and unexplained mystery. The world of the romances is a world of abstractions in which there seem to be no definite places, or times, or politics, or problems of existence. There is a complete detachment from ordinary life. The world of Romance is the opposite of the world of the Novel, and some modern critics dismiss it out of hand as escapism. But it had a longer run than the Novel has yet had, and it may be that one day it will been enjoyed again. At any rate, people other than scholars and students are at least aware of one English romance, usually called *Sir Gawain and the Green Knight*.

A small volume, known to scholars as MS. Cott. Nero A x., contains this poem and three others, generally known as *Pearl*, *Patience* and *Purity* (or *Cleanness*). Not a line of any of these poems is found in any other manuscript. They are all in the same dialect (most likely that of fourteenth-century Cheshire), and may be by the same author. *Pearl*, a poem of 1212 lines, is quite unique in English. The poet employs an extraordinarily complex technique, using both rhyme and alliteration, and a 'catch-word' system that

makes the first line of each twelve-lined stanza repeat a word in the last line of
the stanza before. To a great scholar of our early literature, H.M. Chadwick,
Pearl was 'bloody nonsense', and it is easy to understand how distasteful the art
of *Pearl* might be to someone of classical training like Chadwick. But to some
other students it is the most beautiful poem in Middle English. *Patience* is a
versified account of the Jonah story: Jonah goes into the great fish's mouth
'like a mote in a minster door'. *Purity* draws on Scriptural stories that
illustrate 'uncleanness'. (An interesting modern treatment of the subject is
Mary Douglas's *Purity and Danger*). The Anglo-Saxon flavour is strong in
both *Patience* and *Purity*, the treatment of the sea and the storm in *Patience*,
and in both poems the Anglo-Saxon tradition of Biblical paraphrase. As for
Sir Gawain, the reader of *Beowulf* will constantly see obvious similarities
between their landscapes, their adventures, and the virtues they celebrate.

The formal perfection of *Sir Gawain* ranks it with other English
masterpieces like Chaucer's 'Nun's Priest's Tale', Pope's *The Rape of the Lock*,
and Coleridge's *Ancient Mariner*. Written in a dialect of the north-west
Midlands, it is too full of strange words ever to be current again. But much of
its excellence comes through in translation. The Green Man of ancient
folkrites has been seen in the weird 'Green Knight' of the poem; see *The Green
Man*, by Katherine Basford (1978), and *The Jack in the Green*, by Roy Judge
(1979). There are two motifs in the story, the testing of Gawain's courage
through the Beheading Game, and of his courtesy and chastity by the Lady of
the Castle. Gawain searches through the wilderness to find the Green Knight,
so that he may offer himself to be beheaded rather than break his word. The
subplot in the forest castle turns on the loyalty due from guest to host. The
perennial power of the poem derives from its focus upon Gawain, a brave man
facing (apparently) certain death. The poem combines the grotesque and
savage with the ceremonious and courtly. Its terse alliterative phrases and its
stress-based metre distinguish it decisively from the French romances.
Because of its dialect it was out of the main current of English poetry, and has
survived by chance. It was forgotten for many centuries. But it has been much
read by poets in the twentieth century. On the verse of Ted Hughes it seems to
have had an almost obsessive effect. Here is the passage (Gawain's journey
through the Wirral) from which Hughes took the title of one of his poems,
and of a book of poems, *Wodwo*. Even the (unfortunately necessary) bracketed
glosses may not spoil it utterly.

Mony cliff he overclambe [scaled] in contrayes strange,
Fer floten [riding) from his frendes fremedly [forsaken] he rides.
At eache warthe other water [ford or stream] the wighe [man] passed
He fonde a foo [foe] him before, but ferly it were [save by some strange chance].
And that so foule and so felle [strange] that foght him behode [he had to fight them].
So mony mervayl bi mount [in the mountains] ther the mon findes,
It were to tore [tedious] for to telle of the tenth dole [part].

Sumwhile with wormes [serpents] he werres, and with wolves als [also],
Sumwhile with wodwos [satyrs] that woned [dwelt] in the knarres [rocks],
Bothe bulles and bears and bores otherwhile [on other occasions],
And etaines [giants] that him amelede [attacked] of the heghe felles [moors];
Hade he [had he not] been dughty and drighe [brave], and Drighten [the Lord] had
      served,
Douteless he hade been ded and dreped [defeated] full ofte.
For werre wrathed [wars troubled] him not so much, that winter [wintry weather]
      was wors,
When the colde cler water fro the cloudes shadde [fell],
And fres [froze] er it falle might [could fall] to the fale [pale] earth:
Ner [almost] slain with the slete [sleet] he sleped in his yrnes [armour],
Mo nightes than innoghe in naked rokkes,
Ther as [where] clatrende fro the crest the colde borne [stream] renne,
And henged heghe over his hede in iise-ikkles,
Thus in peril and paine and plites [woes] full harde
Bi contray [through the country] cayres [travels] this knight, till Cristmasse even.

Sir Gawain was perhaps written by a knight or squire in a great house, a
master of courtly manners and the skills of hunting. *Pearl* suggests a learned
clerk or trained rhetorician. The poet may have been moved to write it by the
death of a little daughter, the lost pearl of the poem. But the Pearl may be an
emblem and the child a personified quality. We are reminded of scholars'
arguments about Dante's Beatrice. Perhaps Margaret was the poet's own
daughter and the sorrow was real. He looked for consolation, as Milton or
Tennyson might, in a poem. But he recollected other symbolic poetry, Dante,
and the *Roman de la Rose*, and the Apocalypse of John. Perhaps he was not a
'symbolic poet', but a personal poet in an age of symbolism? No one knows.

With these poems the Middle English phase of English literature comes to
maturity. Too much has been lost for a coherent account of it to be given, but
Gawain is usually aligned by scholars with other long poems in alliterative
metre belonging to the mid-fourteenth century, some love romances, some
'histories', some political satires, some religious legends. These works used to
be described as 'the Alliterative Revival', but this presupposes that the
alliterative style had ever died. It seems plausible to conjecture that the
Anglo-Saxon kind of verse had continued unbroken in the west and north of
England, the difference from Anglo-Saxon being merely due to changes in the
language. This kind of verse went on in Scotland till early in the sixteenth
century. On the other hand, London and the east preferred syllabic verse and
rhyme. Chaucer's Parson says he is a southern man and cannot do the
alliterative style, 'run ran ruf by lettre'. The future of English verse, till about
1920, lay with Chaucer.

Notable among the poems of the 'Alliterative Revival' is *Le Morte
D'Arthur*, used by Malory. The greatest of them is *Piers Plowman*. This poem
was very popular. Sixty or so manuscripts are extant (though, strangely, it was

not printed till 1550). The author, Willian Langland, or Langley, was born in 1331 or 1332 somewhere near the Malvern Hills in Shropshire, and was educated in the school of the Benedictine monastery at Malvern. He probably took minor orders. By 1362 he was in London, poor, and writing his poem. His first version was the A-text (2567 lines). The poem's major editor, W.W. Skeat, distinguished two other principal versions or texts, the B-text (7242 lines) and the C-text (7357 lines). Modern scholars have added further refinements, but the general picture is the same: periodic enlargements and reconsiderations of the poem by the author during his life. The facts about Langland are almost entirely derived from his poem, and scholars have warned us of 'the autobiographical fallacy' here (as with Chaucer). It might all be fiction. Earlier in ths century J.M. Manly elaborated a theory that there was no 'Langland' but five separate authors, working in succession.

Today it is widely considered that there is only one author and he is the 'Long Will' of the poem. Possibly Langland was a very short man, or dwarf, cf. Robin Hood's 'Little John', or Sapper's 'Tiny Carteret', both huge. However that may be, he had visions, which he expressed through literary conventions, compared by scholars to the tradition of the *Roman de la Rose* and other allegorical poetry. The Dreamer falls asleep on Malvern Hills and sees a picture of the world as 'a fair field full of folk' placed between Heaven and Hell. It is like the 'General Prologue' of Chaucer, a survey of the estates of the realm. It is also a company of sinners, brought to penitence and led on a pilgrimage to Saint Truth by Piers (Peter) Plowman. The poem exists to exalt Christian charity and the way of life of Jesus Christ. The pilgrimage takes place in the mind of the Dreamer. The B and C texts fall into four great divisions, the Vision of Piers Plowman, and the lives of Do-well, Do-bet, and Do-best, which show man's effort to answer the command 'Be ye perfect'. The Dreamer finally witnesses the crucifixion of Jesus, the building of Holy Church, and the assault of Antichrist. Meanwhile we are given glimpses from time to time of the aging Dreamer's life on earth.

Langland's verse is concise, colloquial, dramatic. It is capable of rhetorical splendour. His alliterative line is not as inferior to Chaucer's metre as it was once said to be. We soon capture the music of his verse, as in the beautiful opening of the poem.

> In a somer seson. when soft was the sonne,
> I shope [clad] me in shroudes. as I a shepe [sheep? or shepherd?] were,
> In habite as an hermite, unholy of werkes,
> Went wyde in this world, wondres to here.
> Ac [but] on a May morninge. on Malvern hulles
> Me byfel a ferly [marvel]. of fairy me thoughte;
> I was wery forwandred. and went me to rest
> Under a brode banke. by a birnes [brook's] side,
> And as I lay and lened. and loked in the wateres,
> I slombered in a slepyng. it sweyned [flowed] so merye.

Piers Plowman combines several literary kinds of the time – the vision, the debate, the encyclopaedic satire and, above all, the sermon. It has been called the quintessence of medieval preaching. It is also a great document of social oppression. But its religious doctrine is old-fashioned and orthodox. Langland (like Shakespeare?) emphatically supports the maintenance of social order, if necessary by force. In the later versions of the poem his hostility to communism has increased. His poem is too scholastic for a popular audience. He uses the technical language of the universities; he has read in the Christian Fathers, and in philosophers like William of Occam. He is a clerk, writing for clerks and cultivated readers.

Yet mingling with his great allegoric figures we find the Shoemaker, the Gamekeeper ('and his wife, drunk'), the Ratcatcher, the Hackneyman, the Tinker, the Rebab (fiddle) Player, the Watchmaker, the Cheapside Scavenger, the Tyburn Hangman. This is the England of the Black Death and the Peasants' Revolt, people like Daw the Ditcher and Rose of the Small Shop, the nun who 'had a child in cherry time', the tears of Hawkin, the ordinary man, with his stained coat. We cannot miss Langland's sense of the injustice done to the poor. He prays to Christ for them.

> Pore peple, thiise prisoneres, lorde, in the put [pit] of myschief,
> Comforte tho creatures. that moche care soffren
> Thorw death, thorw drouth. all her [their] dayes here.
> Wo in wynter tymes. for wanting of clothes,
> And in some tyme selde [seldom] soupen to the fulle;
> Comfort this careful, Cryst, in the ryche [kingdom],
> For how thou comfortest all creatures, clerkes bereth witnesse.

Law is a mockery unless it is the expression of justice. In the England of Richard II ('the kitten', as Langland calls him) justice is constantly violated. There is a force in man that impels him to steal his due from others. It is covetousness, the desire for reward ('meed') that is undeserved, contrary to that right reason which is fundamentally part of the nature of created things.

Yet how *can* man be just? This question dominates the whole poem. The Pardon that Saint Truth gave Piers Plowman cannot save men. Piers tears it up (we think of Luther). Without God's mercy it is useless, indeed it is a condemnation, for the just man falls seven times a day. Only one power can keep justice among men. In the vision of the Harrowing of Hell Lucifer himself is blinded by its light. It is the light of Charity. The terrible scenes of Langland's London are its negation. Piers, painted with blood, comes with his cross before the common people, 'like in all limbs to our Lord Jesus'. Whether Love will triumph is a question the poem leaves open. Against the lust for Meed, which leads to injustice, oppression, chaos, is set the aspiration of Love, fair shares and unity in the Common Barn of the People of God. By the end of the poem Piers has vanished, and in the last lines we leave Conscience vowing to travel through the wide world to look for him. It is natural to ask who or what Piers is, but no simple answer can be given to this question. Piers is a 'constitutive symbol': his significance is slowly unfolded in the course of the poem. He is the Plowman, who becomes Peter (i.e. the Church) and finally Christ and King. The poem lacks a climax. Langland, most unvisual of visionaries, does not bring before us the promised scene in which Christ is to joust in 'Piers's armour' (human nature). He describes Christ's Crucifixion straightforwardly, in the manner of a Miracle play. But whatever its structural defects, *Piers Plowman* is one of the major long poems in English, surpassed by none in its sublime indignation and passionate charity.

Geoffrey Chaucer (?1340–1400) never mentions Langland, though he could have seen Langland's poem, and the Ploughman of his 'General Prologue' is perhaps Piers Plowman, a mystical figure. He seems much nearer to us, more accessible, than Langland, but this may be an an illusion: the difficulties of *Piers Plowman* are obvious, on the surface; the difficulties of Chaucer may lie deeper. Chaucer is best read in his own English. Despite scholarly demurs, a more or less modern pronunciation (making due allowanace for the sounding of final -e) does not greatly denature his verse. Of course Chaucer can yield much in modernized versions. Dryden, Wordsworth and Nevill Coghill all tried their hands. But (although Dryden and Wordsworth were poets) they lost Chaucer's quality.

Though so apparently accessible now, Chaucer was in many ways a typical medieval poet. He was a translator, editor and compiler. He was a master of 'rhetoric', which in the Middle Ages included all modes of literary expression: 'figures of speech', allegory, digressions, illustrations, and rules for presenting material in a clear, comprehensive and interestingly varied way. (Langland would have benefitted from this kind of training). In the record of his life Chaucer appears as a courtier, diplomat and public servant in three reigns (Edward III, Richard II and Henry IV). As a young man he served as a soldier and was taken prisoner in France. On one occasion a lady with the attractive name of Cecily Chaumpaigne accused him of *raptus* – the meaning of the word is uncertain. Twice in the performance of his duties he was assaulted and robbed. He sometimes lost his post, or was in trouble for debt. Chaucer's social position is impossible to express in Victorian or modern terms. His work was that of a *douanier*, or customs inspector, yet his wife was a lady-in-waiting whose sister was a mistress and later the third wife of John of Gaunt, uncle of Richard II, and he himself as a young man had been a page at the court of Prince Lionel. His friends included French poets (Eustache Deschamps) and English (John Gower). From his writings we know that he was an astronomer and mathematician, well versed in medicine and the other sciences of his time. He read fluently in French, Italian and Latin.

We do not know any of the inner facts of Chaucer's life, but this is true of all the great English poets until Milton. He portrays himself in his poems as shy and timorous, a lover of solitude, kneeling in adoration of daisies. There are hints of unhappiness in love. In some of the poems he depicts himself as bookish, but in *The Canterbury Tales*, when Our Host of the Tabard asks him for a tale, he says he only knows one ('Sir Thopas'). The relation between this *persona* and the historical Chaucer is totally obscure. We do not know whether the 'Chaucer' of the poems is a humorous exaggeration of traits that his friends would have recognized in the man they knew, or whether the joke is that the real Geoffrey Chaucer was notoriously unlike that. So in one sense it can truly be said that we know nothing of Chaucer; but in another sense we know a great deal. There is a recurring tone in his poetry that is absolutely individual and unmistakable:

A marchand whylom dwelt at Saint-Denys,
That ryche was, for which men held him wys [wise].

An early admirer called Chaucer the English Dante. Like Dante, Chaucer raised the prestige of the language he wrote in. He seems to have decided from the first to write in English, whereas his friend Gower wrote his major works in French and Latin and did not attempt an English poem (the *Confessio Amantis*) till the late 1380s.

Chaucer introduced the fashions of Western European poetry into English. He was the heir to allegory and vision poetry, Dante's *Divine Comedy*, and the *Roman de la Rose*. Several of Chaucer's poems show the influence of these dream-poems, such as his *Book of the Duchess*, *House of Fame*, *Parliament of Birds* and *Legend of Good Women*. All are charming, in spite of the phosphorescent nimbus of scholarship which now surrounds them. They contain much humour. In the *House of Fame*, for example, an eagle carries the poet through the heavens. The eagle turns out to be a forerunner of Arthur Eddington or Fred Hoyle, proud of his ability to explain physics to the plain man.

The older literary historians divided Chaucer's work into a French, an Italian, and an English period, but it seems simpler to distinguish between a younger and an older Chaucer, though it must be remembered that the chronology of many of his works is uncertain. The turning point may have been his prose version of Boethius's *Consolation of Philosophy* (early sixth century AD), one of the most widely studied books of the Middle Ages. (Skeat believes that Chaucer's version was made between 1377 and 1381). Today many readers think of Chaucer as primarily a comic writer, but his contemporaries saw him as a philosopher; and at times he is a tragic poet, aware of the dark side of life. It is true that he has little to say of the great calamities of his century, the Black Death and the Hundred Years' War and the 'cherles rebelling' (as he calles the Peasants' Revolt). But he did take note of the disasters of contemporary individuals, Bernabò Visconti, Pierre de Lusignan, Pedro of Castile. And he was to live to see the downfall of his own king, Richard II, in 1399. Still, there is no evidence that the themes of his poetry were influenced, much less determined, by the politics of the time.

In his translation of Boethius, Chaucer had explored the problems of human freedom and divine foreknowledge, of Fate and Fortune. In *Troilus and Criseyde* he brought these concerns into a poem which joyfully celebrates a lighter theme, the code of practice of romantic love. This theme was dear to the audience to which an illuminated manuscript shows Chaucer reading, the 'yonge fresshe folk' of Richard II's court, and his poem seems designed to teach court manners and the *ars amandi*. Modern readers often assume that Pandarus, the go-between of the story, is a comic character, and there are comic touches in the scenes in which he appears; but it is a mistake to suppose that Pandarus is meant to play a part like that of the vulgar birds in the *Parliament*, who scoff at *fin amour* (or 'courtly love', as modern scholars call it). Pandarus would probably have been seen by Chaucer's readers as a fine gentleman and courtier. If he is long-winded and leisurely in his recital of 'olde ensaumples', so was Chaucer himself. (*Troilus* is much longer than its source, Boccaccio's *Filostrato*, which supplied only one-third of Chaucer's poem). Pandarus may joke at the lovers' expense, but he sings the praises of courtly love. What Pandarus preaches, Troilus practises. Love gives him a new beauty of character, makes him a knight second only to Hector, compassionate in distress, sparing the 'smale bestes' in his hunting. Book III brings the consummation of Troilus's love. But in Book IV Fortune turns her wheel. Criseyde is sent to join her father in the Greek camp, and, parted from Troilus, betrays him with Diomede. There are extenuating circumstances: she is 'with women fewe among the Greekes stronge'. Chaucer altered the character of Criseyde. Unlike Boccaccio's heroine she is not fickle but fearful. Weakness, not wickedness, turned her to Diomede in search of the protection Troilus had given her in Troy. Most of the last Book is devoted to the grief of Troilus. It is a sustained lament, and the poem closes with an appeal to the young to renounce earthly love – a conclusion found problematic by some modern readers.

Chaucer's masterpiece is *The Canterbury Tales*, one of the greatest English books. It belongs, or ought to belong, to the literature of everyone. Its framework, as everyone knows, is a pilgrimage to the shrine of Thomas Becket at Canterbury, and the structural device is a story-telling contest. The plan of collecting tales and uniting them by a central idea was not new. Long ago the (Moslem) Middle Ages had seen *The Thousand and One Nights*, and in Chaucer's time there was Boccaccio's *Decameron* (which he seems not to have known). The beginning and the end of Chaucer's great work are clearly marked by the 'General Prologue' and the 'Parson's Tale'. But Chaucer wrote less than half the number of the tales promised in the Prologue. Only 24 survive, three of them interrupted by other pilgrims, and one (the Cook's) unfinished. It is not clear that Chaucer ever settled down to a final ordering of the tales. There are signs that he considered different plans. Chaucer was an excellent narrative poet. The *Tales* shows an extensive range of the forms of story-telling known in his day. Some of the tales may have been written before the general framework was devised, but most of them seem to be mature work. The only clear string of connection from first to last is the Host, soliciting or censuring tales, praising or abusing. The most remarkable and original feature of the *Tales* is not the tales themselves, good as many of them are, but the 'head-links', the by-play between the pilgrims. Chaucer would have had little to learn from the drama or the novel. To ask which is the best tale is a pleasant but unanswerable question. We do not know to whom the Host awarded the promised prize (a supper). 'The Knight's Tale' is the most ambitious, an attempt to fuse epic and romance. 'The Nun's Priest's Tale' is the most perfect in artistry. 'The Miller's Tale' is the funniest, a demonstration that beauty is compatible with gross and naive farce. 'The Pardoner's Tale' is a small masterpiece of narration, casting a surprising light on its grotesque narrator.

Chaucer is above all a creator of characters. 'Chaucer's characters', said the poet William Blake, 'live age after age. Every age is a Canterbury pilgrimage; we all pass on, each sustaining one of these characters; nor can a child be born who is not one of these characters of Chaucer'. Blake had in mind the characters in the 'General Prologue'. As a creator of character, Chaucer passes the supreme test: he can make nice, good people interesting. Troilus, Criseyde, Pandarus, 'Chaucer' himself are just as interesting as the oddities and scoundrels of whom he shows us many. His charity is impartial.

> He was, an I shall yeven him his laude [give him his due],
> A theef, and eke a somnour, and a bawde.

As a poet Chaucer can strike with all his force in a single line:

> Hyd, Absolon, thy gilte tresses clere.

or

> The smiler with the knyf under the cloke.

One of his chief gifts as a poet is his power to capture the inwardness of physical sensation, not only in itself, but in the individual's attitude to it, as when we are told of the Friar:

> Somewhat he lipsed for his wantownesse,
> To make his English swete upon his tonge.

He can show a thought taking shape in the mind, as when the young monk in 'The Shipman's Tale' is embarrassed by the lustful thought that comes into his head as he jokes with his friend's wife.

> I trow, certes, that oure goode man
> Hath yow laboured sith the night began,

That yow were nede to resten hastily.
And with that word he lough ful murily,
And of his owene thought he waxe al reed.

By a simple observation the poet brings home to us Griselda's love for her child:

And in hire swough [swoon] so sadly [firmly] holdeth she
Hir children two, when she gan hem t'embrace,
That with great sleighte [skill] and great difficultee
The children from hire arm they ganne arace [tear away].

Chaucer belongs among the great observers of mankind, from the Knight to the Ploughman. He presents the human scene on a large scale, and dispassionately, but with humour. He was not a crusader like Langland, he was an entertainer, but he taught while he entertained, as in our time the scholarship of D.W. Robertson has proved. Only two things deter Chaucer's recognition as the greatest English poet: his dialect is obsolete, and he is fundamentally unromantic. But in its broad amenity his work has no superior in English literature.

John Gower (1325–1408) was once famous for three books: *Speculum Meditantis* (written in French), *Vox Clamantis* (in Latin), and *Confessio Amantis* (in English). The first two show what an impressive man he was, but he is remembered not for those works, in which he tried to set the world to rights, but for the *Confessio Amantis*, in which he tells stories about love. Like *The Canterbury Tales* it is a collection. The connecting idea is an ingenious one: the lover makes his confession to a priest of Venus, who asks him about his possible sins against love; the tales illustrate these. If Gower's trilingual writings show the uncertainty of the linguistic situation for writers at that time, his language in the *Confessio*, like Chaucer's, shows the development of an assured and cultured English, replacing French as the medium of polite literature. Gower's verse is very regular, but he combines the accentual and syllabic in a thoroughly English way. Gower's literary personality is elusive: C.S. Lewis in *The Allegory of Love* (1936) and Christopher Ricks in *The Force of Poetry* (1984) have both written well about it. Gower is very like the late Victorian poet William Morris in many ways. They are both quiet poets and storytellers, and both are undervalued to-day for similar reasons.

For convenience the successors of Chaucer in the fifteenth and sixteenth centuries may be dealt with here. First, Chaucer's personal disciples. Thomas Usk (d. 1388) wrote a curious rhythmical prose in his *Testament of Love*, anticipating the Euphuism of the sixteenth century. Thomas Hoccleve (*c*.1368–*c*.1450) was once known as the first autobiographical poet in English. This claim has been challenged on the ground that the profession of autobiography is merely a conventional trope in medieval poetry, but Professor John Burrow has recently come to the defence of the traditional view. (A critical doctrine which insists that a medieval poet could not be autobiographical, even if he wanted to, is surely suspect.) John Lydgate (c. 1370–1450) is known as 'the Monk of Bury'. He was in fact a court poet to the Lancastrian dynasty, who had many noble patrons, and spent most of his life in London. He followed in Chaucer's footsteps, by adding many new words, taken from French and Latin, to the language, and coined the word 'aureate' for the resulting enrichment of style. He saw himself as consolidating Chaucer's achievement in establishing a high style for English poetry. There is controversy about whether he understood Chaucer's metre; his own verse appears to stumble frequently. Lydgate's output was enormous. Few besides his eighteenth-century editor Joseph Ritson can have read it all, and Ritson called Lydgate 'a voluminous, prosaic, and drivelling monk'. This is too harsh. The personal notes that come through in (e.g.) *The Temple of Glass* suggest someone much more sympathetic. Still, nothing can make Lydgate a great poet. He was mainly a compiler and translator.

The great successors of Chaucer were the Scottish poets. Scottish writers are equally annoyed at being included in, or excluded from, English literature, but there is no need to enter that quarrel here. At that time Scottish literature was simply the northern branch of English. Its difference from the literature of the south originated in the English government's policy in the 1290s, when the machinations of Edward I unintentionally brought into being the first (and still perhaps the most) self-conscious nation of Europe. John Barbour's *Bruce* (1370) is a mythical history and an expression in epic of the new national feeling. It is the Scottish equivalent of Layamon's *Brut*. Anthologists are fond of the passage beginning

> A! fredom is a noble thing!

taking it to be a manifesto of Scottish nationalism, but Barbour here is talking about the blessings of the unmarried state. The great period of Scottish poetry begins with the Chaucerian school. *The Kingis Quair*, so called because of its attribution to James I of Scotland (1394–1437), is written in the Chaucerian stanza, thereafter called 'rhyme royal' in his honour. Robert Henryson (?1425–?1500) is best known for his *Testament of Cresseid*, in which he shows the retribution that befell the faithless heroine, which Chaucer had forborne to tell. In Henryson's fine sequel she is afflicted with leprosy. Troilus, riding past, glances down at her leper's cup and clapper.

> And with ane blenk it came into his thocht
> That he sumtime her face before had seen.

William Dunbar (?1460–?1520) was the most versatile and varied of the makars (as the old Scottish poets are called). He wrote mellifluous allegories in the tradition of Chaucer, Gower and Lydgate, but he was also a master of the flyting, or comic abuse, which has always delighted Scottish poets. In the 'Treatise of the Two Married Women and the Widow' he plays off a charming garden scene against the cynical conversation of the women. In other poems he attacks the corruptions of friars, the pretensions of the vulgar, the foulness of the Edinburgh streets. He writes of the humours of life at court, or complains of his headache, or longs in winter for the return of spring. His rollicking dance-rhythms and eldritch humour are seen in the macabre 'Dance of the Seven Deadly Sins'. Of all old Scottish poems the best known is his 'Lament for the Makars'. It has been criticized for showing the medieval obsession with death; but death is still quite common today. In devout poetry Dunbar's poem on Christ's Nativity can stand comparison with Milton's, though its verse-music and its spring colouring are totally different. His poem on Christ's Resurrection, beginning with the tremendous line

> Done is a battel on the dragon blak

has no rival in English on this subject. Dunbar ranks second only to Burns among Scottish poets. He has something in common with Burns, especially the Burns of 'Tam O'Shanter'. The medieval poet he most resembles is François Villon, though none of his poems is as great as the French poet's 'Ballade des pendus'.

High among the makars stands Gavin Douglas (?1475–1522). His *Eneados* (before 1512) is the first complete vernacular translation of Virgil's *Aeneid*, the first translation of any great classical poet into English, the largest scale achievement in the whole of Scottish poetry. Douglas created a Scottish poetic diction drawn from many sources. His *Eneados* is 'better that the original', said Ezra Pound, 'because Douglas had heard the sea'. Douglas's Virgil is very medieval, part seer, part sorcerer. Douglas himself is more like Chaucer in spirit than any of the other 'Scottish Chaucerians'.

Finally, the name Sir David Lindsay (?1490–1555) should be mentioned here. He is best known for his *Satire of the Three Estates*, successfully adapted at the Edinburgh Festival in 1948, but his finest poem is *Squire Meldrum* (after 1550). For some reason textbooks are apt to describe it as a burlesque, but it is in fact a romantic biography of a real person, full of the spirit of medieval chivalry.

Scottish poetry of the late Middle Ages was colourful and self-confident, already beginning to run to the over-elaboration and excess of an exuberant literary period, like the late Elizabethan age in England. English poetry of the same time – Lydgate, Stephen Hawes and others – was unadventurous. Much of it is no more than a repetition of the allegorical tradition, and its instability of metre makes it very hard reading. Between Chaucer and Wyatt the best things in English poetry are anonymous, lyrics like 'I sing of a maiden', 'Adam lay ibounden', 'Maiden in the mor lay' or 'The Nut-Brown Maid'.

It is convenient to discuss the Ballads here, though many of the best are dateless. Inexplicably, some countries of Europe have a ballad tradition, others have not. A ballad is a narrative poem, with no indication of personal authorship. The story is told in an objective manner, without general reflections or expressions of feeling, and with the minimum of connecting links. Stock epithets are used: 'golden', 'silver', 'rose-red', 'lily-white'. Ballads often have repeated lines and refrains, suggesting a chorus accompanying the narrative of a solo speaker. They were meant originally to be sung, and are connected with dancing, as their name implies. They have been handed down by oral tradition among unsophisticated people, in rural communities, in conditions which ceased to be general after the fifteenth century. The earliest example of the ballad manner in English is the snatch called the 'Canute Song' ('Merrily sang the monks of Ely . . .') recorded by one of those monks c.1167. The most important ballad source is a folio volume written c.1650, discovered by Bishop Percy, from which he drew his *Reliques*, printed in 1765, adapting the ballads to eighteenth-century taste. Other collectors, including Walter Scott, gathered more material. F.J. Child's definitive collection (1882–98) contains 305 ballads, and these are represented by over 1300 versions. No definition of poetry based on the *mot juste*, the single, unique, irreplaceable word, can apply to ballads. Yet some of them are among the greatest poems ever composed.

Among these are the ballads of domestic tragedy, such as 'Edward', or 'Lord Randal' (which has many versions) – tragedies of mother and son, or of the false mistress or wife or servant. Others turn on true love and faithfulness, like 'Child Waters', or on fickleness and fate. Some deal in the matter of romance, stories of elopement and pursuit. Others are pure fairytales, like 'Earl Mar's Daughter.' The lament 'Sir Patrick Spens' is known wherever English poetry is read. Ballads involving ghosts and the otherworld include 'Thomas the Rhymer' and 'The Wife of Usher's Well'. Ballads of a more epic kind are found among the 'Border Ballads' – i.e. the border between England and Scotland – such as the two probably dealing with the same fight, 'Cheviot' and 'Otterburn'. In the Elizabethan age Sir Philip Sidney's heart was moved by the 'trumpet sound' of what may have been 'Cheviot', and in the eighteenth century Addison praised a version of it known as 'Chevy Chase'. The great figure of the epic ballads is Robin Hood, with 36 ballads extant about him. His poet invites us to the sunny glades of Nottinghamshire.

> When shaws be sheen and swards full fair,
> And leaves both large and long,
> It is merry walking in the fair forest
> To hear the small birds' song.
>
> The woodwele sang and would not cease,
> Sitting upon the spray,
> So loud he wakened Robin Hood
> In the greenwood where he lay.

The finest of the ballads recalls us to the elemental facts of human existence, day and night, the wild moors and the wind, and the sea.

> O they rade further and further on
> An they waded rivers abune the knee;
> And they saw neither sun nor moon,
> But they heard the roaring of the sea.

(from 'Thomas the Rhymer')

In some ballads the dominant emotion is the pain of separation, when the souls of the departed are drawn back by the longing of those on earth who loved them.

> Lie still, lie still, but a little wee while,
> Lie still but if we may;
> Gin [if] our mother should miss us when she wakes
> She'll go mad ere it be day.

Others, such as 'Lord Thomas and Fair Annet', or 'Burd Ellen', speak only of the passions which terminate in this world. 'Clerk Saunders' brings together the human world with the world beyond the grave.

> Is there ony room at your head, Saunders?
> Is there ony room at your feet?
> Is there ony room at your side, Saunders,
> Where fain, fain I wad sleep?

Quiller- Couch's *Oxford Book of Ballads* (1910) is a permanent addition to English culture. James Kinsley's replacement of it (1969) caters for a more modern taste, including the comic and bawdy, and makes room for some later, 'literary' ballads also.

Another book which the lover of English poetry should have is Carleton Brown's *Religious Lyrics of the Fifteenth Century* (1939). It includes 'I sing of a maiden' from the Sloane manuscript. In rapt contemplation the poet sees not a mother or the birth of a child, but the arrival of one 'begotten by his Father before all worlds'. The whole mystery of the Incarnation is implicit in a few simple lines, succeeding where ambitious poems like those of Crashaw fail by their frothy churning up of sentimental and self-regarding emotion, and even the great Milton in *Paradise Regained* is inhuman and frigid.

The other achievement of anonymous poets in these centuries is the religious drama. This falls into three categories, the Mysteries, the Miracle Plays, and the Moralities. The Mystery cycles are associated with Chester, York and Wakefield. (The 'Ludus Coventriae', despite its name, is thought to come from York). The cycles present the whole of time, from the Creation and the Fall of the Angels to the Day of Judgment. They derive from the liturgy of the Mass, and centre on the Incarnation of Christ. Old Testament scenes are shown as prefigurings of Christ's coming. The Mysteries were presented by craft guilds, usually round about the feast of Corpus Christi (established 1311). The characteristic power shown in some of them has led to the identification of individual playwrights by descriptions, such as the York Realist or the Wakefield Master. The Miracle plays are not grouped in cycles. They are single plays on Biblical topics, or the lives of saints. Of the earlier Moralities, the best known is *The Castle of Perseverance* (stress on the second syllable); of the later ones, *Everyman*. The Mystery cycles and Miracle plays are often revived and received with enthusiasm. In them comedy, tragedy, everyday life, and religious sublimity come together. The Moralities are more problematic. T.S. Eliot praised *Everyman* as 'the one English drama within the limits of art'. Two comments may be made on this. First, *Everyman* may not be English at all; the original play may be Dutch. Second, if it is English it is exceptional in English literature in being entirely abstract. Its theme is that of Tolstoy's story 'The Death of Ivan Ilyich', but its effect is in stark contrast with Tolstoy's story, since it lacks the appeal of the particular and individual. Everyman himself, Death, Fellowship, Kindred, and Good Deeds are mere wooden figures. The puzzling thing is that, in spite of that, the play moves audiences deeply.

Some writers of religious prose from these times are still read. The recluse Richard Rolle (?1300–49) is one of them, and so is Walter Hylton (d. 1396), whose *Ladder of Perfection* is more modern in style than Rolle. *The Cloud of Unknowing* (anonymous; affinities with Hylton) probably belongs to Chaucer's time, but it deals with states of mind and soul into which Chaucer never enters. The literature of mysticism is a wild flower which can spring up anywhere. It is a conversation with the reader which soars above the time and place. The anchoress Julian of Norwich (c.1342–1442), in her *Revelations of Divine Love*, shows acquaintance with Hylton, and a fervent piety of her own.

In this same time our Lord showed me a spiritual sight of his homely loving . . . a little thing, the quantity of a hazel-nut in the palm of my hand . . . I thought: What may this be? And it was answered generally thus: It is all that is made. I marvelled how it might last, for methought it might suddenly have fallen to naught for little. And I was answered in my understanding: It lasteth, and ever shall, for that God loveth it.

In this century the words 'all shall be well, and all manner of things shall be well', with which Christ reassured her, were to be used in Eliot's 'Little Gidding.' In her own time Julian had a visitor one day called Margery Kempe. Margery's autobiography was discovered and first printed in 1936. It was taken down from her dictation. 'This creature' (as she calls herself) confesses her bodily and spiritual difficulties with great frankness, and narrates her pilgrimage to the Holy Land. Her weeping and noisiness made her much disliked, but she was quite fearless, and convinced of divine inspiration. She had read Rolle and Hylton, and herself had a personal experience of religious ecstasy. Though a turbulent character, Margery Kempe was no heretic or Lollard, but extremely orthodox. Her confession is the first of its kind in English, anticipating those of George Fox and John Bunyan.

Other prose of the age is less lively. Chaucer's prose is not up to the standard of his verse. Wyclif's translation of the Bible is historically important, but it is not great literature as Tindale's is. The letters of the Paston family in Norfolk are valued as historical documents rather than literature. More entertaining than any of these is *The Travels of Sir John Mandeville* (*c.*1350). Mandeville became a household word in many languages. Then it was discovered that 'Sir John' never lived, and his travels never happened. His alleged personal experiences were compiled out of books. Whoever the author was, he achieved one of the most successful literary frauds ever known. There are said to be 300 manuscripts. The *Travels* are, in fact, the first and one of the best examples of the prose of pure entertainment (prose was usually employed for edification and instruction). The author (Jean d'Outremuse, or another) added permanently to our mythology, with the Fountain of Youth, the Great Cham, the Lady of the Sparrowhawk, and Prester John.

Tudor prose was founded by three men of affairs who took to literature late in life: Berners, Caxton and Malory. Lord Berners (1467–1533) made an original adaptation of Froissart, treating history as heroic romance. He also wrote the extravagant fairytale kind of romance, 'Arthur of Little Britain' and 'Huon of Bordeaux'. He introduced Oberon the fairy king into English literature, and he was the first to use the ornate style that later became fashionable and culminated in *Euphues*.

William Caxton (1422–91) is, historically speaking, the most important person in English literature. At this time there was no standard form of the English language, and a famous story may be worth retelling here. Some British merchants sailed from London and put in at the Kentish coast. What happened next (in Caxton's spelling) was that

. . . one of theyme named Sheffeldies, a mercer, came in-to a house and axed for mete; and specyally he asked after eggys; and the good wyf answerde, that she coude speke no frenshe. And the merchaunt was angry, for he also coude speake no frenshe, but wolde have hadde 'eggys' and she vderstode hym not. And thenne at laste another sayd that he wolde haue 'eyren', then the good wyf sayd that she vnderstod hym wel. Loo, what sholde a man thyse dayes now wryte, 'egges' or 'eyren'?

A century later this contretemps would have been unlikely, and Caxton's work was largely responsible. Caxton had become rich in the textile business, and in middle age took to translating European works into English. Not satisfied with the then common method of circulating such works (scribes copied them), he went to Cologne to learn the use of a printing press. In 1475 he issued the first book to be printed in English, a romance, the *Recuyell of the Historyes of Troye*. Over fifteen years he published about 100 books, mostly translations. He had to decide what was meant by English, and he chose the language of London and the court – the King's English. Because of the success of Caxton's books it became the language of Shakespeare and the basis of Modern English.

Greatest of the books Caxton printed was *Le Morte D'Arthur*. Sir Thomas Malory has been identified with an actual person of that name, the ruffian from Newbold Revel, but his book is remote and impersonal, belonging to no age or condition of ordinary life. It is better that 'Malory' should remain mysterious (although he does ask us to pray for his soul). The Knight Prisoner seems to have finished his Arthurian romances in 1469–70, and they were printed by Caxton in 1485. For centuries this was the only text. Then, in 1934, Walter Oakeshott discovered a manuscript in Winchester College library, contemporary with Caxton's text but independent of it. This establishes that the *Morte* was not originally meant as a single work; its apparent unity is due to Caxton. The standard modern edition by Eugene Vinaver is called *The Works of Sir Thomas Malory*. Malory apparently began by making a prose version of the alliterative poem *Morte Arthure*, but most of his sources were French Arthurian romances, composed in great cycles. Vinaver shows how Malory broke up their complex narratives into single tales. He was less interested in theological significances than the French writers, and more interested in earthly emotions and motives. His stories are various, and so are his characters. He shows us the religious austerity of Galahad, the worldliness of Gawain, the romantic chivalrousness of Tristram. Dinadan too has his place, as a sardonic commentator. There is more unity in the last four parts of the work, which tell of the unlawful love of Lancelot and Guinevere and the destruction of the Round Table. Lancelot is a tragic figure, like Homer's Achilles, or Emily Brontë's Heathcliff. His tragedy is summed up in his farewell to Guinevere.

God defend but that I should forsake the world as you have done. For in the quest of the Sangreal I had that time forsaken the vanities of the world, had not your love been.

We owe the reading 'love' (for Caxton's 'lord') to the Winchester manuscript.

Malory's work has not always met with approval, and its moral code has been questioned. In the sixteenth century the classicist Roger Ascham attacked if for 'manslaughter and bold bawdry'. In the nineteenth century Tennyson disapproved of its record of 'a time/That hover'd between war and wantonness'. In our own time the Marxist critic Ralph Fox, a brave man who died fighting for the Spanish Republic, rebuked Malory (while admitting his genius) for escapism, which held up the development of the realistic novel, a genre in which Marxists have always felt happier than in the mysterious world of Arthur. However, Malory's work remains the finest literary treatment of that world (Tennyson is too Victorian-decorous-erotic, T.H. White too boyish, Charles Williams too cryptic). He is the belated last great writer of the Middle Ages.

T W O

The sixteenth century

English literature in the sixteenth century has usually been seen as having two phases. In the first and longer of these (1500–80) it was worthy but unexciting, with no masterpiece. In poetry it was what C.S. Lewis called 'the Drab Age'. Then in the 1580s and 1590s came a 'Golden' period of great vigour, usually known as the Elizabethan age, though Elizabeth I had come to the throne as long ago as 1558 (and her own poetry is certainly 'Drab' enough). This outburst of first-rate literature included our greatest writer, Shakespeare. The traditional view of the century was expounded with great vigour by Lewis in his influential volume in the *Oxford History of English Literature*. But readers more attuned to twentieth-century literature than Lewis have come to be less sympathetic to that view. Shakespeare still holds his place, but the verbosity of the Elizabethans (from which he is by no means free) is now censured, and for Lewis's 'Drab' and 'Golden' some would substitute 'Plain' and 'Decorated', and are not too enthusiastic about the 'Decorated'. It is true that the writers of the early sixteenth century can also be very tedious, and the interest of most of them is merely historical, but here and there we find a few things that have turned out to be particularly attractive to twentieth-century readers.

Some of these are in the work of John Skelton (?1460–1529). He is one of the few poets of his time who is still read with interest today by people other than professional scholars or students. Skelton is an oddity; he is unlike anyone else. He has no influence on the poets who came after him, and was largely neglected until two twentieth-century poets, Robert Graves and W.H. Auden, drew attention to his work, and submitted to his influence. Skelton's most ambitious poem was the Morality play, *Magnificence*, which is very long, but at times very lively. The hero, Magnificence, is a colourful figure, perhaps suggested by Skelton's enemy Cardinal Wolsey. Skelton had the intriguing idea, not much used by dramatists, of differentiating his characters by giving them different metres. His other work falls into four categories:

1. *Aureate poetry*, in the tradition of Lydgate and other fifteenth-century poets. A good example is his poem on the death of Edward IV. The king himself speaks:

> Now there is no more but to pray for me all.
> Thus say I, Edward, that late was your king,
> And twenty-two years ruled this imperial,
> Some unto pleasure and some to no liking,
> Mercy I say for my misdoing . . .

It is all very medieval, awkward and lumbering, but it has a ring of reality absent from anything written in commemoration of (say) Winston Churchill or John F. Kennedy.

2. *Lyric poetry*. Skelton's short poems addressed to young women are charming:

> Ennewéd your colour
> Is like the daisy flower
> After the April shower,
> Star of the morrow gray.
> (from 'The Garland of
>   Laurel')

Perhaps he wrote 'Woefully arrayed', a lyric monologue put into the mouth of Christ on the Cross.

> Thus naked as I am nailéd, O man for thy sake!
> I love thee, then love me; why sleepest thou? awake! . . .
> Thus tuggéd to and fro
> Thus wrappéd all in woe,
> Whereas man never was so . . .
> Woefully arrayed.

3. *Poems in rhyme royal. The Bouge of Court* (1498–9) – 'bouge' perhaps means bag or purse – is a dream-allegory, satirizing court intrigue. *Speak Parrot* (1521) is extremely obscure. It is written in a kind of code, like some of Dylan Thomas's poems. Many readers today enjoy it as a kind of nonsense verse.

4. The poems in a hopping and jumping metre, called after him the '*Skeltonic*'. It is used in *Philip Sparrow* (before 1509), a mock-heroic poem expressing a child's grief for her pet, in a mixture of English and Latin (the technical term for this is 'macaronic'). *Colin Clout* (1522) is another attack on Wolsey. *Elinor Rumming* is like a grotesque cartoon, about a hideous alewife and her customers. With Skeltonics the poet added a new species to light

verse, as individual as nursery rhymes, or the limerick.

> Maude Ruggy thither skipped,
> She was ugly hipped,
> And ugly thick lipped,
> Like an onion sided,
> Like tan leather hided.
>   (from *Elinor Rumming*)

Christina Rossetti in *Goblin Market* (1862) combines the helter-skelter effect of this style with high poetry, but Skelton rarely does this. He likes to use it for abuse:

> Dundee, Dunbar,
> Walk, Scot,
> Walk, sot,
> Rail not too fast!

Skelton's style seems to the product of his own odd mind and temperament. It is artless and incoherent.

> I purpose to shake out
> All my cunning bag
> Like a clerkly hag.

He has no message, no comprehensive vision of life. He excels in lampoon, satirical doggerel, invective, caricature. Of all the considerable poets in English his verse has the least resonance, but it may appeal to many modern poets and lovers of poetry more than the big boomy lines that came later from Spenser, Milton, Tennyson etc. We like the Skeltonian staccato.

Skelton had no classical (or 'humanist') training – which might have pulled some of his more chaotic poems together – and he was untouched by the two great spiritual movements of his time, today, though not then, called the Renaissance and the Reformation. But at the beginning of the century England was drawn into their vortex. The revival of learning began as an Italian movement, but spread later to Northern Europe, where its leader was Erasmus (?1466–1536), by birth a Dutchman, but in his culture a citizen of Europe. Erasmus's Latin textbook on good manners, *De Civilitate* (1526), was once known to every educated person. It is said that by the beginning of the eighteenth century 128 editions of it had been published. Samuel Johnson, though himself an old savage, recommended it highly. In the fifteenth century cultivated Englishmen had known about Italian humanism, but they contributed little to it themselves. Now such men as Thomas Linacre (?1460–1524), William Grocyn (?1446–1519), John Colet (?1467–1519) and John Fisher (1459–1535) determined to bring England into the revival of learning, and to see to it that the revival should be Christian (they distrusted the pagan elements in the Italian Renaissance). Erasmus was brought to Cambridge, from 1511 to 1514, to lecture on Greek. His great friend was Sir Thomas More (1478–1535), the 'man for all seasons', the victim of Henry VIII, associated with Fisher in his tragic death, the symbol in every age of the integrity of the individual conscience. More was at the heart of the English Renaissance. He had been a pupil of Linacre and Grocyn; he was a disciple of Colet. He was a patron of letters and the arts, and his house became a sort of private university. As a thinker extolled both by papal Rome and by Bolshevist Moscow, More is indeed a remarkable figure. His character, however, is not easy to make out, and some aspects of it are by no means attractive. To the student of English literature he is only a background figure. His poems in English are not very good.

The work of More that conquered Europe was *Utopia* (1516), written in Latin. It added a word to the world's vocabulary, but not with the meaning intended by More; 'Utopia' means, not 'good place', but 'no place'. It is best read either in Latin or in a modern English version; the sixteenth-century translation by Ralph Robynson makes More's thought seem more 'period' that it is. At this time of his life More allowed himself some daring speculations. The literary ancestor of the book is Plato's *Republic*; its innumerable successors include Morris's *News from Nowhere* and Wells's *A Modern Utopia*. More's book is interesting for its ideas rather than as literature. Much of his later work consists of brutal polemics against Protestants, especially Tindale. Like similar things in Milton's prose writings, they are a disgrace to him and to Christianity. The only work of More which evokes a sympathetic feeling is the *Dialogue of Comfort against Tribulation*, written by him when awaiting execution (and probable torture as well).

Other men of this time, though less famous than More, had a greater part in the making of English culture and literature. Sir Thomas Elyot (1490–1546) was one, with his *Book named the Governor* (1531). ('Governor' means 'member of the ruling class'). Another was Thomas Wilson (1525–81), with his *Art of Rhetoric* (1551). 'Rhetoric' means not what it often does today, i.e. empty ranting without argument, but the art of persuasion by words (there is no reason why it has to be illogical). These writers were inspired by Erasmus in his *Adagia* and *Colloquia*, in which he used the writings of antiquity to instruct and edify his contemporaries. The classics were to be the basis for gentlemen's schooling and the proper models for writing in the vernacular. Some of this worked out well, some of it did not. The bad side of it was pedantry, and cruelty to children (Dame Grammar's emblem is, ominously, the birch). The school and college plays which drew on classical sources are usually unreadable today. The attempt to make English literature obey classical (or, more strictly speaking, Roman) rules was not successful, and classical form – with the great exception of Milton – has had little influence on English writers. But there was a good side too. If the classics could not supply form, they could supply matter abundantly. The great men of antiquity became familiar figures. Classical allusions abound in the work of Shakespeare, a popular writer (they are much more frequent in his work than they are in scholarly Milton's). Classical myths, legends and anecdotes were the common property of English readers down to the 1950s. Modern educationalists may deplore the old curriculum and the way it was taught, but it is worth a moment's reflection that its ascendancy coincided with all the great works of English literature and the centuries when England was a great force in the world. Today England, in regard to the classics, is in the position of a recently independent Third World country which has been dominated by the imperial power's literature and has now to work painfully towards its own, though its standards and values are still bound up with the older one. We still use words like 'poem', 'lyric', 'epic', 'drama', but without being sure what they mean.

A masterpiece of the Renaissance, much admired at this time, was the *Cortegiano* (1528) by Baldassare Castiglione, which introduces us to the Italian court of Urbino, and the discussions of courtiers, prelates and fine ladies. It was 'translated' into very slapdash English by Sir Thomas Hoby in 1561 (under the pleasant title *The Courtyer of Count Baldesar Castilio*). There were further editions in 1565, 1577, 1588 and 1603. Elizabethan courtiers were fascinated by the concept introduced into European culture by Castiglione, *sprezzatura*. (Hoby's word for it is 'recklessness'). 'Lifemanship' is the modern equivalent, but that brings a touch of humour into the idea which Castiglione did not intend. His concern was with the educated humanist, the civilized gentleman, and there is a metaphysical background to his discussion of the good life. Hoby was more down to earth. What he was really interested in was court advancement. The nearest modern analogy to his work is the early novels of Aldous Huxley, intended to give the middling reader glimpses of the cultured conversation of the day (and very odd some of it is). Some Englishmen viewed these Renaissance developments with caution. The educator Roger Ascham (1515–68) had admired the *Cortegiano*, and despised medieval literature as unclassical (and immoral). But in his *Schoolmaster* (published posthumously in 1570) he inveighed against the 'Englishman Italianate', and fought against the importation of Romance words into English. Ascham is apt to get snarled up in his sentences – English prose was in a chaotic state at this time – and he has many quirks and prejudices, but it is impossible not to like the crusty old fellow. Now and again scattered readers today discover with pleasure his quaint work *Toxophilus* (1548), ostensibly a defence of the virtues of the English longbow.

Tudor poetry in the plain style was dominated by Wyatt and Surrey. Both were court poets in an age when the court was a dangerous place. Sir Thomas Wyatt (1503–42) was involved with the king's second wife, Anne Boleyn, before her marriage, and, himself a prisoner, witnessed the execution of her alleged paramours. The Earl of Surrey (?1517–47) witnessed the execution of the king's fifth wife, Catherine Howard, who was his cousin, and a few years later was himself executed on a trumped-up charge of treason. Wyatt and Surrey are always linked as poets, since their work appeared posthumously in an anthology of 1557 called *Songs and Sonnets* (generally known, after its compiler, as *Tottel's Miscellany*). In 1589 an Elizabethan critic, perhaps named George Puttenham, described them as 'the two chieftains' in 'the new company of courtly makers' in Henry VIII's reign. Puttenham found 'little difference' between them. Other Elizabethans placed Surrey above Wyatt: after all, Surrey was an earl, Wyatt was only a knight. Modern opinion favours Wyatt.

Neither Wyatt nor his immediate circle issued an authoritative edition of his poems. For centuries they were known only in the form in which Tottel printed them, until in 1816 G.F. Nott published an edition based on two manuscripts contemporary with the poet. Then it was seen that Tottel (or his editor) had altered many lines to make them metrically regular. Since then other manuscripts containing poems by Wyatt have been found. Controversy continues about Wyatt's metrical irregularity, complicated by the uncertainty of his canon. Authoritative guidance about these problems can be found in H.A. Mason's *Humanism and Poetry in the Early Tudor Period* (1959) and *Editing Wyatt* (1972).

Wyatt's poetry falls into five categories, all of which contain strikingly good work, as well as very inferior stuff.

1. *Sonnets*, mostly translated or imitated from Petrarch and his Italian followers.

2. '*Epigrams*' — not quite what we understand by this term — short poems, usually on personal themes.

3. Some longer *verse translations*, including the Penitential Psalms, in Dante's *terza rima*.

4. *Verse satires* (also in *terza rima*).

5. A number of '*balets*' or song-like poems. It is natural to think of these as songs, since the poet refers frequently to his 'lute', but this appears to be a poetic convention.

The metrical problem does not arise with the lyrics in the last category. These include some of the most beautiful poetry of its kind in English. The note is of quiet, resigned sadness. Wyatt's subject is the pain of love, unrequited, or thwarted, or betrayed.

> And wilt thou leave me thus?
> Say nay, say nay, for shame,
> To save thee from the blame
> Of all my grief and grame [pain];
> And wilt thou leave me thus?
> Say nay, say nay!

or

> Once, as me thought, fortune me kissed,
> And bade me ask what I thought best,
> And as I should have it as me list [as it pleased me],
> Therewith to set my heart at rest.
>
> I askéd nought but my dear heart
> To have for evermore mine own;
> Then at end were all my smart,
> Then should I need no more to moan.

or

> What earthly thing more can I crave?
> What would I wish more at my will?
> Nothing on earth more would I have
> Save that I have, to have it still.

To the scholar, Wyatt is mainly of interest as the first Italianate English poet since Chaucer (Gower seems not to have known Italian). To common readers – and Wyatt has some – he is the Tudor poet who speaks to us with a personal voice, as most sixteenth-century poets do not.

Surrey was the product of the new teaching of classical literature initiated by More and Colet, Cheke and Ascham. Thomas Warton in 1781 called him 'the first English classical poet'. His poems are chiefly translations from Latin and Italian. The most ambitious is his version of Books II and IV of Virgil's *Aeneid*, in which he introduced blank verse into English. This was a memorable development: the drama of Marlowe and Shakespeare and their successors, Milton in *Paradise Lost*, and great numbers of Romantic and Victorian poems and plays, use this metre. Curiously, it fell into disuse in England in the early twentieth century, but American poets have found new music in it: Frost, Robinson, Stevens, Eliot (in the greatest passage of 'Little Gidding') and Robert Lowell have all used it with much effect. But again curiously, it has not been much used for poetic plays lately. Surrey was, then, a pioneer; but he was less a master of this metre than his successors. He may have adopted it for a humanistic, anti-medieval reason (rhyme was thought by some classicists to be barbarous). His blank verse is stiff and apt to stop too regularly at the end of lines. His translation of Virgil is less lively than Gavin Douglas's (to which he seems to owe something).

The link between Surrey and Wyatt may be more religious than technical. Surrey admired Wyatt as a moral figure. His poetry is less rugged than Wyatt's, and his dream world is different: it was a green and sunny landscape, inspired by southern England, and enriched in the poet's mind by images from Italy and ancient Greece. His poem on Windsor, which reflects it, is a lament for his lost boyhood. Another good poem, in which Surrey's aristocratic timbre appears attractively, is his elegiac sonnet on his friend

Clere. Other sonnets use the motifs of Petrarch, for Surrey, like Wyatt, is Italianate. His style often anticipates Sidney. Surrey is, in fact, more like an 'Elizabethan' than a 'Drab' poet, and unfortunately he has the Elizabethans' characteristic fault of prolixity.

Surrey, like Wyatt, was touched by the Reformation. So too was the finest masterpiece of the early phase of the English Renaissance. But this is in prose, – the work of Thomas Cranmer (1489–1556), archbishop of Canterbury, tool of Henry VIII and victim of Mary I. He was either a master of English, or a committee chairman who knew great prose when he saw it. In either case he must receive credit for the first *Book of Common Prayer*, issued in 1549. It was revised in 1552 and again in 1559. The Prayer Book of 1662 is substantially the same as the 1559 version. Behind the Prayer Book are the medieval English prayers and aids to devotion of the laity. What Cranmer and his colleagues did was to superimpose the grandeur and sonority of Latin, Ciceronian prose upon the simplicity and straightforwardness of ordinary English. For generation after generation the cadences of the General Confession reverberated on English ears.

Almighty and most merciful Father, We have erred and strayed from thy ways like lost sheep, We have followed too much the devices and desires of our own hearts, We have offended against thy holy laws, We have left undone those things which we ought to have done, And we have done those things which we ought not to have done, and there is no health in us.

Everyone had to go to church in the sixteenth century, and the Prayer Book became a great influence on English speech and writing, and on English feeling. Finally, in 1974, Parliament permitted the modern clergy to use alternative versions.

The chief work of Reformation literature is the English Bible. Two great names here are William Tindale (d. 1536) and Miles Coverdale (1488–1568). Tindale was a violent pamphleteer. He was also an inspired translator, fixing the character of English versions of the Bible for ever. Like many of the writers and preachers of his day he had a sure feeling for the popular style. The second edition of Coverdale's version (published in 1537) was the first complete Bible to be printed in England. The Prayer-book Psalter is his work, an abiding testimony to his literary power.

The great age of Biblical translation, which began with Tindale, ended with the so-called Authorized Version (in fact it was never 'authorized') in 1611. It owes much to Tindale and Coverdale. The A.V. has a unique place in English literature. Its influence can be seen from Bunyan to D.H. Lawrence, from Blake to T.F. Powys. The writings of unbelievers like Ruskin and Kipling, Swinburne and A.E. Housman, are saturated with it. But it is little read today: the church of England is abandoning it in worship: scholars ignore it because it is archaic and inaccurate, and *literati* ignore it because it is religious. Modern translations of the Bible continue to be made by men of learning and piety and sensitive literary feeling, but they have not succeeded in giving the twentieth century a religious language. It may then be worth recording that English did once have a language in which it does not seem absurd to say that we hear the voice of God.

> Where was thou when I laid the foundations of the earth?
> Declare, if thou hast understanding.
> Who hath laid the measures thereof, if thou knowest?
> Or who hath stretched the line upon it?
> Whereupon are the foundations thereof fastened?
> Or who laid the corner stone thereof;
> When the morning stars sang together,
> And all the sons of God shouted for joy?
> Or who shut the sea with doors,
> When it brake forth, as if it had issued out of the womb?
> When I made the cloud the garment thereof.
> And thick darkness a swaddling band for it,
> And set bars and doors,
> And said, Hitherto shalt thou come, but no further:
> And there shall thy proud waves be stayed?
>   (Job 38. 4–11)

Whether the Bible can survive only as English literature is doubtful. But while English is still read it is possible to enjoy the matchless simplicity of the story of Abraham and Isaac (Genesis 22. 1–14) or the 'still small voice' (I Kings 19. 11–12), the cloudy fulminations of the Prophets, the 'new heaven and new earth' of Revelation. The book of Job stands with Shakespeare at his greatest. The book of Ruth has the pure simple effect Wordsworth partly attained in 'Michael' and Tennyson missed in 'Dora'. The book of Jonah effortlessly relates fantastic comedy to divinity. As pure poetry the Psalms have never been surpassed, with the grandeur of the 18th, and the 22nd with its serenity as of George Herbert. In quite another vein are the inside story of King David's court, or the sexual longings of the Songs of Songs, or the tale of Amnon's passion for Tamar (2 Samuel 13. 1–22), or the atrocious story of the Levite's concubine (Judges 19): the strong meat of human existence. In the New Testament the A.V. leaves Paul's style its contortions, but it can rise also to his intense humanity and moments of radiance. And it has given familiar form in English to the inimitable sayings of Jesus, emerging from the unpretentious, unliterary prose of the Gospels. In the end it is impossible to separate the A.V.'s imperishable expression of human emotions from its command of rhythm.

> And the king was much moved, and went up to the chamber over the gate, and wept; and as he went, thus he said, O my son Absalom, my son, my son Absalom! would God I had died for thee, O Absalom, my son, my son!

The Protestant classic of this period, read alongside the Bible by people who read no other book, was the work which became known as *The Book of Martyrs* (1563), by John Foxe (1517–87). It could be compared to *The Gulag Archipelago* in our time: detailed stories of persecution and suffering. Mary Tudor became for all time 'Bloody Mary'. There is no doubt that Foxe's propaganda fed the flames of anti-Catholic hatred, and its stress on physical cruelty brings it close to pornography. But it has a better claim to remembrance: it tells the story of ordinary men and women defying their oppressors.

Other Tudor prose writers characteristic of their time are the chroniclers and antiquarians who wrote to glorify England: Edward Hall (d. 1547) and Raphael Holinshed (*Chronicles of England, Scotland and Ireland*, 1577, enlarged 1586). They helped to establish the 'Tudor myth' of English history, much drawn on by poets, including Shakespeare. He no doubt also knew the *History of King Richard the Third* (first printed 1543), perhaps the work of Thomas More, and perhaps based on first-hand evidence (that of More's early patron, Cardinal Morton) which introduced the terrible figure of the Crookback. Shakespeare also perhaps knew George Cavendish's *Life and Death of Cardinal Wolsey* (though it was not fully published till 1667) – a little classic in its own way, the first biography in English with claims to be a work of literature.

Shakespeare, and other writers of his time, rarely remind us that this was an age of maritime adventure: the feeling expressed in the Victorian painter Millais's picture 'The Boyhood of Sir Walter Raleigh' is rather hard to document in the writings of the Elizabethans themselves. The only great name here is that of Richard Hakluyt (?1552–1616) – his name is pronounced 'Hacklewit'. 'Industrious Hakluyt', as Drayton called him, was a man of one idea, which brought about his great collection, *The Principal Navigations, Voyages , and Discoveries of the English Nation* (first edition 1589). Virginia Stephen (one day to be Virginia Woolf) as a girl made a special trip to the London Library to get Hakluyt's *Voyages*, enraptured by 'those large yellow pages', dreaming of 'those obscure adventures'. With them may be mentioned Samuel Purchas (1575–1626) with his *Pilgrims*, to be a source one day for Coleridge. Another book that some people still like is *Coryat's Crudities*, the curious autobiography-cum-travel-book of Thomas Coryat (?1577–1617). 'Crudities' – cf. French *Crudités* – is Elizabethan for titbits. How much reliable information there is in these works it is hard to say, but they are splendid escapism.

Meanwhile, in the verse of the middle sixteenth century, the humanist training enabled poets to write less chaotically than the late medievals. Metre becomes regular, and the poems hold together. Latin texts were studied at grammar schools and universities, and there were manuals of rhetoric. Besides Wilson's of 1553, already mentioned, there were those of Cox (1524) and Sherry (1553). The poets of this time were competent, but heavy in the hand. 'Poulter's metre', a six-foot line followed by a seven-foot line, introduced by Wyatt, was his worst legacy to English poetry. It leads to thumping rhythms and over-emphatic alliteration, which the reader of sixteenth-century verse soon learns to dread.

> Till tides of turning time shall toss such fishers on the shelf.
>
> (Gascoigne)

Tudor poets of the time of Edward VI (1547–53) and Mary I (1553–58) and the earlier years of Elizabeth I, worked in a variety of forms, moral poems, satires and epigrams; and they introduced new material from the Continental Renaissance. They were serious men, but relentlessly platitudinous. They, have, however, been defended by the great American critic Yvor Winters as establishing a tradition of strong plain writing in English, and he has undoubtedly found good poems through sifting the work of Gascoigne, Googe, Turbervile etc.

The most ambitious project of the age in poetry was *A Mirror for Magistrates* (1559), a collection of versified legends from English history. It was very popular in its day, and was issued with enlargements several times down to 1621. Thomas Sackville (1536–1608) was the liveliest contributor. But only scholars read the poem now. Still read now and then for pleasure is Thomas Tusser's *Hundred Points of Good Husbandry* (1557). It is a collection of versified maxims. His little verse-autobiography is touching. He was miserable at his school (Eton) and happy at his university (Cambridge). Some of us would give the whole of the *Mirror for Magistrates* for the glimpse Tusser gives of his hateful headmaster, Nicholas Udall.

> From Paul's I went, to Eton sent,
> To learn straightways the Latin phrase
> When fifty three stripes given to me
> At once I had.
>
> For fault but small, or none at all,
> It came to pass, thus beat I was,
> See, Udall, see! – the mercy of thee
> To me, poor lad!

The Elizabethan age gets much of its glamour from figures like Sir Walter Raleigh (*c.*1552–1618), but his contribution to literature is not easy to determine. Many poems are attributed to him on dubious authority, including excellent pieces like 'The Lie' and 'The Passionate Man's Pilgrimage' (which begins 'Give me my scallop shell of quiet'). The authentic canon is dominated by the 'Cynthia' fragment, which, with three other poems, survives in Raleigh's own hand. Entitled 'the 11th and last book of the Ocean to Cynthia', it was not discovered and printed till the nineteenth century. It is connected with that strange cult of the Queen which pervades the Elizabethan age. In this period she was the 'White Goddess' who, according to Robert Graves, inspires all true poets at all times. The prosaic realities of Raleigh's relationship with Elizabeth are not known, and his 'Cynthia' lines are fragmentary and monotonous, though they have some memorable moments. Raleigh wrote some strong prose in his pamphlets about the ship *Revenge* and Sir Richard Grenville (1591), and the discovery of Guiana (1596), describing his first expedition to that area in 1595. His *History of the World* (1614) is most readily accessible in the excellent selection from it made by C.A. Patrides in 1971. Raleigh is more important as a participant in history than as a writer. John Aubrey said of him: 'He was sometimes a Poet, not often'.

About Raleigh's friend and protégé Edmund Spenser (?1552–99) all that Aubrey could find out was that 'he was a little man, wore short hair, little band and little cuffs'. Spenser has always been regarded as one of the leading English poets, but he must be the least read of them today. He made his first impact with *The Shepherd's Calendar* (1579), dedicated to Sir Philip Sidney. It consists of a series of eclogues or pastoral poems, one for each month of the year, together with a prose commentary by one 'E.K.', unidentifed. A young poet was expected to start with pastorals, with their purling streams and shady groves, lovelorn shepherds and enchanting shepherdesses, and Spenser provides these, and the appropriate melodious idealizing and lyrical passages. But Spenser had also inherited a tradition in which pastoral was used as a cover for satire and topical comment, and his shepherds discuss, for example, the errors of the Church of Rome.

Spenser's life-work, *The Faerie Queen*, was begun before 1580, but none of it was published for ten years. He was not a full-time poet like Wordsworth or Tennyson, but a busy civil servant, who started his career under the patronage of Leicester and Sidney, and became, in 1580, secretary to Lord Grey of Wilton, who was going to Ireland as Lord Deputy. Apart from occasional returns to his native country he was to spend the rest of his life in Ireland. He was rewarded with Kilcolman Castle and an estate of 3000 acres in County Cork. Spenser's feelings about the native Irish people were not friendly. He favoured Lord Grey's stern policy towards them. He thought of them as an American frontiersman thought of the Comanche. His prose work, 'View of the Present State of Ireland', shows the hard side to the mind of this gentle poet. But he gives unforgettable glimpses of the horrifying misery of these starving, dehumanized savages which show how deeply they impinged on his imagination. (These were to appear, in nightmare symbolic form, in the siege of the House of Alma in Book II of the *Faerie Queen*). Spenser, like Swift, is one of the English writers whose work is dominated by Ireland. It is clear that he hated the Irish and they hated him, but as C.S. Lewis (himself an Irishman) remarked, that is not an un-Irish characteristic. He came to love his Irish home and took an interest in the native culture. He had some Irish poems translated for him, and praised them, though as a good humanist he had some criticisms to make of them on stylistic grounds. More than one reader has seen in the endless vistas of the *Faerie Queen* a fantasy-reflection of the sad dissolving loneliness of the Irish landscape, as Spenser rode about it on horseback, weaving his stanzas.

Much of Spenser's work was occasional, done to order, and it includes many poems that are read only by scholars. Like another Edmund in English literature, Edmund Burke, he might be more admired if he had written less. The work he put his heart into was the *Faerie Queen*, and he is not done a grave injustice if we read only that. There are, however, one or two other things of his that should be mentioned. The *Amoretti* (1595) is a collection of sonnets. The theme is love, the key is rapture, varied by indictments of the cruel fair or sighs for the absent beloved. Sonnet LXXV is lovely. It begins:

> One day I wrote her name upon the sand,
> But came the waves and washéd it away.

It compares well with poems on this theme by Landor and Housman. Spenser was probably more 'sincere', i.e. autobiographical, in the *Amoretti* than Petrarch with his Laura, Sidney with his Stella, or Shakespeare with his Lovely Boy. The best remembered of Spenser's minor poems is the *Epithalamion* (1595) – as the title is spelt by all except C.S. Lewis, who spells it *Epithalamium*. Written in celebration of the poet's second marriage, it is composed on a simple but ingenious plan, based on the events of the wedding day from dawn till night. He makes a majestic use of the bridal ode to depict on a miniature scale the whole Spenserian cosmos. Spenser was the first English poet to suggest the effect of instrumental and choral music.

> Open the temple gates unto my love,
> Open them wide that she may enter in . . .
> Bring her up to th'high altar, that she may
> The sacred ceremonies there partake,
> The which do endless matrimony make;
> And let the roaring organs loudly play
> The praises of the Lord in lively notes;
> The whiles, with hollow throats,
> The choristers the joyous anthems sing,
> That all the woods may answer and their echo ring.

A companion poem, the *Prothalamion* (1596), written for the double marriage of the two daughters of the Earl of Richmond, is most remembered for its beautiful refrain: 'Sweet Thames! run softly, till I end my song'.

Spenser was in London in 1596 for the publication of a revision of Books I–III of the *Faerie Queen* (first entrusted to the printer in 1589) and of Books IV, V and VI. This, it turned out, was to be all that there was of his great poem. What seems to be a fragment of another Book was published as 'Two

Cantos of Mutabilitie' in the posthumous 1609 edition of the poem. Spenser returned to Ireland in 1597. His life was to close tragically. His castle was burnt down in 1598 during a rebellion of the Irish. Spenser fled to England with his wife and children. He died the next year, and was buried in Westminster Abbey.

Spenser's *Faerie Queen* is the chief poem of the English Renaissance. In writing it he had two principal aims. One was to write a British epic, but not on the classical model of Homer or Virgil. His ambition was, it seems, to 'overgo Ariosto' – Ludovico Ariosto (1475–1533), author of the *Orlando Furioso*, an extraordinary work which provoked and puzzled Italian neo-classical critics, for Ariosto notoriously broke all the rules, yet his poem was obviously delightful. Spenser took over the Italian poet's gloomy forests and magic castles, knights riding and fighting, fair ladies in captivity or flight, true lovers and lustful seducers, sorcerers, giants and monsters. Ariosto's intention was in part humorous, and it is not known how far Spenser understood this. As with D.H. Lawrence, his admirers insist that he had a sense of humour, but the fact that they have to insist is significant; no one has to insist that Chaucer, Shakespeare or Dickens had a sense of humour. Spenser's fantastic world derives its unity of atmosphere from a slightly archaic diction and the leisurely movement of the 9-line intricate stanza invented by him, and called after him 'Spenserian'; it rhymes ababbcbcc, always pausing at the six-foot line, or alexandrine, at its close. Spenser's other aim was didactic, 'to fashion a gentleman or noble person in virtuous and gentle discipline'. In the hero – Arthur, before he became king – he meant 'to portray the image of a brave knight, perfected in the twelve private moral virtues, as Aristotle has devised'. The poem was to be in 12 books, one for each virtue. Thus Spenser wove an allegory in the medieval fashion into his chivalrous Italianate romance. Arthur is Magnificence, the perfection of all the virtues. He had a vision or dream of the Faerie Queen. Captivated by her beauty he went in quest of her through Faerie Land. 'In that Faerie Queen', says Spenser in his published letter to Raleigh, explaining his plan, 'I mean glory by my general intention, but in my particular, I conceive the most excellent and glorious person of our sovereign the Queen, and her kingdom in Faerie Land'.

Only six books of the poem were to be completed. In the poem as we have it Arthur is not prominent, and the Faerie Queene does not appear at all. The virtues Spenser celebrates are chiefly exhibited in the quests and struggles of various knights. He does not tell the stories one after another, but employs the polyphonic method of narrative adopted by Ariosto. A story is often interrupted when new characters appear on the scene, and not resumed till much later, if at all. Spenser's Faerie Land is a completely imaginary world. He anticipates William Morris, Lord Dunsany, William Rice Burroughs and J.R.R. Tolkien in his total unrealism. Coleridge speaks of 'the marvellous independence and true imaginative absence of all particular time and space in the Faerie Queene'. Read day after day, said the American poet Wallace Stevens (1878–1955), 'it comes to possess the reader and . . . naturalizes him in its own imagination and liberates him there'. The poem should not be read in small print and double columns. The Roche and Phillips edition (Penguin 1978), slowly perused over a long vacation, is the best for the general reader who has somehow 'never got round to' reading the famous poem.

Scholars argue endlessly, and enjoyably, about the 'meaning' of this or that episode in the *Faerie Queen* and indeed about its purport as a whole. As a rule they beg the question of its readability and value. Various objections are commonly made to the poem. One is to its archaism. This complaint was made early: 'Spenser, in affecting the ancients, writ no language,' said Ben Jonson. But the archaism consists in little more than a few odd spellings and word formations. To eliminate them would be to lose some of the charm of Spenser's poetry, but it would not denature the *Faerie Queen* as modernizing the *Canterbury Tales* denatures Chaucer.

Some readers find the knightly adventures uninteresting, and too many of them are similar: combating knights-errant, banging spear on shield, vile witches and loathsome monsters. And compared with men and women we meet in Shakespeare's plays, or in the work of the great novelists, Spenser's faerie knights are pale figures. We are surprised at the floods of gore they shed in battles. Who would have thought they had so much blood in them?

This objection might have been decisive some years ago, when the realistic novel was accepted as an absolute. But the *Faerie Queen* is not a novel – nor a drama. It is more like a book of fairytales. If you enjoy 'Bluebeard' you will enjoy Spenser's House of Busirane. In fairytales we do not object to the anonymous, impersonal quality of the characters; indeed it is required by the genre. In the twentieth century writers like William Golding, Samuel Beckett or Harold Pinter have accustomed us to a kind of art different from naturalistic fiction.

The allegory bothers some readers. 'It will not bite us', said Hazlitt; all the same, many of us do not like to have our thoughts clamped down to a single conceptual framework. But Spenser lived in an age when allegory was everywhere, in the visual arts, in the Morality plays, in pageantry, in heraldry, in the symbolism of Church and State. It was second nature to him. We need not suppose that he inverted the proper method of art, by proceeding from concept to image, instead of the other way round, since for him concept and image may often have presented themselves simultaneously in his great allegorical tableaux, such as the Bower of Bliss. The topical element in the allegory (what Spenser calls his 'particular intention') is more problematic. Much of it is fugitive. The Faerie Queen, Gloriana, 'is' Elizabeth. (But Elizabeth 'is' also Belphoebe, Mercilla, and aspects of other characters.)

Arthur 'is' perhaps Leicester. The identification of the wicked witch Duessa with Mary Queen of Scots was made so early that it may be taken as likely.

In her trial before Mercilla we can't help thinking of Elizabeth and Mary. But earlier Duessa 'is', more interestingly, the Church of Rome (opposed to Una, who 'is' the Church of England). And some of the incidents in the 'political' Book V clearly glance at incidents in Raleigh's career. Again, the suggestion of topical politics in the poem would once have been more an objection than it is now. To some modern minds this provides the connexion with the real world which they find otherwise hard to grasp in Spenser.

The Faerie Queen is a work of its time in its prolixity. Elizabethan poets ran riot with words, and Spenser was an amplifier, leisurely of set purpose as Chaucer was leisurely by temperament. There is some bad writing in the poem, and some of the bad taste of the Renaissance, a sort of stucco quality from which a medieval poem like *Sir Gawain* is totally free. But Spenser often writes well. He rescued English poetry in a clumsy epoch. He can be mellifluous, as in the Bower of Bliss:

> So passeth, in a passing of a day,
> Of mortal life the leaf, the bud, the flower . . .

Usually his style is businesslike. He is a visualizer who brings objects clearly before the reader, while at the same time drawing out their moral overtones:

> . . .the rich metal lurked privily,
> As faining to be hid from envious eyes;
> Yet here, and there, and everywhere, unwares
> It shewed itself, and shone unwillingly:
> Like a discolourd Snake, whose hidden snares
> Through the green gras his long bright burnisht back declares.

Spenser's virtues as a stylist are the typical virtues of prose. He writes lucidly and progressively, he develops and organizes his argument. A good example is Artegall's reply to the communist Giant of the Scales in Book V (whatever we think of the argument itself).

The Faerie Queen contains a considerable variety of stories and tableaux, ranging from the Chaucer-like comic horror-story of Malbecco and Hellenore to the vision of the naked Graces dancing round Mount Acidale. All but aficionados will re-read it only selectively. (Readers who seek a 'shortened course' might well omit Books III, IV and V). *The Faerie Queen* seems to suffer from its dual aim. Those who love Spenser for his revelation of spiritual truth are bored by his framework of knightly adventure and his insistence on action, while those who like adventures are bored because he is so descriptive and meditative. For the former kind of readers the great Spenser is above all in the Mutability Cantos and other 'philosophical' passages in *The Faerie Queen*. In real life Spenser was a man of action, like his contemporaries

Drake and Hawkins and Raleigh, and at times the background of his poem fades into the Irish landscape, with the evil savages lurking in the undergrowth, while Grey and the rest become Justice and Courtesy riding along in mail armour to overcome iniquity. Spenser exalts the active virtues. But his poem is most often quoted for lines which celebrate death and its inviolable rest. The old man who entices Redcrosse in the Cave of Despair is a repulsive figure, but the music of his temptation is seductive.

> He there does now enjoy eternal rest,
> And happy ease which thou dost want and crave,
> And further from it daily wanderest.

This is indistinguishable in feeling from those lines in the Mutability Cantos in which Spenser himself speaks of the heaven for which he yearned:

> For all that moveth doth in change delight,
> But thenceforth all shall rest eternally
> With him that is the God of Sabbaoth hight:
> O thou great Sabbaoth God, grant me that Sabbath sight.

The other chief figure in the English Renaissance, apart from Shakespeare, is Sir Philip Sidney (1554–86), a friend and patron of Spenser. The Elizabethans regarded him as the greatest writer of the age, though almost none of his work was printed in his lifetime. Many of them saw him as the perfect man, Castiglione's Courtier, combining the virtues of the public servant and soldier with the learning and culture of the man of letters. This ideal picture was completed when Sidney went out to serve the Protestant cause in the Low Countries as Governor of Flushing and was mortally wounded at Zutphen. His biographer Fulke Greville is the authority for the story of his death at Arnhem and his refusal of the cup of water ('Thy necessity is greater than mine').

As a poet, Sidney belonged to the circle which includes Spenser, Gabriel Harvey, and Dyer (of 'My mind to me a kingdom is'). He made metrical versions of the Psalms which were admired well into the seventeenth century – Crashaw praises them – but his reputation now rests on the sonnet sequence *Astrophel and Stella*, published posthumously in 1591. This was very popular, and gave rise to countless imitations. The sonnets have been traditionally associated with Sidney's love for Penelope Devereux. A pun on 'rich' suggests a reference to her marriage to Lord Rich; but it is hard to smelt out literal autobiography from the sonnets. In real life Penelope did not marry Sidney after her divorce from Rich, but her old love Charles Blount. As for Sidney, his imagery and verbal devices are taken from Italian poetry, and there can be no doubt that he was making a contribution to a European literary movement of the time, Petrarchism, which was then in vogue, like Existentialism after 1945. But the argument used by some scholars – 'derivative: therefore insincere' – is a *non sequitur*. No one can read the sequence without recognizing that some of the poems express the feelings of a man tortured by sexual obsessions, and admitting it: 'Art not ashamed to publish thy disease?'. The poems often touch on other matters, news of the day, court gossip, how to write sonnets. When they are love poems, they often start from the common experience of any courtly love affair: tokens of favour or disfavour from the beloved, the kiss she gives him, her going away, Astrophel's performance in a tournament while Stella watches him. The chronology of the sequence is uncertain. The poems turning on the conflict between Reason and Desire have been thought earlier than those which more single-mindedly express passion. But the poems recur again and again to the conflict. No safe conclusion can be drawn about the real or even the fictitious story. It might have been artistically more satisfying if the sequence had ended, like Chaucer's *Troilus*, with the renunciation of earthly love as a snare and a delusion, in the sonnets 'Thou blind man's mark' and 'Leave me, O love, which reachest but to dust', and it is true that they are sometimes attached to it in popular collections.

However that may be, one thing is certain: for the first time in 200 years England had a master of poetic technique. Sonnet 31, addressed to the moon ('With how sad steps') and sonnet 39, ('Come Sleep, O Sleep') are lovely urbane poems, obviously in the mainstream of English poetry. Sidney has the power of a real poet, of seeming to say all that needs saying about a subject in the simplest possible words:

> My true love hath my heart, and I have his.

Sidney is also admirable in his songs. The Elizabethan period was a great age of English music, and the lyrical Sidney invites musical setting in 'Only joy, now you are here' or 'Who is it that this dark night'. Such songs rank with those of Campion and Dowland.

Sidney's most extensive work in prose, the romance *Arcadia*, is more problematic. Discussion of it is complicated by the need to disentangle just what is meant by 'the *Arcadia*'. Briefly, the situation is this. There were two versions of the *Arcadia*. This has been known since 1907, when the first version, now known as *Old Arcadia*, was discovered. The *Old Arcadia* was completed by 1581. It was revised by Sidney *c*.1583–4, and this version is the *New Arcadia*. This revised version was printed in 1590 and 1593, and appeared with Books III to V of the *Old Arcadia* added. This composite work was 'the *Arcadia*' till the twentieth century. There are inconsistencies among the versions, which makes the 'critical heritage' rather an incoherent one. Like most of the new departures in Tudor literature, the *Arcadia* owed its origin to foreign stimulus, the old Greek romance of Heliodorus, called the *Ethiopic History*. Underdowne's English version was published *c*.1569. Sidney knew of Heliodorus, whom he praises in the *Apology for Poetry*. He includes poems from time to time, some of them of great merit.

How good is the *Arcadia*? Many of us rely (as with Spenser) on the guidance of C.S. Lewis here and if you like Lewis you will enjoy looking at Sidney and Spenser through his eyes. But when he is away, many of us find them rather disappointing. We have the impression that Lewis somewhat overrates the *Faerie Queen*, and that he greatly overrates the *Arcadia*. As far as the *Arcadia* is concerned, he bullies us a little, saying that it is the real test of a reader's depth of sympathy with sixteenth-century literature. The uninstructed reader's impression after its first few pages, with their very long, shapeless, shambling sentences, is that any good writing which may later appear in the work will be there by accident, and this impression is not greatly changed for those who persevere further. There is also a good deal of the wordplay that bores most of us in Shakespeare's plays, and it is not compensated for, as in Shakespeare, by other merits. It is true that the *Arcadia* is sometimes misjudged, by those who have not read it, owing to the mistaken belief that is is 'pastoral'. This belief may have arisen because of the title, or the lovely phrase often quoted from the book, 'a shepherd boy piping as if he would never be old'. The *Arcadia* is not about shepherds piping. It is about (among other things) rape, transvestism, murders, humanistic eloquence, Calvinist theology, politics, and even clowning. But the mannerisms of style through which all this is presented suggest radical immaturities. Of course a gifted man like Sidney does not fail to achieve some good passages. It is enjoyable to find him looking at girls with a courtier-connoisseur's eye.

Philoclea who blushing, and withal smiling, making shamefacedness pleasant, and pleasure shamefaced, tenderly moved her feet, unwonted to feel the naked ground, till the touch of the cold water made a pretty kind of shrugging come over her body, like the twinkling of the fairest among the fixed stars.

And if Sidney did not write good prose in the *Arcadia* it was not from incapacity, as we see from his letter to Molyneux:

I assure you before God, that if ever I know you do so much as read any letter I write to my father, without his commandment, or my consent, I will thrust my dagger into you. And trust to it, for I speak in earnest. In the meantime farewell. From Court this last of May 1578,

By me
PHILIP SIDNEY

The prose of the *Arcadia* is an acquired taste, and readers must consider what C.S. Lewis says in defence of the book and decide whether they think it worth acquiring.

Sidney's best prose is surely in the *Defence of Poetry*, or *Apology for Poetry* as it is sometimes called (the latter title is convenient, to distinguish it from Shelley's *Defence of Poetry*, written in 1821). In this courtly little book, published posthumously in 1595, English literary criticism makes its first bow, and very impressively. The *Apology* was once said to have been provoked by Stephen Gosson's *School of Abuse* (1579), an attack on poets — and play-actors – by an ostensibly repentant ex-playwright, and dedicated to Sidney without his permission. Whether that is so or not, Sidney's 'ink-wasting toy', as he deprecatingly calls it, is quite unpolemical and good-humoured. It has been shown to owe much to Italian Renaissance critics, but Sidney made their neo-Aristotelian theories his own, and his personal taste comes through. There is no better introduction to Renaissance literature in existence. Sidney makes many profound remarks, for example, 'Now for the poet, he nothing affirmeth, and therefore never lieth'. The *Apology* has left us with a complete literary theory in miniature, one that could be accepted by an intelligent person today.

The Italianate literary movement of Sidney and Spenser broadened into a flood of writing of all kinds. There is now so much 'poetry' (in Sidney's sense, i.e. imaginative literature, as we should call it) that writers who would have stood out as major in sparser periods can here rate hardly more than a mention. The much-revising Michael Drayton (1563–1631) is one of them. His long literary career includes successes in several different forms and styles. But perhaps only once does he reach the level of the supremely great, in a sonnet which must, alas, have come to the minds of many English men and women at one moment in their lives.

> Since there's no help, come let us kiss and part.
> Nay, I have done, you get no more of me,
> And I am glad, yea, glad with all my heart,
> That thus so cleanly I myself can free.
> Shake hands for ever, cancel all our vows.
> And should we meet at any time again,
> Be it not seen in either of our brows
> That we one jot of former love retain.

The remaining six lines are not quite at that level: we move into the style of Rupert Brooke, from a great poem to a merely good one. There was a great outburst of sonneteering in the last years of the century. The Italianate verse-pattern had been introduced by Wyatt, but his sonnets are usually so bungled that they could not have influenced anyone. The chief influence on the Elizabethan sonnet was Sidney. The greatest and most mysterious of the sonneteers, however, was the greatest writer of England, and probably of the world. No wonder so many readers have turned eagerly to the Sonnets in the hope of finding out something about Shakespeare's life and personality, as if they were a collection of intimate letters, like those of Keats. Perhaps some of them are. Perhaps some situation of real life may have been behind sonnet 144, about the 'two loves . . . of comfort and despair', 'a man right fair' and 'a woman colour'd ill'. The woman may be the black mistress who appears in a handful of the sonnets, disliked by the poet but irresistibly attractive to him. His love for her is felt to be an ignoble emotion, but one he cannot overcome. About the man everything is disputed. Is he the man who in sonnets placed early in the sequence is urged to marry and beget a son? Is he the 'Mr. W.H.', the 'only begetter' to whom the printer (T. T.) dedicated the sequence? About the man we are told nothing, except that the poet loved him. This love appears as a transcendent experience, something which transformed the poet's whole vision of the world, and could not be assimilated to the categories of everyday life. Here and there traces of a story appear. It is hinted that the friend stole the poet's mistress. A rival poet competes for the young man's favour. But many of the Sonnets have no dramatic intensity. They are meditations on themes of universal appeal. Often the personal reference is of the most formal kind; the ostensible subject, the poet's love for his friend, appears only in the closing couplet, if at all. The themes are of universal interest, the transience of beauty, the destructiveness of time, the immortality of poetry, and (in sonnets placed late in the sequence) the ravages of lust, and the self-deceptions of passion.

This impersonality and lack of particularity allows the reader of the Sonnets great freedom to make them his own. The Sonnets seem to be a collection of occasional verses. Of the 154, about 50 are of the highest excellence. Whether Shakespeare was responsible for the order of the sequence is unknown, nor is it known whether he approved of its publication (in 1609). Imaginative people do not read them to discover Shakespeare's feelings, but to clarify their own.

> So you are to my thoughts as food to life,
> Or as sweet-season'd showers are to the ground.

Was this written to a 'patron'? Who cares? In Shakespeare's plays human passions are shown in close-up. In the Sonnets they are distanced and framed by convention and craftsmanship. The moods expressed range from the serenity of 18 ('Shall I compare thee to a summer's day?') to the hell and degradation of 129 ('The expense of spirit in a waste of shame'), the lofty reflection of 60 ('Like as the waves make towards the pebbled shore'), the sigh of despair of 66 ('Tir'd with all these, for restful death I cry'). This is not Robert Lowell, or Sylvia Plath: we are not given the raw material of the poet's feelings, to give what shape to it we can; the best of the Sonnets send us not to the poet's secrets, but to ourselves and the world. The 'I' of the poems is the ideal reader, pensive and grieving in 30 ('When to the sessions of sweet silent thought'), self-abnegating in 71 ('No longer mourn . . .). They could not have this effect if Shakespeare had not remained a secret man. About the whole sequence there hangs a mystery which cannot be dispelled.

The more philosophical of the Sonnets are a reminder that Shakespeare, as if to show that nothing was beyond his range, was also the author of 'The Phoenix and the Turtle', in which the transcendent power of love is treated with the abstruseness of the Metaphysical Poets, and the accent of mystical religion is heard as it is in Shakespeare's Spanish contemporary, St John of the Cross.

The flood of 'Petrarchan' sonneteering subsided after the 1590s, but the English sonnet has continued. In the seventeenth century Donne and Milton were the greatest masters of the form. Donne did not use the sonnet for love-poems (he may have associated it with the courtly romanticism against which he was reacting) but he turned it into powerful religious drama in his *Holy Sonnets*. Milton used the sonnet for quiet private meditations (as in 'On his Blindness') and dignified public statements (as in 'On the Late Massacre in Piedmont'). For most of the eighteenth century the sonnet was neglected: Gray's sonnet on the death of West is the only well-known one, and it is Gray's only sonnet. The sonnet was revived at the end of that century, and in the next Wordsworth, taking his cue from Milton's sonnets, favoured it for many kinds of occasional utterance, public and private. Keats and Shelley were notable sonneteers of that time. In the Victorian age D.G. Rossetti was the master sonneteer; E. B. Browning the most popular; and Meredith in *Modern Love* wrote a novel in sonnets (of 16 lines each, instead of the usual 14). The linguistic and rhythmic audacities of the strange poet Gerard Manley Hopkins, who favoured this form, moulded the English sonnet into yet another shape. In the twentieth century, W.B. Yeats wrote one unforgettable sonnet, 'Leda and the Swan'. W.H. Auden introduced an original variation of the form, making it accommodate a miniature essay, or character sketch. Poets as various as the dithyrambic Dylan Thomas, the sardonic, plain-spoken Philip Larkin, and the esoteric Geoffrey Hill (b. 1932), have all added to the continuing history of the English sonnet. From the formal point of view Petrarch has prevailed over Shakespeare throughout these centuries; the intricate Italian pattern has been more popular than the simpler Shakespearean model (three quatrains and a final couplet, rhyming a b a b c d c d e f e f g g).

Another Elizabethan form, the mythological romance or 'epyllion' (plural 'epyllia') has lasted less well. The form derives from the *Metamorphoses* of the Roman poet Ovid (43 BC – AD 18), translated into hard vigorous English (in 1565–7) by Arthur Golding. Pound greatly admired Golding's work, and his own *Cantos* represent the last phase of this tradition. The most famous Elizabethan epyllia are the unfinished *Hero and Leander* of Christopher Marlowe, and Shakespeare's sparkling *Venus and Adonis* and (much inferior) *Rape of Lucrece*.

In this period the lyric poet and the composer join hands as never before or since. Thomas Campion (1567–1620) was both. Forgotten after his own day until the end of the nineteenth century, his five books of lutesongs are treasured. He is among the few English poets who have succeeded with unrhymed quantitative verse on the Greek and Roman model: 'Rose-cheek'd Laura' is a lovely example. Campion argued for 'classical' verse and against rhyme (in 1602), and his arguments were answered wisely by another poet, Samuel Daniel, but the best answer is Campion's own rhyming poetry.

All that I sung still to her praise did tend.
Still she was first, still she my songs did end.
Yet she my love and music both doth fly,
The music that her echo is, and beauty's sympathy.
Then let my notes pursue her scornful flight;
It shall suffice that they were breathed, and died for her delight.

This was a time of abundance of airs and madrigals, and songbooks of Dowland, Byrd, Morley, miscellanies like *The Phoenix Nest* (1593), *England's Helicon* (1600) *Poetical Rhapsody* (1602). (Will Bob Dylan or the Beatles last as long as the best of these?). Some of the finest songs are in plays. Lyly's are exquisite; Greene and Peele and Dekker are worthy rivals. Shakespeare's songs are in a class by themselves, not only because of their beauty, but because of their appropriateness in their dramatic contexts, as Auden showed in an essay in *The Dyer's Hand* (1962). The Elizabethan nest of singing-birds could not go on performing for ever, and in the seventeenth century new voices were heard: the harsh argumentative tone of Donne, the clattering satirical talk of Joseph Hall and John Marston, the astringent note of Ben Jonson. The cawing of rooks broke in upon the singing of larks.

Elizabethan prose is more of an age, less for all time, than the best of the poetry, and much of it is too incoherent to be read except in small samples. That a style was needed was clear to John Lyly (*c*.1554–1606) who won fame for *Euphues* (1578) and its sequel (1580), but they will never be read again. They added a word to the language, 'Euphuism'. The definition of Euphuism is disputed, but at any rate it is a highly artificial style, with many antitheses and literary allusions, and insistent alliteration; it is also sententious. Shakespeare laughs at it in *Henry IV, Pt I*.

There is a thing, Harry, which thou hast often heard of, and it is known to many in our land by the name of pitch; this pitch, as ancient writers do report, doth defile; so doth the company thou keepest; for, Harry now I do not speak to thee in drink, but in tears, not in pleasure but in passion, not in words only, but in woes also.

But Shakespeare himself was long in shaking off the Euphuistic influence, if ever he wholly did so. The *Euphues* books are less works of fiction than treatises on the education of a gentleman. More in the tradition of *Arcadia* are romances like Greene's *Pandosto* and Lodge's *Rosalind*, both sources for Shakespeare. There was also realistic fiction: Nashe's *Unfortunate Traveller* (1594), Thomas Deloney's *Jack of Newberry* (1597): and modern readers still enjoy the 'cony-catching' pamphlets for their descriptions of low life in London. There was much pamphleteering at this time, the 'Marprelate', tracts attacking bishops, the abusive polemics between Nashe (with Greene till his death in 1592) and Gabriel Harvey and his brother Richard. It is now difficult to make out just what they are fighting about. At any rate this development of vigorous vernacular writing did much to steer English prose away from Latin rhetorical models. The great exception is the *Ecclesiastical Polity* of Richard Hooker (?1554–1600), the classic apologia for the Anglican middle way between Catholicism and Protestantism. Hooker's project has an ironical sound today, as we look at Ulster, but he was a great man, and there is no stronger 'prose of thought' in the language.

There is not much thought in Thomas Nashe (1567–1601), miscellaneous writer and picturesque literary personality. He wrote in many genres – satire, prose romance, controversy . . . His subjects are the excuse for exuberant effusion. Nashe boasted that he could get 'juice from flint'. What he valued was the 'extemporal vein'. He should interest modern critics, since a typical modern definition of literature ('the use of language for its own sake') perfectly fits Nashe. He is also a master of the alienation effect, as when he retells the story of Hero and Leander in *Lenten Stuff*:

. . . but as on his blue jellied sturgeon lips she was about to clap one of those warm plasters, boisterous woolpacks of ridged tides came rolling in, and raught him from her (with a mind belike to carry him back to Abydos). At that she became a frantic Bacchanal outright, and made no more bones but sprang after him, and so resigned up her priesthood, and left work for Musaeus and Kit Marlowe.

('Musaeus' was supposed to be the original poet of the Hero and Leander story). Nashe is a writer of remarkable power, but perhaps only touches greatness in his poem 'In Time of Pestilence', from *Summers Last Will and Testament*. These are the best known lines:

> Brightness falls from the air,
> Queens have died young and fair,
> Dust has closed Helen's eye . . .
> Mount we unto the sky;
> I am sick, I must die –
> Lord, have mercy upon us.

The horrors of the Plague haunt Elizabethan literature. The description of the nightmare adds a terrifying paragraph to Thomas Dekker's *The Wonderful Year* (1603). This is the dark side of a great period of literature, the period of Elizabethan drama. 'Elizabethan drama' is the accepted term, though many of the best plays belong to the following reign of James (VI of Scotland and I of England), 1603–25, and a few to the reign of his son Charles I (1625–49). The sudden appearance of this great theatrical, dramatic and literary form represents the supersession of a native religious drama dominated by the Catholic Church, by the secular entertainment of a Protestant society, though one still linked with the Old Religion in much of its language and habits of thought and feeling. In pre-Shakespearean drama the most characteristic form of the early period is the Interlude, as in John Heywood's *Play of the Weather* (1533). The effect of classicism then made itself felt. The closet plays of the Roman poet Seneca (d. AD 65) gave the Elizabethan drama melodramatic situations, stories of ghosts and revenge and savage passions, interwoven with sententious moralizing and Stoic philosphy. The first original English tragedy on this model is Sackville and Norton's *Gorboduc* (performed 1561). This quaint old play has not survived in the repertory, but it anticipates much in Shakespeare: high tragic action, fate and retribution, a ghost, a play within a play, and, above all, blank verse – a great invention which replaced the thumping poulter's metre as the norm of English versification. In comedy from the 1550s academic writers drew on the Roman dramatist Plautus (*c.*254–184 BC). *Gammer Gurton's Needle* depends on situation and action; odious but clever Nicholas Udall's *Ralph Roister Doister* pours out verbal absurdities, the doggerel and nonsense which were the froth on the wave of the Elizabethan linguistic revolution. Both plays suggest college lawns and light summer drizzle, but they can provide some entertainment for an audience which comes to them with low expectations. The other chief pre-Shakespearean genre is the chronicle play, or historical interlude, as in John Bale's *King John*: another link with Shakespeare, this time his plays on English history.

The main period of Elizabethan drama began with the writers known as the University Wits, who flourished in the 1580s and 90s. John Lyly, author of *Euphues*, sacrificed plot, character and action to dialogue. As a prose stylist in his comedies he ranks with Congreve and Shaw. Some of the graver writers of the day disapproved of Lyly's success. 'Playing with words and idle similes,' said Drayton. 'A mad lad, as ever twanged,' said Gabriel Harvey, 'sometimes the fiddlestick of Oxford, now the babble of London'. This type of writer is recognizable down to our own day, but Lyly excels all his successors. *Endimion* (1591) is a graceful, stylized little masterpiece of moonlight and playfulness.

George Peele (?1558–?1597) seems to have been a short-lived, passionate, feckless man. His plays are rarely performed now, and he is remembered most for pure poetry, rather than plot or characters. Here is part of a spell from *The Old Wives Tale*:

> Gently dip, but not too deep,
> For fear thou make the golden beard to weep,
> Fair maid, white and red,
> Comb me smooth and stroke my head,
> And every hair a sheaf shall be,
> And every sheaf a golden tree.

As a word-musician Peele ranks with Poe and de la Mare and Edith Sitwell. Yet as a playwright he was capable of fearful ranting. Robert Greene (*c.*1558–92) in *Friar Bacon and Friar Bungay* (*c.*1591) handles the necromancer theme used by his friend Marlowe in *Dr Faustus*, but in a more light-hearted manner. The relation between the two plays is not known.

Greene has more readers today for his pamphlets, which describe the low life of the time, and the posthumous *Greene's Groatsworth of Wit* (1592 – though perhaps not in fact by him) in which he appears in the role of the penitent sinner. It is of historical interest chiefly because it (almost certainly) refers to Shakespeare as 'an upstart crow beautified with our feathers'. This has been thought to mean that Greene was accusing Shakespeare of plagiarism. But perhaps what he resented was the presumptuousness of a player without an Oxford or Cambridge degree (Greene himself had both) thrusting himself into competition with the University Wits. Also associated with the Wits (though perhaps not a university man) was the mysterious Thomas Kyd (1558–95). He is thought to be the author of *The Spanish Tragedy* (?1589), the first known English play to naturalize the dramatic horrors of Seneca in a form which conquered the popular stage. It was the first revenge drama, a prototype of what is now called 'the serious thriller'. (William Empson wrote one of his best essays on it.) Kyd may have been the author of a lost play on the Hamlet story which influenced Shakespeare. He was a friend of Marlowe and played some part in the darker side of Marlowe's life.

With the cruelly brief career of Christopher Marlowe, born in 1564, the same year as Shakespeare, and killed in a Deptford tavern in 1593, began the great period of English drama. Much about Marlowe's life and death is disputed, and the most recent scholarship emphasizes our almost total ignorance about them. His work also presents many problems. His major plays are *Tamburlaine the Great* (in two parts), *The Jew of Malta*, *The Tragical History of Dr Faustus*, and *Edward II*. They may have been written between 1587 and 1593. Marlowe was the first major poet of the English drama. Ben Jonson spoke of his 'mighty line'. Here are a few examples.

> Batter the shining palace of the sun . . .
>
> Adding this golden sentence to our praise
> That Peter's heirs should tread on emperors . . .
>
> Infinite riches in a little room . . .
>
> And ride in triumph through Persepolis . . .
>
> Was this the face that launched a thousand ships,
> And burnt the topless towers of Ilium?

It is easy to see why *Tamburlaine*, which introduced this style, made such an impact. But the mighty lines often bear little relation to the total structure of the plot or the character who speaks them. Bajazet and Tamburlaine, Faustus and the Jew of Malta, even the cowardly and feeble Edward II, are all capable of the Marlovian fortissimo. The versification is often splendid but soon becomes monotonous, because of the regular end-stopping, (i.e. the sense is frequently completed at the end of the line). Elizabethan dramatists often did this, as in *Hamlet*:

> Angels and ministers of grace defend us!

but Shakespeare, unlike Marlowe, more often continues the sense into the next line, as in:

> But look, the morn in russet mantle clad
> Walks o'er the dew of yon high eastward hill.

Marlowe's characteristic movement is quite different:

> Now clear the triple region of the air,
> And let the majesty of Heaven behold
> Their scourge and terror tread on emperors.
> Smile, stars that reigned at my nativity,
> And dim the brightness of your neighbour lamps!
> Disdain to borrow light of Cynthia!

Marlowe's genius seems sometimes epic, sometimes lyrical, rarely dramatic. When he is dramatic he is a maker of scenes rather than whole plays. The last scene of *Dr Faustus* is among the most compelling in English drama:

> O I'll leap up to my Christ: who pulls me down?

But as a whole the play makes the impression of a glittering façade behind which is nothing but dust and rubbish. Even allowing for textual corruption, it is impossible to agree with Goethe's strange comment: 'How nobly it is all planned!'.

Marlowe's characters are as much personifications as those of the Morality plays. His genius did not lie in the evocation of individual human beings, and his best character is not a human being at all, but Mephistopheles:

> Why this is hell, nor am I out of it.

Marlowe was the quintessential Elizabethan in his passion for excess. After this stage direction 'Enter three Jews' Barabas exclaims:

> Why how now countrymen?
> Why flock you thus to me in multitudes?

'Three' has become 'multitudes'. *Edward II* has been seen as a hint that Marlowe, had he lived, might have developed in a more Shakespearean direction, and certainly it is better constructed than his other plays. It must not be forgotten that he died at 29.

Some of Marlowe's best poetry is in his translations from Ovid, and Lucan. The unfinished narrative poem *Hero and Leander* (ably completed, in a more corrugated style, by George Chapman) shows sustained poetic power. He blends force and sweetness in the rhymed couplet in a way that had never been done before; he is the poetic ancestor here of both Dryden and Keats. This puts him in the main stream of English poetry, in view of his own debt to

Spenser. To come to the voluptuousness of *Hero and Leander* from Spenser's Bower of Bliss is like coming from Botticelli to Titian.

Marlowe's rhetoric was much imitated by other Elizabethan dramatists, but soon came to be parodied and mocked. Shakespeare makes the empty braggart Pistol use 'Marlowe's mighty line'. But in *As You Like It* the love-lorn Phebe quotes the most famous line from *Hero and Leander*:

> Who ever loved, that loved not at first sight?

and here there is no mockery of *Hero and Leander*, or of the 'dead shepherd' who wrote it.

Shakespeare's plays are an institution of the English-speaking world. No players are regarded as great unless they have appeared in them with success. But William Shakespeare (1564–1616) made no effort to win recognition for his work. Like J.S. Bach, his immense strength functioned without self-consciousness, and like Bach he is impossible to generalize about: he is all trees and no wood. Little is known of Shakespeare's life. He was the son of respectable parents in the country town of Stratford on Avon. He was a married man and a father. He was a member of a company of London actors under noble and (in James I's reign) royal patronage. He enjoyed at least enough financial success to buy a good house in his native town and to spend his later years there. Most of what is known about him is only known because he was a frequent litigant, so that to write his life is like trying to write a modern man's life solely on the basis of his income tax returns.

Shakespeare did not himself issue a collected edition of his plays. Individual plays were published during his lifetime, and scholarship has done much to establish which among these (the so-called Good Quartos) best represent what he wrote. But the chief authority for the text and canon of his plays is the collected edition known as the First Folio (1623), published after his death by his fellow-actors Heminge and Condell. The editors of the Folio did not arrange the plays in order of composition but (roughly) according to genre – Comedies, Histories, Tragedies. There is still much dispute over the dates of many plays. Internal evidence is sometimes helpful, but it must be remembered that in some cases the extant texts may have been revised by Shakespeare himself. It was once widely held that the plays were of composite authorship. Elizabethan dramatists did collaborate, Beaumont with Fletcher, Middleton with Rowley. The play of *Sir Thomas More*, which survives in manuscript, is clearly the work of several playwrights, one of whom may be Shakespeare. Some of his earlier plays especially have been thought to be reworkings of plays by other dramatists, while among the later plays non-Shakespearean material has often been seen in *Measure for Measure*, *Macbeth*, *Timon*, and *Henry VIII* (with great probability in the last three). However – a fact rarely mentioned – Leonard Digges, who knew Shakespeare personally, says in his tribute printed at the beginning of the Third Folio that

Shakespeare did not collaborate with other writers. As for the suggestion that the plays are wholly, or mainly, the work of some other writer, it is not worth discussing. No convincing reason has ever been given for doubting the good faith of the Folio editors. The Baconian theory necessitates belief in the existence of a vast conspiracy, involving the participation of some people whose known character makes it out of the question.

Shakespeare established once and for all the major note of English poetry. Some of his plays were clearly written in haste and contain bad writing, sometimes due to mere carelessness, sometimes to his passion for quibbling and wordplay – here he is very Elizabethan. Shakespeare wrote excellent prose, the best prose of his time. But most of his plays are in verse. His good verse is in two styles. Here is an example of the first:

> Five hundred poor I have in yearly pay,
> Who twice a day their wither'd hands hold up
> Toward heaven, to pardon blood; and I have built
> Two chantries, where the sad and solemn priests
> Sing still for Richard's soul.
>
> (*Henry V*, IV.1.)

This style seems to occur more in Shakespeare's supposedly earlier plays than in the later ones, and it appears at its best in eloquent oratorical speeches, like those of Antony in *Julius Caesar*:

> If you have tears, prepare to shed them now.
> You all do know this mantle: I remember
> The first time ever Caesar put it on;
> 'Twas on a summer's evening, in his tent,
> That day he overcame the Nervii.
>
> (*Julius Caesar*)

If Shakespeare had always written like this, it would not be absurd to call him an exact and lucid writer. But no one could call him that, and the reason is to be found in his second style:

> She is that queen of Tunis, she that dwells
> Ten leagues beyond man's life, she that from Naples
> Can have no note, unless the sun were post,
> The man i' the moon's too slow, till new-born chins
> Be rough and razorable, she that from whom
> We were all sea-swallow'd, though some cast again,
> And by that destiny, to perform and act
> Whereof what's past is prologue, what to come
> Is yours and my discharge.
>
> (*The Tempest*, II.1.)

This rapid, elliptical style, leaping from one thought or image to another before the first is fully uttered, is typically Shakespearean. Some of his most miraculous passages are in this style, but it should not be forgotten that Shakespeare can write magnificently in the first style too. In fact most of the styles of English poets are echoed or anticipated in Shakespeare.

Shakespeare is best read with nothing but the text and the reader's imagination. But the reader should imagine the play as being performed in a theatre, however hazily his conception of it may resemble the stage of Shakespeare's time, in so far as scholars have been able to reconstruct it. There is much controversy about the Elizabethan playhouse, and particular points must be referred to specialists. Three things need above all to be realized.

1. The plays were played fast ('the two hours' traffic of our stage').

2. There was no approximation to the ideal of the naturalistic theatre, the effect of a real-life room with one wall removed. An Elizabethan play was a narrative for voices. Sometimes the characters' speech is realistic, but often it is not; the dramatist may be doing other things with it, such as telling the story, or creating 'atmosphere'.

3. There was not much in the way of scenery; so the scene could change rapidly, unlike Victorian productions of Shakespeare, with their long pauses between acts. But the costumes were splendid, and much use was made of music. Shakespeare is encrusted with stage traditions. To mention one among thousands, 'Thisbe' falls on the scabbard instead of the sword in the Mechanicals' play in *A Midsummer Night's Dream*. This is a piece of business which may go back to Shakespeare's own time.

For literary and dramatic interpretation it is widely agreed that the outstanding Shakespearean critics in English are Johnson, Coleridge, and A.C. Bradley. In more recent times George Wilson Knight (author of *The Wheel of Fire*, 1930) was the most original and inspired. At present there is no critique recognized as the most distinguished representation of modern views, but the Pole Jan Kott has had a great deal of influence on productions with his *Shakespeare our Contemporary* (English translation 1964). Equally challenging, and superior in scholarship, is A.P. Rossiter's *Angel with Horns* (1961).

Shakespeare is difficult to compare with other writers, English or otherwise. He is perhaps unique in being both a great classic and an author whom people actually like (it is hard to imagine anyone *liking* Aeschylus or Dante). His status in literature is also peculiar. He is 'the Janus of poets', said Dryden. At his best he is the best of poets, at his worst the worst. The great detractors, from Robert Greene to Tolstoy, agree about his main fault: his bombast. There are a few English authors who seem to have no counterparts in other literature; among them are Swift, Keats, Jane Austen, and Dickens. Shakespeare has qualities in common with all of these, but he is unlike them in the range of his art. Unlike any of them he can write *both*

> Night's candles are burnt out, and jocund day
> Stands tiptoe on the misty mountain tops
> > (*Romeo and Juliet*)

and

> . . . This house is turned upside down since Robin Ostler died.
> Poor fellow! never joyed since the price of oats rose; it was the death of him.
> > (The Carriers in *Henry IV*, Part I)

Shakespeare was not 'a bright particular star', but a constellation. Most writers, even major ones, have only one masterpiece (at most), but Shakespeare has about twenty, and many of us are Bardolaters (to use Bernard Shaw's word) who would add even more names to the list.

The Comedy of Errors is widely agreed by scholars to be Shakespeare's earliest play. It is worth reading. Shakespeare the poet is present, and there is some sense of character. But the business of the twins (Shakespeare introduces two pairs) has lost its power to entertain. Duly cut, and with ballet, comedy tricks, and music added, it can work, if the Dromios are good. *Titus Andronicus* is Grand Guignol. There are some fine lines of poetry, but the characters are puppets, except Aaron the Moor. It is a revenge play, Tamora against the Andronici, the Andronici against Tamora. It outdoes *The Spanish Tragedy* in horrors. If it is by Shakespeare it is anomalous; Professor Alfred Harbage has shown that it violates all the moral conventions observed by Shakespeare in other plays. But no other good reason has ever been given for excluding it from the canon. *The Taming of the Shrew* is still popular. It touches the relationship of the sexes at its liveliest point, the mixture of antagonism and affection, though Shakespeare's later treatment of this theme in Benedick and Beatrice may be preferred. The best productions make us feel that the Man and Woman have come to love each other and accept the fact, and suggest a growing attachment under the Man's roughness. Katharina's speech of submission, the greatest defence of Christian monogamy ever written, is usually delivered ironically to-day, but it is doubtful whether Shakespeare's audience would have seen irony in it. As in many of Shakespeare's plays the setting is Italian. But the Induction is deeply English, and greater than anything in the play itself:

> Christopher Sly, old Sly's son of Burton Heath, by birth a pedlar, by education a
> card-maker, by transmutation a bear-herd, and now by present profession a tinker.
> Ask Marion Hacket, the fat ale-wife of Wincot, if she know me not.

But after a single intervention Sly drops out of the play. *The Taming of a Shrew*, a strange play the relation of which to Shakespeare's is not known, finds more work for him to do.

The Two Gentlemen of Verona also seems to be early. The poetry suggests *Venus and Adonis*, and the Sonnets, in lines such as 'The uncertain glory of an April day'. Proteus is a stuffed shirt, and Speed a wisecracking puppet – but it is to be feared that the dramatist thought him a pretty wit. On the stage, with music, costumes, and a good clown for Launce, it may pass, but would probably not be remembered without Shakespeare's name. *Love's Labour's Lost* is full of topical allusions and in-jokes that have lost their point, but it is often revived with success. It is not clear who the main character is; probably Armado the Spaniard. The pageant at the end can be made funnier than its counterpart in *A Midsummer Night's Dream*. The humour of Costard is kindly; where Sir Nathaniel fails in the part of Alexander he says:

There, an't shall please you, a foolish mild man; an honest man, look you, and soon dash'd. He is a marvellous good neighbour, faith, and a very good bowler; but for Alisander – alas! you see how 'tis – a little o'er parted.

(i.e. the part is a bit too much for him.) The clouding of the scene at the end is a masterstroke. And after all the literary fancies and ingenuities the play ends with the lovely naturalness of 'When icicles hang by the wall'.

Romeo and Juliet is one of the masterpieces of Shakespeare's early maturity. He never wrote anything better than the Balcony scene. The play has many affinities with Shakespeare's comedies, and it could be described as a comedy that ends unhappily. With the death of Mercutio ('A plague o' both your houses!') the lightness goes out of the play. (There is an old tradition that Shakespeare said he had to kill Mercutio or be killed by him, which only makes sense if he himself played the part.) The play captures audiences with its swiftness of movement, the impatience of the lovers, the suddenness and brevity of their love:

> 'Tis like the lightning which doth cease to be
> Ere one can say, it lightens.

In *A Midsummer Night's Dream* Shakespeare created a new kind of play. It is a poem of the imagination. Oberon and Titania live in a vast universe: Oberon arrives from the steep of India. The atmosphere is pervaded by the 'watery' moon and allusions to waves and weeping and wet flowers. It is a world of moist earth and darkness, like Keats's *Nightingale* Ode, until in Act IV dawn comes and the hounds of Theseus set the forest ringing. The Mechanicals' play is like a parody of *Romeo and Juliet* done with affection in the style of bumbling old plays in which Shakespeare himself may have acted. The end of the play is inspired. The commonsense of daylight has banished the fantasies and delusions of the night. But the Fairies are given the last word. Perhaps after all it is not they but Theseus and his court, and we the audience, who are unreal shadows.

With three plays on the reign of Henry VI Shakespeare set his decisive stamp on the English chronicle play, if indeed he did not invent it, as even the cautious Professor F.P. Wilson thought probable. The verse of the plays is like Marlowe's, but already Shakespeare, a practising actor (as Marlowe was not) has learned the value for dramatic speech of breaking up the end-stopped verse and making the passage, not the line, his unit. These plays are the tense saga of an age of civil war, with a topical message for contemporaries. The Jack Cade scenes seem the most alive; Cade himself, with Dick Butcher, Jack the Weaver, and the two anonymous rebels (we have only the actors' names, Bevis and John Holland) are more lively than the nobility.

From the long tale of national disaster and the conflict of factions Richard Crookback emerges brilliantly as a character. Richard is witty. In his repartee, as in his wooing of Anne, he carries the audience with him in *Richard III*. Like many of Shakespeare's best drawn characters, he is consciously histrionic. The play anticipates the great tragedies but does not rank with them, because Richard, unlike Hamlet or Othello or the Macbeth of the early acts, is a murderer who delights to kill. Like *Richard II* and *Henry V* the play is primarily a star vehicle, and it is more popular than either.

Richard II is a historical chronicle, treated with lyricism. In the first half the poet-king speaks with the usual Shakespearean official rhetoric, but faced with his rival Bolingbroke he changes to an elegiac note. In the abdication scene in Act IV he takes the role of Christ. (The theme of a prince dethroned was then a tricky one, and the first three quartos omit this scene.) The mirror episode shows his self-pity. He is an Elizabethan poet, making his prison a symbol as he composes a poem in the Metaphysical style, taking a cue from the music he overhears. From the beginning of Act IV onwards the play seems to go off the rails, and it is obscure. The most reasonable interpretation is that Richard has been a bad king who brought his fate on himself. But his memory goes on in the historical plays as sympathetic, in what Hotspur says of him in *Henry IV*, in Henry IV who ousted him and can never forget it, in Henry V's efforts to atone. The *Richard* plays are like concertos: *Richard II* for violin, *Richard III*, a great theatre melodrama, for brass and percussion.

Henry IV is in two parts: Hal is the hero of both. If someone knew nothing of Shakespeare and asked which was his best play, *Henry IV* would be a good choice. In Part I the balance is held between the Boar's Head tavern and the scenes of politics and war; the magnificence of Hotspur is thrown into the scale against Falstaff, with Prince Hal squarely between the two of them. But in Part II the Falstaff scenes are richer, with Doll Tearsheet, a fuller treatment of Quickly, Pistol, Falstaff's new page, and Justice Shallow's orchard, which represents the rural heartland of England. Hal is a hero, but drawn with some realism, while Falstaff, his 'misleader', is an old scoundrel drawn with some tenderness. Falstaff speaks for the irresponsible sensual man. He is a mimic and parodist, but he has his own style, short-breathed, with short phrases. The drift of *Henry IV* is steadily towards Hal's regeneration as Henry V; Falstaff, a titanic figure of comedy, is from the structural point of view merely an interlude. But things do not quite work out like that. Part II is not such a good play as Part I. The remnants of the Hotspur rebels are tame and colourless. The shabby trick extinguishing the rebellion is given to Prince John, of whom Falstaff says:

Good faith, this same young sober-blooded boy doth not love me, nor a man cannot make him laugh, but that's no marvel, he drinks no wine.

These scenes are dead wood in the play. Hal can't be mixed up in them. Falstaff and Hal appear together only in one scene in which Hal's share is very minor. To keep the balance steady Hal has a moving scene with his dying father. But our hearts are with Falstaff; the high-minded moral precepts which Henry IV and Hal exchange do not prepare us for the denouement, the rejection ('My king! my Jove! I speak to thee, my heart!'). Two-thirds of the play is Falstaff's, full of gusto. For the rest, the rebellion scenes are wearisome, and the King's scenes at best a dignified pause from laughter; and the end is anti-climactic. The *Henry IV* plays are not as popular in the theatre as the star vehicles. There is no single leading part: the honours are divided between Falstaff and Hotspur, with Hal a close third.

In *Henry V* the Hostess's account of Falstaff's death closes the account on the mighty comedy of *Henry IV*. Pistol, Bardolph, and Nym remain, but look shrunken and pathetic without their master. The Choruses, and other stirring speeches, make *Henry V* a great poem of war, but it lacks dramatic thrust; only an emotion outside the play, English patriotism, holds it together (the French and the Welsh were always good for a laugh). Henry V was a national hero because he defeated the French army and refused to do his French lessons, so Shakespeare confines himself to undercurrents of realism; the common soldiers like Bates and Williams have their say, and the ruthlessness of Henry's character is not glossed over.

As a pendant to the two history cycles may be mentioned *King John*, not one of Shakespeare's successful plays. He seems not to have made up his mind whether John was a Richard III or a Richard II; in the first half John is the former, in the second half the latter. There are two terrific moments. One is the fascination John uses on Hubert to incite him to murder Arthur, with the sudden:

> . . . Thou art his keeper.
> *Hubert.* And I'll keep him so
> That he shall not offend your majesty.
> *King John.* Death.
> *Hubert.* My lord?
> *King John.* A grave.
> *Hubert.* He shall not live.

And there is a great death scene, with the fever raging in the poisoned king. This is fine material for an actor, but no pattern for a play.

Shakespeare's comedies all have a continuous stage history. *The Merry*

Wives of Windsor would be no-one's choice for his best play, but it is useful to librettists making an opera on Falstaff. In this play Falstaff is turned into a farcical puppet (the opposite of what Dickens did with Pickwick). Shakespeare brings back some old characters and introduces some new ones, notably the Wives themselves, unlike anything he did before or since. He seems to dally with his new creatures instead of getting on with the job – traditionally, a royal command – of showing Falstaff in love, but eventually does so, and manages some amusing plot incident and salty dialogue. But he is not engaged as a poet; the young lovers, Fenton and Anne, are untinged with romance. Finally Shakespeare salutes the Knights of the Order of the Garter and brings his characters home to 'laugh this sport o'er by a country fire,/Sir John and all.'

The Merchant of Venice is one of the major plays. It has all the elements of successful theatre. Its dramatic potentialities have been exploited by producers in every imaginable way. There have been magnificent Shylocks and Portias (what are really needed are magnificent Salarios and Salarinos). Bassanio has reminded some critics of the Man in the Sonnets, and the Poet's attitude there may be reflected in Antonio's. Bassanio is the romantic lead. He is sometimes seen as a fortune hunter: 'her sunny locks/Hang on her temples like a golden fleece.' But the noble verse he is given suggests that Shakespeare did not regard him in this way. The play is not profoundly realistic: Venice is fabulous, Belmont fairytale. Its dramatic force comes from Shylock, the underdog out for revenge. Shylock must have been borrowed from Marlowe's Barabas, but he is never allowed to say such things as Barabas says. He is never wholly unsympathetic. The Holocaust has made the character difficult to present to-day. In the past the part has been treated very variously: Dogger at the beginning of the eighteenth century made the Jew a comic figure; Macklin made him realistic; Kean made him savage; Irving went for pathos. This playgoer's vote would be for a tragic Shylock, but not the sympathetic kind of tragedy: a tragedy of terror, not pity. But as with the other two great Jews of English literature, Fagin and Svengali, there are many problems here in securing steady canons of literary judgment.

The other comedies are more balanced; they have no Shylocks. But they are less thrilling. In *Much Ado About Nothing* (mostly in prose) Shakespeare makes the Hero/Claudio plot acceptable by attaching a realistic subplot and playing up the comedy. The 'Dad's Army' characters, Dogberry, Verges, etc. are usually misplayed. There is a good deal of commonsense about Dogberry:

Dogberry. You are to bid any man stand, in the prince's name.
Watch. How if 'a will not stand?
Dogberry. Why then, take no note of him, but let him go, and presently call the rest of the watch together, and thank God you are rid of a knave.

The constables are quiet, serious, proud of their office. While the clever souls are led astray, they arrest the right people (though for the wrong reasons). With Beatrice and Benedick Shakespeare made a new dramatic instrument for the English language, never surpassed even by Shakespeare himself; only Congreve and Sheridan at their best can equal it. Few actresses are up to the rapidity needed for Beatrice: 'a star danced, and under that was I born.' Her lines always have that dancing gleam. 'Would it not grieve a woman to be o'ermastered with a piece of valiant dust? to make an account of her life with a clod of wayward marl?'.

As You Like It revolves round the myth of the Golden Age, i.e. the belief that country life is more natural than court life, shepherds are innocent, the vices of the civilized disappear 'under the greenwood tree', wickedness and injustice die in the fresh air. Wordsworth appears to have held these views, but Shakespeare's attitude is more detached. The heroine, Rosalind, at first seems to belong with the disillusioned critics, 'melancholy' Jaques and cynical Touchstone. But she is herself a woman in love, and she criticizes the critics. Rosalind is a very difficult part: there is a danger of brassiness. She has to convey tenderness as well as ardour. *As You Like It* is full of music; everyone sings, men, women and boys. The play harmonizes like a madrigal or rondo.

Twelfth Night also is full of music, but Orsino's musicians play him melodies with 'a dying fall'. Feste sings:

> What is love? 'tis not hereafter,
> Present mirth hath present laughter,
> What's to come is still unsure:
> In delay there lies no plenty;
> Then come kiss me, sweet and twenty,
> Youth's a stuff will not endure.

Malvolio is the outsider, like Shylock. Andrew and Toby are too inarticulate to formulate the reason for their opposition to him, but they have one: he threatens their 'cakes and ale' philosophy. His exposure and baiting present problems to the modern audience, like Molière's *Le Bourgeois Gentilhomme*: 'class' comedy seems cruel. This aspect of *Twelfth Night* is one of the few moments when Shakespeare seems like Ben Jonson. But the warmth and sweetness of the play as a whole mark it firmly as Shakespearean, and it remains very popular.

The tragedies by common consent are Shakespeare's greatest achievement. *Julius Caesar* is one of his most readable plays, and it always grips those with an interest in politics and great affairs. It can be seen as centred on the conflict of three contrasted men: Brutush, Cassius, Antony. What will come to the top in the new order which will follow Caesar's fall? Not the people, volatile as usual; not the confused liberalism of Brutus; not the passionateness of Cassius; not the popular arts of Antony, master of 'the media' of his day; but the cool, keen ruthlessness of Octavius, whom we shall meet again in *Antony and Cleopatra*. Shakespeare shows his respect for Plutarch by subduing his own racy style to the dignified atmosphere of marble statues and the well-turned phrases of public men. Brutus is an orator not only in the Forum but in his private tent. He is no Henry V: his intellectual consideration of other men stifles his powers and makes him ineffective in action. Unusually in Shakespeare, the play portrays only a male world: the pleas of Portia and Calpurnia are put aside. Shakespeare diverges from Plutarch in the character of Caesar, with his deaf ear and falling sickness, his changes of mind, his love of flattery, his superstition. Shaw saw this as a travesty and in his own *Caesar and Cleopatra* presented Caesar as a Great Man, but Shakespeare's Caesar is truer to what we know of modern tyrants.

With *Hamlet* Shakespeare created by anticipation a large part of Romantic and Modern literature. By now he was skilled in the art of burying his intentions deep, and *Hamlet* is a play of questions: everything on earth, and in heaven and hell besides, is questioned, except the duty of a son to avenge his father. Shakespeare has rehandled an old melodrama and turned a saga figure into a protean and unpredictable character like the Essexes and Raleighs of his own day. The 'variety' of *Hamlet* which Johnson praised comes in part from its discursiveness, as the Prince turns over the thoughts of Montaigne on the human condition, or Quintilian on the player's tears, or reflects on drinking-customs or fashions in handwriting, or jokes with the Gravedigger in the strangest 'comic relief' ever written. '*Hamlet* without the Prince' is a byword for absurdity, and the part is notoriously a supreme opportunity (or temptation) for the actor. But in fact it is tantalizingly elusive, because Hamlet is not a well focused character; he so often speaks for all of us that it is difficult to see him in profile. More firmly drawn are the Ghost – the best in all drama – the dark soul of King Claudius, the small tragedy of Ophelia, a flower swept away in the waters, the amusing portrait of Polonius, drawn with the incisiveness of Jane Austen. Not all is well. The 'Knife and Fork' (i.e. Rosencrantz and Guildenstern) had to wait for Tom Stoppard to make them interesting; the Queen is there to react rather than to act; and Horatio, after a promising beginning, dwindles to an 'Is 't so, my lord?', 'My lord –' etc. But there is not much dead wood in *Hamlet*. English Literature may be too great to have one single greatest work; but if it has one this may be it. But perhaps it appealed more to the nineteenth century than it does to the twentieth.

Othello has more dramatic thrust than *Hamlet*, which is leisurely. Shaw found the fury of Othello's jealousy 'ridiculous' – *he* would! *Othello* is a study in primitive passion. The racial aspect is important, though Shakespeare does not concern himself with ethnological accuracy. Othello is the blackamoor, the African, the Ethiopian, like Aaron with thick lips and woolly hair, or like Morocco in *The Merchant of Venice* who apologizes for his 'complexion' which repels Portia: 'The shadowed livery of the burnished sun'. The play doesn't work unless it is made clear that Othello was very conscious of how the world would judge his marriage, and the high probability of Desdemona's infidelity. Iago must have spoken for many Europeans:

When she is sated with his body, she will find the error of her choice; she must have change! she must!

The part of Othello is difficult for the actor. The Moor is first above passion ('Keep up your bright swords, or the dew will rust them'), and then its slave ('I will chop her into messes. Cuckold me!'). The sardonic vivacity of slanderer Iago makes his role an easier one. Othello's agony is so fully revealed that he cannot be judged from the outside. The heart of it is 'To be *discarded* thence!' His final rehabilitation is a wonderful stroke of theatre. He has sunk so low that it seems impossible – until you see it done. *Othello* is the most harrowing of Shakespeare's plays. Johnson found the scene of Desdemona's murder 'not to be endured'.

King Lear is often said, especially in the twentieth century, to be Shakespeare's greatest play. It is interpreted by many critics as showing the spiritual rebirth of an arbitrary and stupid tyrant. But Goneril in the first half gets a lot of audience sympathy, and the storm scenes, centred on the storm in Lear's soul, though tremendous to read, are difficult to stage. (And don't they evoke terror rather than pity?) The quietness of Lear's scenes with Cordelia, the exquisite simplicity of the writing, perhaps bring the audience round to Lear's side. But by then the structural problems of the play are felt by the playgoer, not only in the study. The audience can readily see the subplot of Gloster's folly and its nemesis as a parallel to the story of Lear, showing us a relentless world in which such things commonly happen. But the attempt to handle two plots adds to the many inconsistencies, especially in the subplot; the developments inadequately prepared, the arbitrary twists. Edgar is the chief problem here. Why didn't he reveal himself to his blinded father when there was no need for further concealment? Why did he then indulge in a series of different impersonations which defeat the actor and baffle the audience? Kent, too, well drawn in the first half, is almost dropped in the second. The Fool is dismissed without explanation. Scholars explain that he is no longer needed, since the mad king has taken over his functions; but he has moved us, and it is strange to let him go without one note of lament.

Shakespeare in his lighter plays is in the habit of sweeping us through an improbable plot. But *Lear* is not a fantasy world. There is emphasis on the gods, the heavens, the eternal vengeance, the justicers above, the stars which govern our conditions. We have to feel that 'this is life'. *Lear* invites the attention of the metaphysician, the theologian, without ever seeming quite to complete its questioning of the universe. In so far as it is coherent it succeeds with straightforward ironies. Lear's homelessness at his daughter's court becomes his homelessness among the elements. The king who thought he needed a hundred knights meets a man who has only a blanket. Mad Lear fantasises about stripping humanity bare. In his torment of mind he grows suddenly and obscenely gross, like Hamlet, Othello, and Timon. Contrary to Bradley's 'redemptionist' view of the play, Lear does not seem very different at the end from what he was at the beginning: he is still self-absorbed, still straining in vain to catch the words he longs to hear from the quiet daughter. But of course there is an immeasurable difference in the attitude of the audience. Perhaps the twentieth century has not gone far wrong in preferring as its tragic symbol, not the glamorous figure of young Prince Hamlet, but the confused, stricken, cursing old man who has made a mess of everything.

Macbeth is one more study of how men throw away their happiness. It has no villain, no Iago or Goneril. It presents evil in itself, rather than evil people. No wonder there are theatre superstitions about it! Anyone who believes in the dark powers (whether literally or not) must feel that no play has evoked them so powerfully. The main problem is the Witches. The producer has to get behind period superstitions to the perennial terror. Three old women suddenly vanish, in an instant.

> Can such things be,
> And overcome us like a summer's cloud.
> Without our special wonder?'

The completeness of the Macbeths' self-identification with evil cannot be denied. Lady Macbeth calls on the spirits of evil to take possession of her. Unlike her husband she could not imaginatively envisage the horror with which her own crime would come to overwhelm her. Her punishment is so terrible – the enactment of damnation in this life – that although she plays an Iago-like part in the temptation and downfall of the hero, by the end of the play no modern audience feels about her as they do about Iago.

Macbeth is the most concentrated and inexorably logical of Shakespeare's tragedies. Its brevity is a function of its impressiveness. However often we may have seen the play the suspense is always felt. As for the hero, we may not 'rejoice in his fall' as Johnson says, but we know too little about him to make us experience a sense of tragic loss. He remains a mystery to himself as well as to us: *why* could he not pronounce Amen? The world of *Macbeth* is a world of strangeness and unnaturalness, covered by 'the blanket of the dark'. The language is pervaded by references to fear and sleeplessness and blood. The crimes of the Macbeths carry their own punishment. The scene of the Lady's sleepwalking is a miniature of the whole play. For the murderers there is no longer any design or sense among the fragments of the past; it is 'a tale/Told by an idiot'. Perhaps that was Shakespeare's own philosophy of life? But the play closes on a different note, 'the grace of Grace'.

Beside the four great tragedies, four anomalous plays – *All's Well that Ends Well*, *Measure for Measure*, *Troilus and Cressida*, *Timon of Athens* – abide our question. They are neither pot-boilers nor masterpieces. *All's Well* is about the pursuit of handsome young Bertram by the lady doctor Helena. She has

caught the interest of Shaw and other feminists. But few care much for
Bertram, or for his friend, braggart Parolles, whose exposure constitutes the
subplot, until his 'Simply the thing I am/Shall make me live' reveals a human
soul as if by a lightning flash. The most sympathetic characters in the play are
the old people, the Countess, Lafeu, and the King. The scenes at Rousaillon
have something of the quality of a 'mood' play by Tchehov. *Measure for
Measure* is linked with *All's Well* by its use of the 'bed trick'. In an
Elizabethan play, said William Empson, it is assumed that a man cannot tell
one woman from another in the dark. We have also to accept the convention of
the Duke's impenetrable disguise, and his unexplained procrastination in
revealing himself and dealing out rewards and punishments. The manoeuvres
of the 'Duke of dark corners' have been explained as an allegory of – or satire
on? – the ways of God to Man, but only three words of the text support this,
when repentant Angelo says '. . . I perceive your grace, *like power
divine*,/Has look'd upon my passes'. In the theatre the incomprehensibility of
the Duke's behaviour is thrust on us. But the first two acts of *Measure for
Measure* are very powerful. Angelo is a victim of 'the expense of spirit in a
waste of shame'. The passion of his lust is set against the passion of Isabella's
chastity. Her part needs great acting gifts. Any hint in the player of smug
self-righteousness wrecks the character and the play. In the second part of the
play there is a steep drop in the quality of both the drama and the poetry.
Angelo becomes a mere tool of the plot. The play swings away from the
Isabella–Angelo story to the comedy of the prison scenes – Lucio, Pompey,
Abhorson – and very good these are. *Measure for Measure* as a whole is
disappointing both as theatre and drama. But there are two great scenes which
gain by stage representation – one in Act II, when Isabella turns with rage and
loathing on Angelo, and the other in Act III, when she finds that her brother
clings more to his own life than to his sister's honour.

   Timon and *Troilus and Cressida* have rarely been thought successful, but
they have elements of strong drama and poignant poetry. Timon's Athens,
unlike Lear's Britain, has no atmosphere. The action is simple: Timon, a
pathological giver, goes to the other extreme of misanthropy. His cursings are
the greatest poetry ever written of that kind, but the lack of effective dramatic
context means that they have only lyric force. There is no reason to think that
an Elizabethan or Jacobean audience ever saw *Timon*. The title rôle, much
loved (and performed) by Wilson Knight, is a great operatic part, unequalled
for pitiless, raging bitterness. But the play falls into two halves which
Shakespeare has made no effort whatever to join. *Troilus and Cressida* also
contains much invective. This is how people are apt to talk in the play:

> How now, thou cur of envy,
> Thou crusty batch of nature; what's the news?

or

Why, thou picture of what thou seemest, and idol of idiot worshippers, here's a
letter for thee.

Ulysses has a great speech, 'Time hath, my lord, a wallet on his back', but it
contains far too many epigrams. He is brilliant on Cressida:

> There's language in her eye, her cheek, her lips,
> Nay, her foot speaks . . .

Troilus and Cressida is a chronicle play with a cynical tang which pleases many
twentieth-century tastes. The main problem the play handles is why Homer's
Troy took so long to capture, why the statesmen are at loggerheads with the
generals. With the political interest is interwoven the old story of the lovers
and the go-between (Shakespeare's Pandarus is degraded in comparison with
Chaucer's). There is some tender poetry of love and longing: no wonder the
play deeply appealed to Keats. But the poetry of revulsion has the last word.
Only the harsh voice of cynical Thersites unites the two themes of 'war and
lechery'.

Antony and Cleopatra has something in common with *Troilus and Cressida*;
in both there is a debunking treatment of famous figures. Its total effect is
much more genial and more spacious. The play is a challenge to the producer:
failure here means complete débâcle. One problem is how to bring out the
contrast between Rome and Egypt, on which the play turns, without
overdoing mere spectacle. Antony's fall has happened before the play begins,
so that there is no dramatic predicament to untangle. The old lion's grandeur
and generosity are expressed less in action than by what is said of him,
especially by Cleopatra:

> His delights
> Were dolphin-like, they show'd his back above
> The element they lived in.

Cleopatra herself has a special style and speech-music, flexible and rippling,
suited to lovers who compete in play-acting and are reconciled as quickly as
they quarrel. The final quarrel leads to Antony's death, but even in his last
ghastly struggle to die he forgives her the lie that caused it. He can endure
anything from one who is the opposite of Octavia, 'holy, cold and still'.
Cleopatra is too rarely at rest to be understood. She is the 'right gipsy',
unstable and wayward, yet everything becomes her. Her death scene uniquely
blends tragedy, sensuousness and humour. Acts IV and V of *Antony and
Cleopatra* are perhaps the greatest height English poetry has ever reached.

Coriolanus is not a play that has been much loved. 'Not worth a damn', said
the great actor Irving. Yet it is well designed as a theatre piece; perhaps too
manifestly so to be a great play. Proud Coriolanus has moving moments, but
he alienates audience sympathy from the start: his refusal of praise seems less
due to modesty than to boorishness. The play has lively political interest and

can easily stir excitement in the age of Communism, Democracy, and Fascism. Coriolanus is not a dictator. He hates and mistrusts the people and the tribunes, but he has no wish to rule them. He is not elated by the offer of the consulship, and cannot bring himself to purchase it by truckling to the voters or using the arts of the demagogue. He is 'a lonely dragon'. 'His nature is too noble for this world' – this is stressed, but it does not bring the audience round to his side. But a powerful case is put against the rule of the Many. In *Coriolanus* no one respects the people. Coriolanus himself despises them. Volumnia advises him to deceive them; the dishonest tribunes manipulate them. They are fickle. Coriolanus screams at them:

> You common cry of curs, whose breath I hate,
> As reek o' the rotten fens . . .
>   I banish you!

Some curious plays remain which are all thought to belong to the sunset of Shakespeare's career. *Henry VIII* has a fuller stage history than *Coriolanus*. It has only about four scenes which are generally agreed to be Shakespearean; its virtues are chiefly of the pageant kind. Prospero's farewell to his art in *The Tempest* is often taken for Shakespeare's own farewell, but if so it was the kind of 'positively last appearance' not uncommon in his profession, for he seems to have gone on writing plays after *The Tempest*, perhaps in collaboration with John Fletcher. *Henry VIII* may be one of these. So also may be *The Two Noble Kinsmen*, which is not in the Folio. (It is pretty bad, whoever wrote it.) *Cardenio* is lost. *Pericles* also is not in the Folio: it appears in the second issue of the Third Folio (1664) with six other plays, all agreed to be non-Shakespearean. But it is almost universally agreed that the last three acts of *Pericles* are by Shakespeare, including the brothel scenes. And in the theatre Acts I and II do not seem very different from the rest. Cerimon's magic reminds us of Prospero's. There is a 'reunion scene' between Pericles and his daughter Marina in which 'the music of the spheres' is heard. Marina has something of the same springtime delicacy as Perdita in *The Winter's Tale*.

Cymbeline, a very strange concoction, is chiefly valued for Imogen, a better representative of women in love than any character in Lawrence's misnamed novel. Imogen's love is a consuming passion, yet it has tenderness, delicacy and reserve. She comes to life in her short queries and interjections: 'O for a horse with wings!' is rapture. Otherwise, the play is unsatisfactory on the stage. Despite the assured writing in the first three acts, Cymbeline himself is wooden and his wicked queen is too like her counterpart in *Snow White*. But Iachimo is lively, especially in the superb prose of the wager scenes. The play begins to falter from III.3 onwards. Guiderius and Arviragus, the noble savages, are tedious, and grow more and more so. Iachimo has gone; Posthumus becomes a stick; and the Anglo-Roman war, full of dumbshow stage directions and long narrative speeches, fizzles out anti-climactically.

Johnson described the various incongruities of the play as 'unresisting imbecility'. Yet *Cymbeline* has quite a full stage history compared with *The Winter's Tale*. In this play the first three acts are stunningly powerful. Jealous Othello *goes* mad, but Leontes's jealousy is madness from the start. A Greek tragedian would have ended the play with the third act, but there is a surprising sequel, with the pastoral scene, and the resurrection of Hermione in the statue scene (like Galatea in the legend), the most wonderful example in literature of wish-fulfilment. Hermione (who is rather like Queen Katherine in *Henry VIII*) is given a deeply felt part. She is sometimes doubled with Perdita, 'her mother's glass', but it is better not to do this: Perdita is only 16, and it is hard to find someone who can play both a greying matron and a girl of whom it is said

> When you do dance, I wish you
> A wave o' the sea, that you might ever do
> Nothing but that.

The Tempest, with the spirit Ariel and the beast-man Caliban, invites allegorical interpretation, but none has been found quite to fit it. If Caliban is the beast in man, forgotten for a moment by Prospero at the pageant, why is he so touchingly susceptible to the wonders and music of the island? *The Tempest* is a tale of separation and suffering resolved in harmony. The mage Prospero has everything under control in his magic island. He is able finally (after some struggle) to forgive his enemies. But there is no suggestion that the wicked pair, Antonio and Sebastian, are redeemed. For Alonso and the good Gonzalo there may be promise of 'the reasonable shore' and 'a clear life ensuing'; but Trinculo and Stephano, who presumably represent vices of civilization, seem unpromising material for redemption. In the end interest is centred on the young lovers, Ferdinand, and Miranda with her cry of 'O brave new world'. ''Tis new to thee', replies Prospero, perhaps without irony: the world *is* new to every generation.

THREE

The seventeenth century

Elizabethan literature was full of fluent prolixity (or 'copy' as it was called then, from Latin *copia*). The beginning of the seventeenth century saw a reaction against this. Epigrammatic Roman poets like Ovid, Lucan or Martial were favoured; in prose, there was a turn away from Cicero towards the concise style of Seneca or Tacitus. The new trend can be summed up in the words of Queen Gertrude to Polonius: 'More matter, with less art.'

One leader of the terse authors was Benjamin Jonson (?1573–1637), always called Ben; since the eighteenth century it has been accepted practice to spell his surname without 'h', to distinguish him from his namesake Samuel. For centuries he has been bracketed with his friend and older colleague Shakespeare. Such pairings are not uncommon in the history of drama – cf. Ibsen and Björnson, Shaw and Galsworthy – and they are invariably detrimental to the lesser partner, who tends to be overshadowed. Jonson's dramaturgy is very different from Shakespeare's, but it has a right to be considered on its own merits. Jonson appears to have been personally unlike Shakespeare, whom his contemporaries frequently call 'gentle'. He seems to have been an aggressive and difficult man. The chief peculiarity of his work is his compulsion to base everything he wrote on an ancient model. 'He is a most learned plagiary of the ancients,' said Dryden, 'you trace him everywhere in their snow'. The Jonsonian note in English drama first appears with the comedy of *Every Man in his Humour*, in which Shakespeare acted in 1598. It was followed by *Every Man out of his Humour*. In these plays Jonson established the word 'humour' in English literature with the meaning 'ruling obsession, or passion'. The 'humour' method of characterization is useful to dramatists and novelists, and it has a sound basis in observation. Many of the people we meet are 'humours' to us, because we know them only in a limited way. 'Humours' are what the novelist E.M. Forster was to call 'flat characters'.

Jonson was the first (and only?) scholarly person in English to write successfully for the theatre. Some of his plays were intended for court audiences, but his best work was written for the popular stage. He himself was an actor, as well as an all-round literary man. His turbulent character broke out several times in the course of his professional life. He was imprisoned for his part-authorship (with Nashe) of a dramatic satire which annoyed the authorities. He was later imprisoned again, with Marston and Chapman, for jokes made in their comedy of London life, *Eastward Ho!*. In 1598 he killed a fellow actor in a duel and was yet again imprisoned, saving himself by a plea of 'benefit of clergy' (i.e. proving that he could read). He was also involved in a theatrical vendetta, the obscure episode known as the War of the Theatres, involving Dekker and Marston. The details are unclear, and suspicion of a publicity stunt is strong. Jonson's contribution to the War was *The Poetaster* (1601), a satire on contemporary writers.

The plays so far mentioned are all very dull and would not be remembered at all if Jonson had not gone on to write his best comedies, in the first decade of the new century: *Volpone* (1606), *The Silent Woman* (1609), *The Alchemist* (1610), and *Bartholomew Fair* (1614). His Roman tragedies, *Sejanus* (printed 1603) and *Catiline* (printed 1611) were theatrical flops in his own time, and are rarely revived. Jonson's later plays are usually dismissed altogether. *The Devil is an Ass* (1616) is always enjoyed by university students when they revive it, but it is not part of the repertory. As for his plays of the 1620s and '30s, they are remembered, if at all, for Jonson's two angry Odes to himself, in which he denounces the 'loathèd stage' he is leaving after the failure of *The New Inn* (1629). In recent years there have been attempts by academic Jonsonians to revalue his later plays upwards, but so far these have had no effect in the theatre. The later plays are said to show traces of Shakespeare's influence. This would be interesting if correct, since Jonson, though he admired and loved Shakespeare 'this side idolatry' both as a man and as a writer, constantly cavilled at what he considered to be the older dramatist's want of 'art'.

It is not always realized that, with all his proclaimed classicism, there was a romantic, fantasizing side to Jonson. He spent a whole night gazing at his big toe and imagining that he was seeing 'Turks and Tartars' fighting round it. In the fragmentary play *The Sad Shepherd* (c.1635) he seems even to be competing with Shakespearean romance.

The fantastic, fairytale side of Jonson comes out also in the court masques. Of these he was the leading writer of the century. A masque is a kind of drama in which music and dance and spectacle predominate over plot and character. Jonson introduced into this form the comic interlude or antimasque. His masques were composed in collaboration with the designer Inigo Jones, until in the reign of Charles I their association broke up in a quarrel. To a twentieth-century observer the great likeness in appearance between Inigo

Jones and Ezra Pound may do something to explain this.

Jonson was the first of the great literary panjandrums, the forerunner of Dryden, of Samuel Jonson, of Henry James, and of T.S. Eliot. Some of his critical ideas are found in *Timber*, apparently his commonplace book. He was made poet laureate in 1616. Between 1618 and 1619 he walked to Edinburgh, where his talk was taken down by the Scottish poet William Drummond (1585–1649). Drummond's account, if authentic (and if not it is amazingly good pastiche) paints a convincing picture of Jonson, crotchety and boastful, pontificating about life and literature.

Among the great English writers Jonson is the least loved, but he is historically important, because he inaugurated the main tradition of English stage comedy. From the formal point of view Shakespearean comedy is a 'sport', while Jonson's influence extends from Restoration plays, and Sheridan in the eighteenth century, down to Wilde in the 1890s and John Arden in our own time. When his admirer the dramatist Henry Fielding turned novelist he brought the Jonsonian tradition into the English novel of the eighteenth century, and so to Dickens, a keen actor, who often performed in Jonson's plays.

Jonson is sometimes dismissed as (in Shaw's phrase) 'a brutish pedant', but his best plays are effective in the theatre. He railed at the popular audience for not appreciating him enough, yet without them he might well have continued to turn out more dreary plays like *Cynthia's Revels*. *Volpone* and *The Alchemist* succeed where *Sejanus* and *Catiline* fail, in creating a world of their own. (Though Jonson knew innumerably more facts about ancient Rome than Shakespeare, Shakespeare's Rome feels like Rome and Jonson's does not.) In *Volpone* it is clear that Jonson's master in English verse was Marlowe. His hard, glittering verse rivals Marlowe's in splendour.

> A diamond, would have bought Lollia Paulina,
> When she came in like star-light, hid with jewels.

But Jonson invented more suitable settings than Marlowe for the antics of his monomaniacs, and he was a much better dramatist. He seems intuitively to have recognized, as Marlowe did not, that a serious or tragic flat character is impossible, so that while critics are still disputing whether *The Jew of Malta* is a tragedy or a farce, there is no doubt about Jonson's comic intention. *The Alchemist* is just a story of con-men and their victims, what the Elizabethans called 'cony-catching', but its theatrical skill and disciplined style make it into a work of art. The nearest modern equivalent to it is the Marx Brothers films: hard-edged (with underlying cruelty), topically allusive, often very fantastic, sometimes very funny. The grotesque characters are not set off against rounded ones, but against colourless ones, i.e. the 'good' characters and the heroines.

From his beloved classics Jonson had learned to extol the virtues of measure and balance and to ridicule the eccentrics who ignore the limits of the human condition, and Professor L.C. Knights's well-known book *Drama and Society in the Age of Jonson* takes him at his word and presents a steady, poised Jonson. It would seem, however, that Jonson's heart was really with characters like Sir Epicure Mammon in *The Alchemist* and the baroque exuberance of his dreams, and with the thieves and fools and mountebanks. From *Bartholomew Fair* the real message seems to be that for anyone to have power over anyone else is folly; the reprisals are only for those who presume to positions of judgement and authority, like Justice Overdo. Subtle and Face get away with their villainy in *The Alchemist*, and Volpone's fate is left to the audience, like that of Barrie's Tinker Bell: if we applaud, he goes free. There is some disarming sly charm in Jonson's work if you look for it.

Jonson's non-dramatic poetry was founded on his reading of Roman poets such as Martial (his favourite), Horace, and Catullus. Some of his finest lyrics occur in his plays – 'Have you seen but a bright lily grow', 'Slow, slow, sad fount', 'Queen and huntress'. The best known, 'Drink to me only', occurs in a collection of verse. Here Jonson has transmuted some uninspired bits of Greek prose into a lovely English song. Many of his poems are occasional, addressed to his friends and fellow-authors: the best known is his tribute to Shakespeare ('He was not of an age, but for all time!'). The epitaph on the boy actor Solomon Pavey, and 'On his First Son', show the capacity on which Jonson prided himself, to say much in little. In 'To Penshurst' Jonson pays homage to a great house, with memories of the Sidney family, and sets his stamp upon a genre, the country house poem, often used by later poets – most memorably by Yeats. Of his moral poems the most moving is the proud 'Farewell to the World of a Young Gentlewoman, Virtuous and Noble'. These are the closing lines:

> No, I do know that I was born
> To age, misfortune, sickness, grief,
> But I will bear these with that scorn
> As shall not need thy false relief.
> Nor for my peace will I go far,
> As wanderers do, that still do roam,
> But make my strengths, such as they are,
> Here in my bosom, and at home.

Despite these and a few other beautiful poems Jonson seems to have been more suited to be a prose author than a poet. The future of his comedy was to lie with prose dramatists and novelists. The bent of his mind was rational and analytical, and he wrote excellent prose, none better in English.

What a deal of cold business does a man mis-spend the better part of life in! in scattering compliments, tendering visits, gathering and venting news, following feasts and plays, making a little winter-love in a dark corner.

(from *Timber*)

Apart from the two or three grand luminaries, Elizabethan, Jacobean and Caroline drama is on the whole mostly inert. The acclaiming tradition about it coming down from Lamb and Swinburne tends to be rather uncritical. T.S. Eliot's *Elizabethan Essays* (1934), his best prose book, must have enticed many readers to this drama by his felicitous quotations, but it is a common experience to come away from it feeling that Eliot has found all the good lines in it that there are.

The sombre tone noticeable in many of Shakespeare's and Jonson's plays after 1600 is very marked in the tragedies of John Webster (dates not known, perhaps 1580–1625). 'Webster was much possessed by death', said Eliot in a poem ('Whispers of Immortality'). He was preoccupied by characters at the point of death, when the sense of the meaning of life, or its meaninglessness, is most tested. Famous for the lurid Italianate horrors and churchyard atmosphere of his plays, Webster in poetry has a thrilling rhythm which compels us to take them seriously; speeches, lines and phrases of *The White Devil* (written 1608–9) and *The Duchess of Malfi* (1613) suggest the presence of a great artist, which the plays as a whole do not quite succeed in doing. A peculiar melancholy, sometimes darkening into horror, sometimes settling down to a note of calm acceptance, is conveyed through the murmured phrases of his characters:

> No, at myself I will begin and end.

or

> While we look up to Heaven, we confound
> Knowledge with knowledge. O I am in a mist.

Webster's dramaturgy was assailed early in the twentieth century by William Archer (1856–1924), the apologist for Ibsen. But to-day Ibsen and Webster seem to have more in common than Archer imagined. The stage conventions they employed were very different, but both were poet-dramatists with a sombre and uncompromising vision of life, which they expressed through poetic symbols.

An anonymous play, *The Revenger's Tragedy* (1607), may be mentioned here. Its sensational crimes and horrors make it ludicrous when acted, and the dramatist's love of railing makes it monotonous. But whatever its dramatic faults it contains passages of macabre poetry which have a closeness of texture unmatched outside Shakespeare.

> Does the silkworm expend her yellow labours
> For thee? for thee does she undo herself?
> Are lordships sold to maintain ladyships
> For the poor benefit of a bewitching minute?
> Why does yon fellow falsify highways,
> And put his life between the judge's lips,
> To refine such a one? keeps horse and men
> To beat their valours for her?

So speaks the hero-villain Vendice, addressing the skull of his murdered mistress. The play was traditionally assigned to Cyril Tourneur (?1573–1626), but is now more often thought to be the work of Thomas Middleton (1580–1627). Middleton's *The Changeling* (1625), with a subplot by William Rowley (?1585–1626), ranks with it and Webster's two best plays as the only Jacobean tragedies worthy of comparison with Shakespeare's. Middleton's plays show a marked psychological interest and a special concern with the emotional problems of women in the kind of situation which Shakespeare evades when he takes Isabella off the hook in *Measure for Measure*. Middleton's *Women beware Women* (written in the 1620s, not published till 1657) is proving to have a lot of life on the stage as well as in the study. His fame is in the ascendant.

The *Malcontent* (1603–4) of John Marston (1576–1634) was a product of the 'Angry' movement of its day; it mingles revenge themes with sardonic humour and verbal grotesquerie. Eliot's essay surely overrates Marston as a playwright, if not as a poet.

Modern producers have rarely attempted to cope with the tragedies, on themes of French history, of George Chapman (?1560–1634). C.S. Lewis describes him as 'unbalanced' and 'Wagnerian'. He is most remembered for his translations of Homer, an attempt to convert the *Iliad* and *Odyssey* into heroic poems as the Renaissance understood them. Chapman has so loaded these poems with moralizing interpolations, tortuous conceits, and Elizabethan fancies, e.g.

When sacred Troy shall shed her towers in tears of overthrow.

that they are now unreadable, except in short passages. Yet it is hard not to feel that his excursions into 'life's rough sea' are Homeric in spirit. A restless and adventurous man, Chapman belongs to the age of the Voyagers. He was an associate of Marlowe and Raleigh in the freethinking circle called the School of Night, and much of his work remains cryptic and obscure.

A few other tragedies of the period may be mentioned. Thomas Heywood (?1575–1641) anticipated Victorian sentimental melodrama in *A Woman Killed with Kindness*. *A Yorkshire Tragedy*, published 1608, and stated in the title to be by Shakespeare, is now argued to be by Middleton. It is a realistic drama of murder in contemporary life. *The Witch of Edmonton* (first performed probably in 1621, not published until 1658) is by various hands. Productions of it should not be missed: in its treatment of the theme of witchcraft it strikes home in a humane way that makes the play still very affecting. The best work of Philip Massinger (1583–1640) was in comedy, but he wrote tragedies also. His blank verse carries further the breakdown of regularity already apparent in Shakespeare's later plays and in other Jacobeans like Middleton and Webster. If not printed as verse it reads as admirable prose, limpid and well-knit. That Massinger should have offered it as verse is a sign of the still continuing prestige of 'poetic drama'. The collaboration of Francis Beaumont (1584–1616) and John Fletcher (1579–1625) produced some plays that were for long more popular than Shakespeare's. *The Maid's Tragedy* (before 1614, perhaps only by Beaumont) is a skilful theatre piece, though fault has been found both with the verse and the characters' motivations. *Philaster* (1620) has been compared with Shakespeare's romances. Jacobean tragedy became Caroline and virtually came to an end with John Ford (?1586–1640) and James Shirley (1596–1666). Of Ford's plays *The Broken Heart* (c. 1630), which turns on a forced marriage, and *'Tis Pity She's a Whore* (published 1633), centring on the incestuous love of a brother and sister, are sometimes revived. (The title of *'Tis Pity* is a misnomer, since Annabella is not a whore.) Ford has his full share of the sensationalism and horrors of the period, but what tends to survive in many readers' memories is not these but the falling elegiac note which makes his blank verse quite distinctive.

> Remember,
> When we last gathered roses in the garden,
> I found my wits; but truly you lost yours.
> (from *The Broken Heart*)

Ford was evidently fascinated by the 'reunion scenes' of late Shakespeare and several times draws on them. Some of his plays are connected with the cult of 'Platonic Love' at the court of Queen Henrietta Maria and take us into very strange territory, both psychological and literary. In Shirley the devices and mannerisms of Elizabethan/Jacobean tragedy have become pastiche. His best work is in his comedies.

Elizabethan/Jacobean comedy includes a few plays that are still performed now and than, chiefly at schools and colleges. *The Shoemaker's Holiday* (1599), by the versatile popular writer Thomas Dekker, is an amiable piece of work about citizen life. *The Honest Whore* (c. 1604–5) shows a genuine interest in making characters credible; *The Roaring Girl* (1604–10), written with Middleton, seems cheerfully to side with its outspoken heroine. Dekker, like Heywood, and many others of the time, was a journeyman playwright rather than an artist, but he wrote serviceable theatre verse and charming songs. No comedy by the saturnine Middleton has become part of the repertory, but a play of his may have suggested Massinger's *A New Way to Pay Old Debts* (published 1633), the best comedy of the age, after the great days. Massinger's presentation of the chief character, the villainous Overreach, has however been criticized on the ground that he is sometimes a flat and sometimes a round character. Beaumont's *The Knight of the Burning Pestle* (?1607) is a burlesque of romantic drama written with such verve that although it is full of topicalities it is often revived. Fletcher's reputation might stand higher if his comedies were revived; they make excellent reading, with good plots, and a more consistently modern kind of English than Shakespeare's. Shirley's light plays, like *The Lady of Pleasure* (1637) are better than his tragedies. His work is proof of the continuity of English drama down to the Restoration period (after 1660), which his comedies often anticipate. Shirley is best known for the song 'The glories of our blood and state' (published 1659). It has an interesting complexity of thought and imagery in lines like:

> Upon death's purple altar now
> See where the victor–victim bleeds!

But as a dramatist Shirley belonged to a time of decline. His *Love Tricks*, a set of parodies of Elizabethan prose and verse, shows that his predecessors had come to sound absurd to him. We are now nearing the year 1642, when the outbreak of the Civil War closed the theatres. After their reopening the Elizabethan flavour in drama had gone for ever.

Great periods of art are always brief, and there is nothing surprising about the swift transition of Elizabethan drama from barbarism to decadence. (Compare the history of the cinema). What matters is the moment of civilization in between: the moment of Shakespeare.

The seventeenth century, said one of its poets, Abraham Cowley, was a 'warlike, various and tragical age'. In politics it was a time of revolution and civil war. Charles I was executed in 1649 and a republic was established. This was followed by the restoration of his older son as Charles II in 1660, and then by the expulsion of Charles II's brother James II in 1688 and the post-revolutionary settlement under the joint sovereigns William III and Mary II. In intellectual life the period was one of questioning and controversy. The outcome was the establishment of modern thought on its two foundations of scientific method and analytical history. The great seventeenth century controversies reflect conflicts between traditionalists and innovators. The appeal to authority was met by the appeal to experience. The atmosphere of the time was disturbed and violent. It was a time of autobiography and self-assertion. 'Every man,' said the poet Donne, 'thinks he has got to be' (i.e. has become)/'A Phoenix'. Men came to blows over questions of church order and liturgy. James I's conception of Divine Right was challenged by new theories of democracy. Against these, in turn, Thomas Hobbes (1588–1679) argued in his *Leviathan* (1651) that the necessity for order overrode all notions of popular liberty; while the aristocratic republicanism of Milton offered yet another alternative for independent minds like his own. Meanwhile for the first time in English history the voice of the English people was heard in public debate on how they should be governed, as their religious passions erupted in the sermons and propaganda, the confessions and wild claims to divine revelation, of the England of the Sects. Here is a 'Muggletonian' Song:

We do believe in God alone,
Likewise in Reeve and Muggleton.
None hath salvation, we believe,
But those of Muggleton and Reeve.
Christ is the Muggletonians' king,
With whom eternally they'll sing.

The turbulence of the age reverberates in the stylistic variety characteristic of seventeenth-century literature. This century saw the establishment of modern discursive prose. but on the way there it exhibited several extreme developments of different ways of writing English. The unreasonable Elizabethans went for a while out of fashion, and the curt Jacobeans reigned in their stead. But in the middle years of the century the old flowery metaphorical language came back again. Sir Thomas Urquhart (1611–60) in his translation of Rabelais (first two books published 1653) outdoes John Florio (?1553–1625), who Englished Montaigne (1603), in linguistic extravagance. Urquhart even outdoes his original, which is saying something.

The French humanist Montaigne (1533–92) gave the name *essai* to the short adventure of ideas which he introduced into European literature. The first English essayist was Francis Bacon (1561–1626). His *Essays* appeared first in 1597 and they were added to and expanded up to their final collection in 1625. Bacon is less meandering than Montaigne; he favours an aphoristic style, like Seneca's: 'To be master of the sea is an abridgment of monarchy.' Bacon was the pioneer of modern scientific thought. As a master of English he is most remembered for particular phrases and sentences: revenge is 'a kind of wild justice'; a married man with children has given 'hostages to fortune'; 'What is truth? said jesting Pilate, and would not stay for an answer'. Bacon *does* stay for an answer; colourful as his writing is, the temper of his mind was utilitarian. Much of his work was in Latin, the language of educated Europe. His only major writings in English, apart from the *Essays*, are the *Advancement of Learning* (1605) and *The New Atlantis* (1626), which describes an imaginary city dominated by scientists. Bacon was a man of the world rather than a spiritual writer like Pascal, but his religion was sincere, and so was his love of the arts. Amid all his sententiousness we are always aware of his passion for virtue and truth. In Bacon the scientific spirit has no cocksureness. It is associated with piety, humility, and wonder.

Seventeenth-century empiricism leads, in *The Anatomy of Melancholy* (1621) of Robert Burton (1577–1640), to a vast exposition of the wild craziness of the human mind. Its framework is that of a medical treatise, and it is full of the science of Burton's day, which now seems very odd. It can be dipped into anywhere. Samuel Johnson, himself a victim of 'melancholy', recommended it as the best of bedtime reading. A great physician of the twentieth century, Sir William Osler, said that Burton had enriched a subject of universal interest with deep human sympathy, 'in which soil the roots have struck so deep that the book still lives'. It is full of prose poetry of the utmost beauty.

Voluntary solitude is that which is familiar with melancholy; and gently brings on, like a siren or shoeing-horn or some sphinx, to that irrevocable gulf.

Another popular genre of the period was the Character. (This means the succinct portrayal of a human type.) The genre derives from the ancient Greek author Theophrastus (d. 278 BC). Of his several seventeenth century English successors the best remembered is Bishop John Earle (?1601–65), with his *Micro-cosmography* (first complete edition 1633). Still lovely and touching is the Character of 'A Child', which ends:

Could he put off his body with his little coat, he has got eternity without a burden, and exchanged one heaven for another.

Much seventeenth century literature can be summed up as quaint science touched with sensitive poetry – a mixture never seen before or since.

The age was one of historians and biographers. William Camden (1551–1625), Ben Jonson's headmaster, has been called the first really critical historian in England. He wrote mainly in Latin, but his *Remains concerning Britain* (1605: later edd. 1614, 1633) is in English. The book was recently re-edited (1985). Camden is a mine of information about all sorts of things British.

A changing conception of history is revealed in the contrast between two leading historians, Raleigh and Bacon. Raleigh's *History of the World* illustrates the view of history as a series of exemplary tragedies penned by the hand of God. His moralizing rises to great eloquence, as in this apostrophe to Death:

O eloquent, just and mighty death! whom none could advise, thou has persuaded; what none hath dared, thou hast done; and whom all the world hath flattered, thou only hast cast out of the world and despised; thou hast drawn together all the pride, cruelty and ambition of man, and covered it all over with these two narrow words, *Hic jacet*.

To go from this to Bacon's *History of Henry VII* is to breathe a more modern air, rational and secular. When Henry VII got from Pope Innocent VIII a Bill diminishing the rights of sanctuary, Bacon says it was granted in return for a complimentary oration delivered by the English ambassadors:

The Pope knowing himself to be lazy and unprofitable to the Christian world was wonderfully glad to hear that there were such echoes of him sounding in so distant parts.

Biography and anecdotal writing flourished at this time. Thomas Fuller (1608–81) of the *Worthies of England* (1661), and the learned John Selden (1584–1654) of the *Table Talk* (published 1689), put much of the English cultural heritage on record. The most attractive of seventeenth-century biographers is Izaak Walton (1593–1683). His *Lives* of distinguished clergy of his time are still read, not for reliable information or character-drawing – Walton is a hagiographer rather than a biographer in the modern style – but for their beautiful English. John Donne to us is a more complex and puzzling figure than appears in Walton's simple portrait of the 'second Augustine', but no modern writer could rise to Walton's closing passage:

He was earnest and unwearied in the search of knowledge; with which his vigorous soul is now satisfied and employed in a continual praise of that God that first breathed it into his active body, that body which once was a temple of the Holy Ghost, and is now become a small quantity of Christian dust. But I shall see it re-animated.

In this century the introspective autobiography became a major genre, with the subtle self-portrait of Sir Thomas Browne (1605–82) in *Religio Medici* (1642); the swashbuckling *Autobiography* of Lord Herbert of Cherbury, not published till 1764, when Thomas Gray and Horace Walpole 'screamed with laughter' over it; the singular religious document of John Bunyan (1628–88), *Grace Abounding to the Chief of Sinners* (1666); and the self-vindication of the Puritan divine Richard Baxter (1615–91) in *Reliquiae Baxterianae* (1696). Most loved of all these 'pictures of a disposition' is Walton's *Compleat Angler* (1653). Its manifest content is a disquisition on angling, but the latent content is political (or anti-political), a plea for peace in an age racked with civil war. As a work of art it has lasted better than the self-consciously saintly portrait of the royal martyr Charles I, in the once bestselling *Eikon Basilike* (1649), supposedly compiled by the king himself, but more probably the work of John Gauden (1605–62). According to John Milton's modern admirer William Empson, Milton, for purposes of anti-royal propaganda, foisted a prayer from Sidney's *Arcadia* into the text and then (in his *Eikonoklastes*, 1649) accused the king of plagiarism. Those were days of dirty work in a bitter, murderous climate.

The seventeenth century left much in the form of memoirs and letters. The best known are the letters of Dorothy Osborne (1627–95) to Sir William Temple (1629–99), whom she was to marry in 1655. It is a familiar irony that Temple was in his day a leading literary figure, while Dorothy Osborne wrote nothing but private letters, but to-day Temple's writings are forgotten and she is still read. There were other notable women writers in the century, and advocates of 'the alternative canon' will have to consider, among others, the eccentric, very likeable poet the Duchess of Newcastle (?1624–74). Her biography of her husband shows perhaps the last survival of the old romantic English medieval chivalrousness, soon to be eclipsed by the swaggering of Dryden's Almansor and the court of *Le Roi Soleil* at Versailles. The memoirist Lucy Hutchinson (b. 1620) in her portrait of her husband (not published till 1806) gives the lie to those who think that seventeenth-century Puritans were all uncouth, ignorant fanatics. Katherine Philips (1631–64) presided over a literary salon and wrote verse under the name of 'Orinda'; her admirers called her 'the matchless Orinda'. But few read her work now. This is not true, however, of the fiction-writer and dramatist Aphra Behn (1640–89). Her life and work have attracted a great deal of attention in this century. She has the Restoration note. But Dorothy Osborne, who was not a 'writer' at all (she thought the Duchess of Newcastle 'distracted'), excels every one of them because she wrote better than they did.

Last night I was in the garden till eleven o'clock. It was the sweetest night that e'er I saw. The garden looked so well, and the jasmine beyond all perfume. And yet I was not pleased.

The Sermon then met the needs now catered for by the theatre, films and television – not to speak of social sciences, psychology etc. Puritans rather than Anglicans made it central in worship. But only the Anglican preachers, such as Andrewes, Taylor, or Donne, are still read, and at that only in selections. Donne's *Devotions upon Emergent Occasions* (1624) has more appeal to-day, the intimate thoughts of a sick man confronting in solitude the ultimates of his faith. Everyone knows, if only from the title of Hemingway's novel, the passage which ends: '. . . send not to know for whom the bell tolls; it tolls for thee'. Another and very different classic of English religious life is the *Centuries of Meditation* (?1634–1704). Unpublished till 1908, Traherne's invocation of an original radiant innocence when 'the corn was orient and immortal wheat' presents the strongest possible contrast to the dark, sin-stricken self-scrutiny of Donne.

The greatest prose artist of the age was Sir Thomas Browne (1605–82). The singularity of Browne is that he has something in common both with the inquisitive savants and scientists of his age and with the other-worldly mystics. He is the greatest master in English of the Decorated style in prose. His organ tones were soon to give place to a more practical style, and his works are now well known only in short passages, which are remembered like poems, for instance (from the last chapter of *Urn Burial* (1658)):

Time, which antiquates antiquities, and hath an art to make dust of all things, hath yet spared these minor monuments.

and

What song the Sirens sang, and what name Achilles assumed when he hid himself among women, though puzzling questions, are not beyond all conjecture.

Browne drew fresh melodies out of the English language by playing off, as Shakespeare had done, its polysyllabic Latin vocables against its plain short Saxon words: 'But the iniquity of oblivion blindly scattereth her poppy.' Browne's thought belongs to a remote epoch. It is hard to remember that he was a contemporary of Hobbes and Descartes. His *Vulgar Errors* (1646) is a quaint display of antiquated learning. *Christian Morals* (not published till 1716) has little to do with its ostensible subject. Browne is remembered for the personal charm of his work. Like Chaucer he makes friends with the reader. In *Religio Medici* he was one of the first English writers to make his theme the studied awareness of his own singularity.

Seventeenth-century poetry might well have figured in textbooks as a silver age, a time of steady continuity between the tradition of Spenser and other reflective Elizabethan poets (Daniel, Chapman, Greville) and the age of Dryden and Pope. But, as sometimes happens, the placid course of English poetry was violently interrupted by the impact of strange unforeseeable genius. John Donne (1572–1631) has more right to be called original than most poets. No convincing precedent has been found for the characteristic style of his poems. By the middle years of the century his was the leading voice in poetry. But Donne himself was an Elizabethan, only eight years younger than Marlowe and Shakespeare. As a young man he seems to have been worldly and discontented, witty and cynical, finding in love affairs a refuge from his external troubles and his innate melancholy. He was more imaginative than any other writer of the day: he is one of the few Elizabethan poets who convey the contemporary excitement about 'the Indias of spice and mine' and the new discoveries in astronomy (he visited Kepler and discussed the new science with him). Donne was adventurous by temperament, sailing with Essex in the Cadiz expedition in 1596, and on the ill-fated Islands Voyage of 1597. On his return he became secretary to the Lord Keeper, Sir Thomas Egerton, but ruined his career by his elopement with Égerton's wife's niece Ann More. 'John Donne – Anne Donne – undone', was his punning summary (which shows incidentally how he pronounced his name). Donne was too poor to be accepted by her family as a suitor. In the 16 years of their marriage she bore him twelve children and died worn-out at the age of 33. For many years Donne's life was that of an unsuccessful place-seeker. Finally King James I, who had been impressed by his prose work *Pseudo-Martyr* (1615), in which Donne urged Catholics to take the oath of allegiance, insisted that he should take orders in the Church of England. His ecclesiastical career finally brought him in 1622 to the Deanery of St Paul's in London. By that time he had become a frequent preacher at court and one of the most famous and learned divines of his day. Donne had been born into a Roman Catholic family (his mother was related to Thomas More), he was brought up as a Catholic, and it has been thought that his adoption of Anglicanism was due to worldly motives. Certainly it is doubtful to what extent he ever became a Protestant.

Most of Donne's poetry was written before he took orders; to use his own expression, it came from 'Jack Donne', not 'Dr Donne'. The chronology of his poems is uncertain. They were nearly all occasional, written to please himself and a few friends, mostly circulating in manuscript and not gathered up and printed till 1633, after Donne's death. Apart from some funeral elegies and verse-letters written for great persons of the day like Lady

Bedford, Donne's only published poems were the so-called *Anniversaries* (1611, 1612), two long verse-meditations in celebration of the deceased daughter of his patron Sir Robert Drury. Readers have been repelled, and mystified, by Donne's evocation of apocalyptic doom and cosmic disaster in his laments for a little girl he had never set eyes on. Professor Rosemond Tuve argued that for a seventeenth-century reader they would have been perfectly decorous; but Donne's friend Ben Jonson thought them in bad taste. Herbert Grierson, Donne's great editor, apologizes for them. But the *Anniversaries* are characteristic of Donne and probably his greatest poems. Their real subject is the fragmentation and division of the human world by the advent of 'the new Philosophy', i.e. modern natural science: a theme of the greatest possible significance to us to-day.

The five poems known as 'Satires' belong to the years before Donne's marriage in 1601: his beginnings as a poet may have coincided with the sudden vogue of satire in the 1590s. These poems are irregular in metre: Donne may have been experimenting with a sort of free verse, based on the rhythms of prose, or talk. Among them is 'Of Religion', which contains the well-known passage which begins 'On a huge hill/Cragged and steep, truth stands . . .' Donne was already caught up with the problem of religious faith. Some of the Elegies may belong to this time. After the fluency and glamour of much Elizabethan verse, poems of Donne like 'The Calm' and 'The Storm' sound consciously 'modern', hard-bitten and disillusioned. So does the fragment of narrative poetry called 'The Progress of the Soul' (written about 1601), misogynistic and cryptic.

Some of the lyrical poems later to be known as the 'Songs and Sonnets' may belong to this time, but others probably belong later, after 1603 ('the King' is mentioned). In these poems Donne shows a force in lyric poetry comparable to Shakespeare's in drama. They are the work of an intellectual, remote from ordinary life. Donne is a self-centred poet, more interested in his own thought-processes than in the emotions they purport to clarify. Dryden and Johnson were to find Donne's love poems frigid, and some of them are little more than exercises in ingenuity. But when he is at his best Donne's power gives a strange intensity to whatever mode he writes in. Some of the poems, like 'The Apparition':

> When by the scorn, O murderess, I am dead . . .

are like little plays. In others, dramatic monologue becomes song, as in 'The Sun Rising':

> Busy old fool, unruly Sun . . .

or 'A Valediction of Weeping'. The surprising comparisons known as 'conceits ' (e.g. two lovers compared with a pair of compasses), the glittering array of sophisms and abstruse arguments, are brought alive by Donne's vehement excitement. His originality impressed his younger contempories, such as Thomas Carew (?1598–?1639), as evidenced by his funeral elegy on Donne:

> The Muses' garden, with pedantic weeds
> O'erspread, was purged by thee; the lazy seeds
> Of servile imitation thrown away,
> And fresh invention planted.

Donne's greatest love poetry seems to have been inspired by an experience which raised him above his normal self and found expression in a few poems that transcend everything else he wrote. This inspiration may well have been his passion for Ann More, for whom he threw away his worldly prospects. Perhaps his mystical poem 'The Ecstasy' was written when it was still uncertain whether she would marry him; he pleads for the physical union that would dissolve their 'loneliness'.

Whether Christianity inspired Donne's poetry quite to the same extent as sexual passion is disputed, but during the years before his ordination Donne wrote some of the finest devotional poetry in the language. After his ordination his extraordinary gift for words was chiefly exercised in his sermons and in the prose *Devotions*. But to those later years belong also the great Hymns, to Christ, to 'God my God in my sickness', and to God the Father.

After his vogue in the first half of the century Donne's place in English poetry became problematic. He was still read, but not rediscovered as a great master till the twentieth century. Among the Elizabethan poets, so heavily flavoured with their period, Donne's voice sounds astonishingly direct:

> 'Tis true 'tis day: what though it be?
> O wilt thou therefore rise from me?
> Why should we rise, because 'tis light?
> Did we lie down, because 'twas night?
> (from 'Break of Day')

Donne influenced many poets in his own century and in this. But none of his followers is really like him. Only William Empson (1906–84), in his earlier poems, sometimes catches the authentic accent of 'the monarch of wit'. (Empson has also Donne's characteristic fault of over-complexity.) Donne lacks the colourfulness and sensuousness of some poets, the grace and charm of others, the broad humanity of the greatest, but he has his own special contribution, his 'naked thinking heart'. The best judgment on his poetry was made by Ben Jonson, who called him 'the first poet of the world, in some things'.

Samuel Johnson called the school of Donne 'the Metaphysical poets'. He remarked that to write on their plan it was at least necessary to read and think. But only a poet with the power of Dante can make great poetry out of abstruse information, and Dante has other strings to his bow. The poetry written in the reign of Charles I (1625–49) is harmed by over-cleverness. The verse of John Cleveland (1613–58) consists of little else. In his own time, and for long afterwards, Abraham Cowley (1618–87) was reckoned the chief Metaphysical poet. His cycle of love poems, *The Mistress*, is made up of endless variations on one theme, like Petrarch's Sonnets. His unfinished Biblical epic the *Davideis* (on king David) is one more casualty on a littered field where *Paradise Lost* is the sole survivor (the Metaphysical style was unsuited to narrative). Cowley's 'Pindaric' odes in irregular verse established a free-ranging form which later poets made much use of, but it is hard to think of any great poetry in this form, unless *The Unknown Eros* (1877) of the Victorian poet Coventry Patmore (1823–96) is an example. Pope said of Cowley:

> Forget his epic, nay Pindaric, art:
> But still I love the language of his heart.

This language is found in Cowley's elegy on his Cambridge friend Hervey, and in his poem on another friend, Richard Crashaw, a Catholic:

> His faith perhaps in some nice tenets might
> Be wrong; his life, I'm sure, was in the right.

Cowley has provided the occasion for the most important modern discovery to be made in seventeenth century poetry. He wrote a political epic, *The Civil War*, of which Book I was published in 1679. It was thought that the other two books were lost. But they were recently discovered and edited. Whether this new find will come to rank with two other twentieth-century discoveries, Traherne's *Centuries of Meditation* and Smart's *Jubilate Agno*, has yet to be seen.

A poet more widely read than Cowley to-day is George Herbert (1593–1634). Herbert came from an aristocratic family; he was the brother of the philosopher-poet Lord Herbert of Cherbury (whose 'Ode on a Question Moved . . .' is much anthologized). George Herbert had a distinguished university career at Cambridge. Then he was ordained and became rector of Bemerton in Wiltshire, where he spent the rest of his life. It was unusual for a man of Herbert's social standing to become a country priest. He differs from other pious writers in his sense of the reality of, and his resistance to, the great world, which is often felt in his poetry. Herbert is remembered for his book of poems *The Temple* (1633). He is at the same time devout and witty.

> The subtle chymic can divest
> And strip the creature naked, till he find
> The callow principles within their nest;
> There he imparts to them his mind,

> Admitted to their bedchamber, before
> They appear trim and drest
> To ordinary suitors at the door.
>> (from 'Vanity')

Some of his verse is in an emblematic tradition widely used in his time, for example by his then very popular contemporary Francis Quarles (1592–1644). A few aspects of his poetry look odd to modern eyes. He compares Christ's graveclothes to a handkerchief to dry our eyes on, the spear piercing Christ's side to the broaching of a cask of wine. He uses acrostics in serious verse. And he became notorious for what Addison in the next century was to call False Wit, as when he shapes some of his poems on the page to look like bells or wings (to-day this sort of thing is called Concrete Poetry).

Yet Herbert's own literary ideal was an unmannered simplicity. He rejected the 'fictions and false hair' of the poets of his time. He can write with great directness.

> But now in age I bud again,
> After so many deaths I live and write;
> I once more smell the dew and rain
> And relish versing: O my only light,
> It cannot be
> That I am he
> On whom thy tempests fell all night.
>> (from 'The Flower')

Herbert has a special appeal to twentieth-century intellectuals, struggling towards the acceptance of religious faith, such as Simone Weil or Thomas Merton. 'The Pulley' and 'Love bade me welcome' have been attractive to many troubled souls. 'The Collar' has a validity independent of theology; the voice that calls 'Child' at the end can be heard, not as coming from an angry God, but from the poet's own adult self. Technically Herbert rivals Donne among the masters of form in English lyric verse. 'The great mine of original stanzaic forms in English is Herbert's *Temple*, which consists of 158 poems, 127 of them stanzaic, 98 of them being metrically unique in English'. (George Watson, *The Discipline of English*, 1978).

Herbert's chief poetic disciples were the Welsh doctor Henry Vaughan (1622–95) and the Catholic convert Richard Crashaw (?1613–49). Vaughan's most remembered work is *Silex Scintillans* (1650, 1655). It is in a vein of mystical piety.

> My soul, there is a country
> Far beyond the stars,
> Where stands a winged sentry
> All skilful in the wars.
>> (from 'Peace')

'They are all gone into the world of light' is a poem of spiritual vision which extends beyond the grave. In 'The Retreat' Vaughan is like Traherne, and like Wordsworth later, in seeing the memory of childhood as a prefiguring of Paradise. Richard Crashaw was the son of a Puritan divine, but was drawn at Cambridge into the High Court movement led by archbishop Laud, and frequented the community of Little Gidding, a lay monastery one day to be celebrated by T.S. Eliot in *Four Quartets*. Crashaw, unlike Eliot, was received into the Roman Church. His piety is that of a fervent devotee. His erotic religiosity suggests the Spanish, Italian and Neo-Latin 'conceited' verse of his time. Like Vaughan he owed much to Herbert; the title of his volume of poems, *Steps to the Temple*, is reminiscent of Herbert's *The Temple*. In 'The Weeper' Metaphysical poetry arrives at the zenith, or nadir, of absurdity, when Crashaw describes St Mary Magdalen's eyes as

> Two walking baths, two weeping motions;
> Portable and compendious oceans.

Crashaw has no sense of humour. He is single-minded in the ardour of his devotion. But despite the walking baths 'The Weeper' is an impressive poem. The tears, flames, floods, doves, primroses and lilies are detached from their normal reference and become the notation of a self-sufficient poetic world. The 'Hymn to St Teresa', completely unvisual, none the less creates a verbal equivalent of Bernini's statue of the saint in ecstasy.

> O how oft shalt thou complain
> Of a sweet and subtle pain!
> Of intolerable joys!
> Of a death, in which who dies
> Loves his death, and dies again,
> And would for ever so be slain,
> And lives and dies; and knows not why
> To live; but that he thus may never leave to die.

Crashaw's only successor was to be the Victorian poet Francis Thompson (1895–1907), with his 'Hound of Heaven'.

Robert Herrick (1591–1674), like most of the great English writers, is in contrast mainly this-worldly. He seems to have made little impression on his contemporaries. He was much admired in the Victorian period and some of his poems are as well known as any in English. 'To the Virgins, to Make Much of Time' stands with Marvell's 'To his Coy Mistress' as the classic English treatment of the *carpe diem* theme ('Gather ye rosebuds while ye may . . .'). Herrick took orders in 1627 and received the remote crown living of Dean Prior, on the fringes of Dartmoor. He bewailed his life in Devon and yearned for London, but the country atmosphere is very notable in his poems. He freshens the old conventions of pastoral, and adds his own urbanity to them. His inspiration came from classical writers, chiefly Anacreon and

Horace, but he acknowledges his discipleship to Ben Jonson. Much of Herrick's poetry is erotic and sensual (as in 'On Julia's Clothes'), dwelling on the attractions of young women. Sometimes he writes a dream-like poetry in which sensation takes on a strange rarefied quality. Herrick is not really very like Jonson or any other poet; he is an original. Perhaps overrated in the nineteenth century, he is underrated now. Herrick wrote a large number of short poems, like Christina Rossetti and Hardy. He has more than one style. In *Noble Numbers* (1648) he leaves his pagan world of fancy and writes as a Christian poet.

The 'Cavalier' poets are also often regarded as in the tradition of Jonson. They rewrote classical commonplaces in terms of contemporary life and manners. Thomas Carew is best known for his lyric poems, especially 'Ask me no more where Jove bestows . . .' His most striking poem is 'The Rapture', too strong meat for the anthologies. His verse-letter to his friend and fellow-poet Aurelian Townshend well conveys the cultured aristocratic atmosphere of the 1630s, the years of 'The King's Peace', brought to an end by the Great Rebellion. Sir John Suckling (1609–42) shows a light-hearted cynicism at the expense of the old cult of courtly love.

> If of herself she will not love,
> Nothing can make her:
> The devil take her!

His good-humoured 'Ballad on a Wedding' is a sophisticated imitation of popular poetry. Four lines from a poem by the Scots poet the Marquis of Montrose (1612–50) epitomize the Cavalier spirit:

> He either fears his fate too much,
> Or his deserts are small,
> Who dares not put it to the touch,
> To win or lose it all.

Richard Lovelace (1616–57) is the representative Cavalier poet, at once chivalrous and sophisticated, reckless and urbane; the living embodiment of *sprezzatura*. 'The Grasshopper' is not really about an insect but about the Cavalier way of life for which it is the metaphor. 'La Bella Bona-Roba' is another poem that is too lively for the anthologies, which prefer 'To Althea, from Prison', and 'To Lucasta'. But these are excellent too, part of the language ('Stone walls do not a prison make . . .' 'I could not love thee, dear, so much/Lov'd I not honour more.') Charles Cotton (1630–87), a friend of Lovelace, is another engaging poet. His three sonnets on girls, the first of which begins 'Alice is tall and upright as a pine', are down-to-earth without brutality.

This period of poetry is one of the most pleasant in English. None of the poets can be called great, but taken together they make up a small volume of work of great charm. The crown of seventeenth-century urbane poetry is the work of Andrew Marvell (1621–78). He is the most admired of these poets to-day, thanks to the advocacy of two American poets, T.S. Eliot and John Crowe Ransom. Marvell's life and work exhibit some of the conflicting features of the age. He was a friend of Lovelace, the chief royalist poet, but he became a servant and friend of Oliver Cromwell, the arch-Roundhead. Marvell was a politician who won a reputation in his time for integrity. He worked under the Commonwealth without hypocrisy, and under Charles II without corruption. His 'Horatian Ode on Cromwell's Return from Ireland' (1650) shows that he could see both what was impressive in Cromwell and what was appealing in Charles I, who

> . . . nothing common did or mean
> Upon that memorable scene

of his execution. In writing of private life Marvell keeps a similar balance. An undercurrent of irony runs through his urgent pleading with his 'Coy Mistress', while a transferred warmth of feeling glows in his vision of 'other worlds and other seas' in the Garden in which he has fled from the pains of love. Marvell favours the dialogue form in his poems. The 'Dialogue between the Resolved Soul and Created Pleasure' conjures up a graceful drama out of the encounter between an idealized Cavalier and an idealized Puritan.

> Courage, my soul, now learn to wield
> The weight of thine immortal shield.
> Close on thy head thy helmet bright,
> Balance thy sword against the fight.
> See where an army, strong as fair,
> With silken banners spreads the air.

The 'Dialogue between the Soul and Body' brings home by successive paradoxes the anguished antinomies of the human condition.

But Marvell is in the main the poet of pure pleasure. He distils a delicious pathos from the Nymph's complaint over her dead Fawn. Most of his best poetry is pastoral; his spokesmen are mowers, shepherds, swains. He is the poet of flowers and fruit, the tulip, pink and rose on parade in 'Appleton House', the 'curious peach' of 'The Garden', the 'orange bright/Like golden lamps in a green light' of his 'Bermudas'. The green garden of a moralized Nature is Marvell's refuge for the mind perturbed by metaphysics and the patriotic statesman afflicted by a time of civil war. Once Marvell had become a committed politician he ceased to write lyrics. His later work consists mostly of topical satires, which did not engage the finer side of his mind. With Marvell the Metaphysical strain comes to an end. In 'To his Coy Mistress' he unites their macabre joking with the timeless good sense of the classicists:

> But at my back I always hear
> Time's wingéd chariot hurrying near,
> And yonder all before us lie
> Deserts of vast eternity.

> Thy beauty shall no more be found,
> Nor in thy marble vault shall sound
> My echoing song; then worms shall try
> That long preserved virginity,
> And your quaint honour turn to dust,
> And into ashes all my lust.
> The grave's a fine and private place,
> But none, I think, do there embrace.

The Caroline poets are typical of English poetry up to that time, in the haphazard, occasional quality of their work. In contrast John Milton (1608–74) is the supreme example in English of the completely dedicated poet. From the early 1620s to 1640 he is the young Cambridge scholar-poet, writing much Latin verse, and first announcing himself among the great English poets with his 'Ode on the Morning of Christ's Nativity' (1629). Here for the only time he adopts the 'baroque', conceited manner used in English by poets like Crashaw and Marvell, but adds to it his own heroic, epic resonance. In the two 'mood' poems 'L' Allegro' and 'Il Penseroso' (1632) he brought new freshness and an English setting to the old motifs of pastoral poetry. In *A Mask* (1634), usually called *Comus*, he wrote the last and best of masques, the only one still read to-day. Like *A Midsummer Night's Dream* it blends English scenery with the mythology of the ancient world, which appealed as much to Milton as to Shakespeare. The poetry of the enchanter Comus has been thought richer than that given to his virtuous antagonist the Lady, but Milton, like Spenser, thought that temptations ought to be tempting. In *Lycidas* (1637) he brought to its final perfection the old tradition of pastoral elegy. *Lycidas* strengthens us for living, not by any 'message', but by its pure beauty. The peculiarity of Milton's early poems is the association in them of learning and poetic craftmanship with ingenuousness. His distinctive quality in his early poetry is his ability to evoke the dawn of life, for most people a vanishing memory by their teens, for Milton a radiance that lingered till his thirtieth year. In *Lycidas* the sky is already overcast.

From 1640 to the restoration of Charles II in 1660 Milton wrote little poetry and much prose. He was an indefatigable pamphleteer, and his pamphleteering was stimulated by events in his private life. In 1643 he married a girl from a royalist family, who almost immediately left him in circumstances that are unknown. Milton then composed the first of his pamphlets arguing for the licitness of divorce. This drew him into controversy with the Stationers' Company, as he had published it without a licence from them. Parliament supported the Stationers, and so Milton addressed to Parliament his *Areopagitica*, a scathing critique of the system of licensing. This is one of the best of Milton's prose works, an impassioned attack on censorship. It contains not only some mystical patriotism and great rhetoric, but some humour too. It has been compared to J.S. Mill's *On Liberty* (1859), the classic apologia in English for tolerance. But Milton was in favour of censorship provided the right people were doing it, and he assisted the passage of a law restricting the Press under the Commonwealth. After the execution of Charles I, acclaimed by Milton as just and 'acceptable', he served Cromwell as Latin Secretary, and defended the republic in tracts which made him famous throughout Europe. Right down to the year of Charles II's return he was writing on behalf of 'the good old cause'. It must be set to the credit of Charles II that he left the old regicide in peace. Milton was now blind. His public career had come to an end in disappointment and disillusion. Milton's twenty years of polemic and controversy had been a loss to literature. A few sonnets, like 'On his Blindness', are among the few masterpieces of that time. Much of his prose was in Latin, and his English prose, except for a few autobiographical passages, is to-day little read; it is often cumbersome and archaic. It is as a poet that Milton is remembered.

In his 'heroic poem' *Paradise Lost* (1667) Milton is the peer of Homer, Virgil, and Dante. Invoking the Muse Urania in fear and trembling, yet borne up by a sublime self-confidence, he offers 'Things unattempted yet in prose or rhyme' and bends his powers to 'justify the ways of God to men'. At the same time he expresses ('obliquely', as E.M.W. Tillyard would put it) the re-interpretation of history which the Civil War and the defeat of the Commonwealth compelled on him. When he came to write *Paradise Lost* Milton had ceased to be a militant revolutionary. Out of the brief biblical story of Adam and Eve he fashioned an epic of temptation and defeat, transformed in the end into the victory of the saving power of Christ and the 'Paradise within'. The first two books show a rhetorical power and towering imagination unparalleled in English poetry, with the speeches of Satan and his followers, the vivid and terrible images of Hell, and Satan's journey through Chaos. In the great invocation to Light at the beginning of the third book the blind poet speaks for the first time of his own plight.

> Thus with the year
> Seasons return; but not to me returns
> Day, or the sweet approach of even and morn,
> Or sight of summer's rose, or vernal bloom,
> Or flocks, or herds, or human face divine

Book III with its Council in Heaven introduces the self-exculpations of God the Father. (The Victorian critic Walter Bagehot put his finger on a weakness in *Paradise Lost* when he said 'Milton made God *argue*'.) Opinions differ about Milton's treatment of Adam and Eve. It is sometimes forgotten that he was daring to deal with 'things unattempted'. Human life in a state of innocence, naked beauty unashamed, is as much beyond our experience as angels and devils. The Eden of Book IV is one of the greatest achievements of the poetic imagination in English. Something of the sweetness and pastoral nostalgia of the young Milton returns here. The middle books are important for the student of Milton's ideas, but the bizarre episode of the War in Heaven, and even the book of the Creation, carry uncomfortable suggestions of Walt Disney. But if the poem falters here (not all would agree) there is a great recovery in Book IX. Milton here shows himself one of the great moral psychologists of literature, as he displays the ingenuity of the Serpent, the vanity of Eve, the chivalrous passion of Adam – which he has imagined with such ardour that for some readers at this point *Paradise Lost* loses its moral balance. The poet is at his worst in what follows. The closing books were structurally necessary, to expound the historic consequences of the Fall, but they make dry reading. But again there is a great recovery in the final pages of Book XII, when the human pair, hand in hand as when we first meet them, are dismissed from the world of innocence.

> Some natural tears they dropp'd, but wiped them soon:
> The world was all before them, where to choose
> Their place of rest, and Providence their guide.
> They hand in hand, with wandering steps and slow,
> Through Eden took their solitary way.

Except for Shakespeare's later manner, Milton's style in *Paradise Lost* is the most elaborate in English poetry. The first impression is of a flowing river of sound. His blank verse is like instrumental music in its aloofness, complication and splendour. But the meaning is all-important, and it is adroitly emphasized by the placing of key words. Some of Milton's single lines have a mighty force by themselves:

> Infinite wrath, and infinite despair.

In such effects Marlowe is his master. But Milton's real unit is the verse-paragraph. In his sustained flights none has equalled him. Controversy about his style has continued intermittently since his own day. What he really writes is not 'Latinisms' (there are far more of them in Ben Jonson) but 'Miltonics'. These have been held to be a bad influence, but this is disputed. In any case, the poem is not uniform in style. It is not all 'magniloquence' (as Eliot called it). It abounds in crisp phrasing, such as 'the bought smile/Of harlots'.

For all his classicism Milton is an intensely subjective writer. His personality pervades everything; that is why he is adored and hated. The historical facts about his life are few and can be variously interpreted. Johnson followed the tradition of Antony à Wood, a writer politically antagonistic to Milton, and wrote deliberately to supplant the 'honeysuckle lives' of Milton, which portrayed him as a pleasant man. But these were by people who knew him. Robert Graves's unsympathetic *Wife to Mr Milton* (1943) is a good novel, but it is not history.

There is no doubt that Milton was egocentric, but this does not inhibit his dramatic sense. Satan is his greatest dramatic creation, and no poet in the world has ever been better qualified to express the heroic defiance of a fallen archangel. But Milton succeeds with other characters too. We always know who is speaking. We come to recognize the self-conscious stiffness of Adam, melting at the crisis into passionate warmth:

> Should God create another Eve, and I
> Another rib afford, yet loss of thee
> Would never from my heart.

We hear the distinctively feminine voice of Eve, the majesty and sarcasm of God the Father, the proud disdain of Abdiel, the affability of Raphael, the sternness of Michael – all held together by the great *continuo* of the verse.

The opening lines of *Paradise Regained* (1671), a shorter (four-book) epic on the Temptation of Christ, suggest that it is a sequel to *Paradise Lost*, but it has proved less popular. Milton's presentation of Jesus is agreeably unsentimental. *Samson Agonistes* (1671) succeeds uniquely where many others have failed, in suggesting in English the effect of Greek tragedy. In the rhythms of Samson's first great speech, as in the intentionally broken rhythms of the Choruses, Milton was experimenting with new measures. This poem's questioning of divine purpose has an agonised urgency which makes the theology of *Paradise Lost* seem light-hearted in comparison. It is not known when *Samson* was written. The use of rhyme is inconsistent with Milton's rejection of it as 'modern bondage' in *Paradise Lost*. And the use of Greek dramatic form is hard to square with the strictures on Greek literature ascribed to Christ in *Paradise Regained*. But many readers find it impossible not to feel the underlying identity of Samson with the Milton of the years after the Restoration, 'Eyeless in Gaza, at the mill, with slaves'.

Milton lived to see *Paradise Lost* acclaimed, and by the wits as well as the Puritans. But it did not become a major influence on English poetry till the eighteenth century. The period between the vogue of Donne and the ascendancy of Pope was dominated by John Dryden (1631–1700). The pattern of Dryden's development is unusual. Unlike most poets his later work is far superior to his early. He did not find his best voice in poetry till he was 50. It is with the great satires on contemporary politics, beginning with *Absalom and Achitophel* (1681), that we first hear the Dryden who is now chiefly remembered. The Second Part of *Absalom* is chiefly by Nahum Tate, but Dryden contributred to it some vigorous verse-portraits, including 'Shimei' (Slingsby Bethell) and 'Og' (Thomas Shadwell). 'Og from a treason tavern rolling home' is a real addition to English comedy. *Absalom* was followed by another topical satire, *The Medal* (1682), and by *MacFlecknoe* (1682), in which Dryden introduced the mock-heroic manner into English poetry; it was to be the model for Pope's *Dunciad*. To the 1680s also belong two treatise-poems, *Religio Laici* (1682), setting forth a plain man's apology for the Church of England, and *The Hind and the Panther* (1687) in which Dryden uses a beast-fable as his allegory in a defence of the claims of Roman Catholicism, to which he had become a convert.

In Dryden's last years he turned mainly to translation. His *Virgil* is his masterpiece here. *Fables Ancient and Modern* (1699) is a miscellany of narrative poems, some original, some translated. Dryden excelled in the commemorative elegy and epitaph. One of his best elegies is that on his younger contemporary John Oldham (1653–83), beginning:

> Farewell, too little and too lately known . . .

His Odes include the poem on *Mrs Anne Killigrew* (1686), and the splendid clangour of *A Song for Saint Cecilia's Day* (1687) and *Alexander's Feast* (1697). His long career closed with his most original poem, the 'Secular Masque' (1700), his ironical farewell to the seventeenth century:

> 'Tis well an old age is out,
> And time to begin a new.

Dryden's verse is little read now, but his place in the history of poetry is secure. He joined a colloquialism like Donne's to a grandiloquence like Milton's, and established English versification on a basis unshaken till modern times. He wrote in many metres, but the metre he made most his own was the heroic couplet. It lends itself, in his hands, to economy of words and rapidity in movement, as in the incisive portrait of a London politician of the time:

> Shimei, whose youth did early promise bring
> Of zeal to God, and hatred to his King,
> Did wisely from expensive sins refrain,
> And never broke the Sabbath, but for gain:
> Nor ever was he known an oath to vent,
> Or curse, unless against the Government . . .
> The City, to reward his pious hate
> Against his master, chose him magistrate:
> His hand a vare [wand] of justice did uphold;
> His neck was loaded with a chain of gold.
> During his office, treason was no crime.
> The sons of Belial had a glorious time:
> For Shimei, though not prodigal of pelf,
> Yet loved his wicked neighbour as himself:
> When two or three were gathered to declaim
> Against the Monarch of Jerusalem,
> Shimei was always in the midst of them,
> And, if they curst the King when he was by,
> Would rather curse, than break good company.
> (from *Absalom and Achitophel*)

In what he called 'the other harmony' of prose Dryden is outstanding. His prose finally superseded the old-fashioned grandeur of Milton and Sir Thomas Browne. Its basis is cultivated conversation, but without the slovenliness of actual talk. Most of Dryden's prose consists of literary discussion. He was pronounced by Johnson to be the father of English criticism. Of all the English poet-critics he suffered least from jealousy. He led a literary revolution, but it was a revolution in the English manner, sparing the opposition.

Literary criticism, often so boring, has never been more delightful than in Dryden's *An Essay of Dramatic Poesy* (1668). The *Essay* takes the form of a dialogue among four speakers, and the setting is 'that memorable day, in the first summer of the late war, when our navy engaged the Dutch'. The sea-battle makes the background to the polite and bloodless conflict of the critics.

. . . the noise of the cannon from both navies reached our ears about the city, so that all men being alarmed with it, and in the dreadful suspense of the event, which they knew was then deciding, every one went following the sound as his fancy led him; and leaving the town almost empty, some took towards the park, some cross the river, others down it; all seeking the noise in the depth of silence.

And soon Eugenius, Crites, Lisideius, and Neander are deep in discussion of the Dramatic Unities. They may all be 'alarmed', and in 'dreadful suspense', but somehow it is not quite like the London Blitz.

Dryden's literary character is puzzling. He can be cheap and vulgar; he can be gentle and dignified. He was thought a turncoat and time-server in his own day, and compared with Milton there is something pliable and opportunist about him. Defoe said that Dryden's genius was

. . . slung and pitched upon a swivel . . . it would turn round as fast as the times, and instruct him how to write elegies to Oliver Cromwell and King Charles the Second with all the coherence imaginable; how to write *Religio Laici* and *The Hind and the Panther* and yet be the same man; every day to change his principle, change his religion, change his master, and yet never change his nature.

Of the other poets of Dryden's time few are remembered. One of the few is John Wilmot, Earl of Rochester (1647–80). His short life was dissolute (but it ended in pious repentance) and some of his poetry is indecent, though modern scholarship has shown that he did not write by any means all of the filth that was ascribed to him. Rochester evidently belonged to the same type of personality as Mirabeau, or Byron, the mocking, intelligent, rebellious nobleman. His 'Satire against Mankind' is powerful, with a bitter Hobbes-like view of 'wretched man', 'From fear to fear successively betrayed'. Rochester has an unexpected sweetness as a lyric poet. 'Absent from thee I languish still' ranks with the best of Carew and the other Carolines. Samuel Butler (1612–80) is remembered for *Hudibras* (in 3 parts, 1663,

1664, 1678). Like Rochester's satires it is a survival from the school of Donne. Butler's octosyllabic banter is directed against those who

> . . . prove religion orthodox
> By apostolic blows and knows,
> Decide all controversies by
> Infallible artillery,
> Call fire and sword and desolation
> A thorough, godly Reformation.

Butler writes against the sectaries as a triumphant royalist, but much of the poem seems to be an attack not just on Puritans but on the whole seventeenth century world of pedantry and eccentricity. In short, Butler is an early 'Augustan'. His famous poem is only enjoyable in bits. The narrative is confused, and much of the satire is too topical. Auden adopted the manner of *Hudibras* for his *New Year Letter* (1940).

The drama of the late seventeenth century is called 'Restoration', though most of the best known plays were written many years after 1660. The rhymed Heroic Plays, advocated and written by Dryden, who carefully distinguished them from tragedies, have not survived in the repertory. They are a sort of opera without music, like the plays of Corneille and Racine, but this genre seems to work in French better than it does in English. Dryden's best serious drama is *All for Love*, in blank verse, where he is using Shakespeare's *Antony and Cleopatra* as a model. Apart from Thomas Otway's melodramatic *Venice Preserv'd* (first performed 1682) no tragedy from this period is often revived.

The stage comedies have lasted better. A critical controversy going back to Jeremy Collier (1650–1726) continues intermittently about their 'immorality'. Collier's objections to them (1698) were repeated in the nineteenth century by Macaulay and in the twentieth by L.C. Knights. Charles Lamb defended the plays as 'a utopia of gallantry', a purely fantastic world. Nearer our time Bonamy Dobrée urged that the best of these comedies represent a serious reconsideration of sex relationships (there is a ring of the 1920s here). The debate continues. Against Lamb it could be said that the plays undoubtedly depict the contemporary smart world; Dorimant, hero of *The Man of Mode* (1676) by Sir George Etherege (?1634–91), was even thought to be a portrait of the Earl of Rochester. Against the realist view may be urged the abundant presence in these plays of traditional, stage types, the playful names ('Sir Fopling Flutter', 'Horner', 'Lady Wishfort') and the artificiality of the plots. Restoration comedy may only bear the same relation to the real London of its day that P.G. Wodehouse's stories do to the English aristocracy, or Raymond Chandler's to life in Southern California.

The comedies of William Wycherley (1640–1716), *The Country Wife* (published 1675) and *The Plain Dealer* (1676) – the latter a very coarse rehandling of Molière's *Le Misanthrope* – are lively, but seem morally unfocused; they are a typically English mixture of cynicism, rough humour, and sentimentality (about young innocent girls). William Congreve (1620–1729) was a geniune artist, whose best work can be enjoyed without historical extenuation. His *Love for Love* (performed 1695) makes a sophisticated use of the conventions of earlier plays, particularly Shakespeare's; a Bardolater should not go back to Shakespeare's 'mad' scenes too soon after seeing *Love for Love*. *The Way of the World* (1700) would be one of the best of stage comedies if it were not for the impenetrable plot. The brilliance of the scenes with the heroine Millamant, and the broader comedy of Lady Wishfort, are first-rate. 'Restoration comedy' may still be a viable form. But its stock of ideas is limited. Venereal disease is funny; impotence is funny; an old man cuckolded by a young man is wildly funny . . . such, too often, are the propositions on which the humour turns. What keeps the plays alive is the well handled intrigue, the stage tricks, the smart repartee, and (especially in Congreve) the flights of fancy and the poetic vitality of the language (the peacock with 'his ogling tail').

Later dramatists, like Vanbrugh and Farquhar, move further towards the world of the eighteenth century novel. Brittle heartlessness and verbal fencing yield to broad farce and warm sentiment. Sir John Vanbrugh (1664–1726), architect and man of many talents, still goes well on the stage, in his *Provok'd Wife* (produced 1697) and *The Relapse* (1697). In George Farquhar (1678–1707) a breath of rural air stirs in *The Recruiting Officer* (1706) and *The Beaux' Stratagem* (1707), both often revived. Malicious wit is replaced by fun: the metropolitan glitter has gone. There is a relaxation of the tense sexual conflict, which prepares the way for the sentimental comedy of Sir Richard Steele (1672–1729), like Farquhar an Irishman and a soldier.

The prose of the theatre is constantly in touch with the general prose of the time. Larger theological and philosophical issues, matters of life and death, now recede in favour of things of everyday concern, political transactions, social contretemps, the performing arts, literary criticism. From now on journalism is all-pervasive. Most of it is of course ephemeral. But the writings of George Savile, Marquess of Halifax (1633–95) find readers in every age, though he was mainly a topical pamphleteer. His characteristic attitude, which resembles that of Montaigne, is stated in his *Character of a Trimmer* (1688). He is one of the best English aphorists:

When the people contend for their liberty, they seldom get anything by their victory but new masters.

There are as many apt to be angry at being well as at being ill governed: for most men, to be well governed, must be scurvily used.

Explaining is generally half-confessing. [Halifax anticipates rude Admiral Fisher's 'Never apologize, never explain'.]

The struggling for knowledge hath a pleasure in it like that of wrestling with a fine woman.

Halifax's *Character of Charles II*, not published till 1750, should not be missed: it is the best prose portrait in existence of the 'merry' king.

In this age of first-rate prose and second-rate poetry the anecdotal writers stand out. Anthony à Wood compiled the first English biographical dictionary, *Athenae Oxonienses*(1691–2). Modern newspaper commentators love to adopt his malicious gossiping style to recount the doings of our own politicians. John Aubrey (1626–97) is even more to modern taste. His *Brief Lives*, besides being invaluable as source-material, e.g. for the life of Shakespeare, are intensely enjoyable reading. No one surpasses Aubrey for quick character-sketching. Here is a glimpse of Hobbes:

He took great delight to go to the book-binders' shops, and lie gaping on maps.

The *History of the Rebellion and Civil Wars in England* (not published till 1702–4), by Edward Hyde, Earl of Clarendon (1609–74) is for the less frivolous. Clarendon writes with the authority of one who was a leading participant in the story he has to tell. His rolling periods and high dignity are not to everyone's taste; there is something of Milton's Beelzebub about him. A faster-moving, more modern style is to be found in Gilbert Burnet (1643–1715) whose *History of My Own Time* (two volumes, 1723 and 1724) may have been inspired by Clarendon's work, but makes livelier reading. We seem to be in the same room as the waspish old Whig bishop.

Surpassing all in personal interest is the diary Samuel Pepys (1633–1703) kept from 1 January 1660 to May 1669. His note is unmistakable:

I went out to Charing Cross, to see Major-general Harrison hanged, drawn and quartered; which was done there, he looking as cheerful as any man could do in that condition.

(13 October 1660)

Among the private journals and personal records in which English literature is rich Pepys's Diary is unchallenged for its candour. Other diarists, Parson Woodforde in the eighteenth century, Dorothy Wordsworth and Francis Kilvert in the nineteenth, also appeal to modern readers, but the spell of Pepys is unique. It is hard to explain. He has no artistry or literary skill: part of the charm of the Diary is its artlessness. It gives us Restoration London in a time-capsule. Pepys's only rival for this period is John Evelyn (1679–1745), his lifelong friend. Evelyn's diaries cover a much longer period, and reflect a more staid and reserved personality. Both are an indispensable source for writers of historical novels.

The prose masterpiece of the later seventeenth century comes out of a very different world. Pepys and Evelyn were gentry: the England of John Bunyan (1628–88), author of *The Pilgrim's Progress* (1678), is the England of the sects. Bunyan, a tinker by trade, was one of many 'mechanic preachers' of that time: his great book had to compete with many didactic allegories now forgotten. He won popular fame in his lifetime, while the Vanity Fair of his day (it included Congreve) laughed at his work. *The Pilgrim's Progress* belongs to Vision literature, like Langland. The book has an important place in the history of English life and character. The tale of the flight of Christian from the City of Destruction thrilled many generations of children who did not recognize the allegory, with episodes such as the pilgrims sinking in the Slough of Despond, the fight with Apollyon 'straddling the way', Giant Despair in Doubting Castle.

The meaning of Bunyan's allegory has often been discussed. Some modern socialists have seen the burden which falls from Christian's back as his poverty. Any serious treatment of human life must recognize the importance of material conditions. But it is surely a banal philosophy which can see no difference between a demand for higher wages and a hunger for the Bread of Life.

The Pilgrim's Progress is open to many objections, both artistic and moral. It contains stretches of sermonizing during which both the allegory and the story are forgotten. Worse still is the religious bigotry which intrudes now and then – horribly in other tales of Bunyan, *The Life and Death of Mr Badman* (1680) and *The Holy War made by Shaddai upon Diabolus* (1682).

It is best to remember the humane things in Bunyan's work, the geniality and humour. His mastery of plain English cannot be overstated. The antithesis of a great stylist like Browne, he used the common language of the English people (now a people that knew the Bible). And he is still a touchstone for great English. There is nothing in the language to surpass, or perhaps to equal, the sublime, yet quiet, exaltation of the closing pages of the second part of *The Pilgrim's Progress*.

After this it was noised abroad that Mr Valiant-for-Truth was taken with a summons by the same post as the other [Mr Honest]; and had this for a token that the summons was true, that his pitcher was broken at the fountain (Eccles. xii.6). When he understood it, he called for his friends, and told them of it. Then said he, 'I am going to my Father's; and though with great difficulty I am got hither, yet now I do not repent me of all the trouble I have been at to arrive where I am. My sword I give to him that shall succeed me in my pilgrimage; and my courage and skill to him that can get it. My marks and scars I carry with me, to be a witness for me that I have fought his battles who now will be my Rewarder'. When the day that he must go hence was come, many accompanied him to the river-side; into which as he went he said, 'Death, where is thy sting?' And as he went down deeper, he said, 'Grave, where is thy victory?' So he passed over; and all the trumpets sounded for him on the other side.

The eighteenth century

In English literary history the eighteenth century means the time from the ascendancy of Dryden to the publication of Wordsworth and Coleridge's *Lyrical Ballads* (1798). There are still some misconceptions about this period. It has been called 'the Age of Reason', but one of the chief features of its intellectual history is a reaction against the excessive claims for what can be accomplished by pure reasoning. A powerful current in its philosophy was the appeal to experience, or empiricism. Another over-simplification is the view that it was 'neo-classical', hedged in by the Rules and the Unities, ossified by 'poetic diction'. But the English eighteenth century was no more neo-classical than previous periods. Ever since the sixteenth century English literature had been heavily influenced by the Classics. Some sixteenth century humanists were more doctrinaire than any eighteenth century critic. English writers such as Dryden, Swift, Pope or Johnson paid little attention to critical prescriptions. Poetic diction (the 'fleecy kind' for sheep, etc.) was largely confined to purposes of epic, as in Pope's translation of the *Iliad*. The best eighteenth century poets write with pungent directness in plain words. One more misunderstanding is reflected in the still popular label for the period as 'the Enlightenment'. This word is best reserved for a European, largely French intellectual movement of the time, anti-Christian, and associated with the French Encyclopaedia and Voltaire. English writers were aware of this movement, and themselves had some influence on it ('British empiricism' was then fashionable in France), but the leading figures in English literature in this period were sincere Christians. The exceptions were writers most influenced by French thought, such as Hume and Gibbon and Bentham.

Of the writers who flourished during Queen Anne's reign (1702–14) Joseph Addison (1672–1719) appeals less to the twentieth century that he did to the eighteenth, or the nineteenth, when Macaulay ranked him above Swift and Pope. His poem *The Campaign*, celebrating the Duke of Marlborough's victory at Blenheim in 1704, and his tragedy *Cato*, were regarded by contemporary critics as major works, and won him fame in his day, but are now unread. He is remembered for the essays and character-sketches in the periodical journals *The Tatler* (1709–11) and *The Spectator* (1711–12). His collaborator, Sir Richard Steele (1672–1719) has been found by many readers a more sympathetic personality than the devious and enigmatic Addison. Both had a hand in the series of 'Coverley Papers', in which these urbane Whig journalists exercise their affectionate humour at the expense of a lost cause, the ethos represented by the Tory squire Sir Roger de Coverley. Addison's social and political purposes have been viewed with suspicion. 'He was the apologist for the New Bourgeoisie', wrote Cyril Connolly, a twentieth century critic, 'who writes playfully and apologetically about nothing, casting a smoke screen over its activities to make it seem harmless, genial and sensitive in its non-acquisitive moments'. Equally witty, and looking with a sharper, more challenging Christian eye over worldly society, is the *Serious Call to a Devout and Holy Life* (1728), by William Law (1686–1761) – despite its title a far from lugubrious work. But the traditional account of Addison is probably correct. He made the familiar essay (i.e the essay which is not contentious or polemical) into one of the major eighteenth century forms. His graceful and easy prose style brought high literature and philosophy within the reach of intelligent non-specialist readers, women prominent among them, all over the nation. His blend of moralizing with entertainment helped to bring together the reading public and foster the taste for the new prose fiction which was to establish itself as the main genre of English literature. His literary criticism encouraged a liberal and catholic taste, favouring the Ballads as well as *Paradise Lost*, and subtly disparaging, as much by its manner as its matter, the schoolmasterly dogmatizing of critics like Rymer and Dennis. He was praised by Johnson for the excellence of his style, elegant without affectation, and conventional without vulgarity. Johnson recommends us to give our days and nights to it as a model. But the turn of Addison's sentences is perhaps too personal to be imitated

The Spectator inspired many successors. The most distinguished was Samuel Johnson's *The Rambler* (1750–2), the production of a more powerful mind than Addison's, but lacking his sparkle and light touch. In Oliver Goldsmith's *Citizen of the World* (1760–2) the essay-formula is enlivened with quaintness and pathos, suggesting a more directly appealing literary personality. Goldsmith in his essays occupies an intermediate place between the amused detachment of the *Tatler* and *Spectator* and the exploitation of personal idiosyncrasy in nineteenth century essayists such as Charles Lamb or Walter Pater.

The other chief prose writer of the early eighteenth century, Jonathan Swift (1667–1745), continues to fascinate modern readers more than any other author of his time. Much of his writing is bound up with contemporary politics and personalities. Like a great deal of Johnson's work, and the work of twentieth century writers like Shaw, Belloc, or Orwell, it belongs to a region in which literature overlaps with journalism, and this means that much of it is now read only by historians. But a few things of Swift have outgrown their original context and taken their place among the classics of invective.

A Tale of a Tub (1704) is, none the less, baffling to a reader who takes it up without advance warning. In part it is a topical work, a symbolic fable designed to defend the Anglican position against Catholics and Nonconformists. But to say no more than that would be to give a very misleading impression. The Tale is an extravaganza of parody and self-parody, a medley of mock-learning, irony, burlesque, buffoonery, and savagery. It defies description. It is the nearest thing in English to the Gargantua and Pantagruel of the sixteenth century French writer François Rabelais, clearly one of Swift's masters in his writing. But Swift's tone of mockery is peculiarly his own.

I am now trying an experiment, very frequent among modern authors, which is to write upon nothing; when the subject is clearly exhausted, to let the pen still move on; by some called the ghost of wit, delighting to walk after the death of the body. And to say the truth, there seems to be no part of knowledge in fewer hands, than that of discerning when to have done.

The mock-heroic literary allegory The Battle of the Books (1704) also requires much annotation. It is a by-product of the great French (and European) literary quarrel of the time between the Ancients and the Moderns. The short satire usually called An Argument against Abolishing Christianity (1711) was provoked by a contemporary controversy about the imposition of denominational tests. It is a small masterpiece of poker-faced irony at the expense of the materialistic and commercial civilization which The Spectator was at the same time blandly applauding. In one of his poems Swift speaks of his 'vein' as 'ironically grave', and the Argument is a sustained tour de force in this style. The implicit premiss throughout is that the only kind of Christianity that any reasonable person would think worth defending is purely nominal. There is greater intensity in a short satire from Swift's later years, generally known as the Modest Proposal (1729), 'modestly' advocating a practical scheme to aid the Irish economy by the slaughter of Irish children. Here again the power of the irony derives from the unquestioned premiss that in economic and commercial affairs 'sentiment' can be ignored, and from the relentless and grisly working out of the detailed advantages of the 'proposal'. This brief work still retains its power to shock the reader into a recognition of the inhumanity of many 'rational' calculations of experts and administrators. It seems actually to have gained in point in our century of Final Solutions.

With the Modest Proposal and other tracts by Swift the sufferings and wrongs and inextricable problems of Ireland first become a prominent theme in English literature. Though of English parentage he was born and educated in Ireland, and he was to become Dean of St. Patrick's Cathedral in Dublin; an ungracious figure, but venerated by the Irish people for his scathing indictment in the *Drapier's Letters* (1724–5), of their exploitation and misrule by the English government.

Swift's masterpiece, *Gulliver's Travels* (1726), takes us beyond Ireland. Purporting to be a factual account of the voyages of 'Captain Lemuel Gulliver', it is written in a sober matter-of-fact prose appropriate to its supposedly level-headed and veracious author. This style of course is designed to enhance the fairy-tale stories of tiny Lilliputians and giant Brobdingnagians, of the flying island of Laputa, and the land of the Houyhnhms, where noble horses rule over the beastly and degraded Yahoos, in whom Gulliver is reluctantly forced to recognize his fellow human beings. The book can be read in various ways. It is said that an Irish bishop at the time 'refused to believe a word of it'. Other readers, particularly children, enjoy it as a fairytale – especially the first two books. The scene of Gulliver's waking up to find himself pinioned by the Lilliputians uses a similar technique to that whereby Lewis Carroll draws us into the world of *Alice in Wonderland*. Adult readers recognize the spice of satire in the story, more narrowly political and topical in Lilliput, broadening out in Brobdingnag with the sage King's indictment of civilized Europeans – on the basis of what he hears about them from Gulliver – as 'contemptible little vermin', and culminating in the scathing pictures of physical and moral corruption presented in the immortal Struldbrugs of Luggnagg and the irrationality and squalor of the Yahoos.

Gulliver's Travels is still one of the most read of the older English books. But there has been some uncertainty about Swift's intentions. His favourite mode is irony, which lends itself to ambiguities and tricks on the unsuspecting reader. He loved hoaxes and disguises. His works were published anonymously, Swift concealing himself behind a fictitious *persona* – 'Drapier', 'Bickerstaff', 'Gulliver' etc. Modern scholars have found recondite allegories and allusions in *Gulliver*, and F.P. Lock in *The Politics of Gulliver's Travels* (1980) has added new interpretations to the critical tradition. But it is difficult to believe that an author who so much cultivated a plain style, and who as a pamphleteer wanted to be understood by everyone, would have been so esoteric. In any case much in the *Travels* surely goes beyond the party-political, even if we discount Macaulay's description of Swift as 'a heart burning with hatred of the whole human race, a mind richly stored with images from the dunghill and the lazar house'.

The general purpose of Swift's satire is not in doubt. *Gulliver's Travels* is an attack on Pride, and in particular on intellectual pride, the extravagance of modern man's claim to rationality, the *hubris* of scientists and philosophers. The terms of the indictment belong to Swift's age, but the theme will always be timely. Swift opposed to human pride what was for him traditional wisdom, the recognition by ancient pagans of man's mental and physical limitations, endorsed by the Christian emphasis on the universality of sin. His targets are those of the traditional satirist; there is nothing new in his diagnosis or his remedies. What makes his book a classic is the fertility of his comic invention – contrary to Johnson's opinion, there is more to this than just thinking of big men and little men – and an intensity of malicious perception in which he has never been surpassed. Swift has been thought morbid, with a depraved imagination, because of his emphasis on the disgusting, and it is true that the reader of Swift's prose (and of his verse) is not allowed to forget for long that men and women, with all their airs and graces, are excreting animals. Some have divined in his writings a hatred and contempt for humanity which border on the pathological. In the nineteenth century Thackeray portrayed Swift as an insane misanthropist. But after two world wars in this century, and the revelations of the inhumanity of modern totalitarianism, present-day readers may not be so ready to dismiss Swift's darker pages as merely the expression of a personal neurosis. And it should not be forgotten that, while some of his writings make disagreeable reading for the squeamish, Swift was essentially a comic writer. His friends saw *Gulliver's Travels* as 'a merry work'.

Swift's ironic habit also appears in his verse, where it is very different from the self-protective irony frequent in twentieth century poetry. He uses irony as an attacking weapon:

> *Libertas et natale solum* ['Freedom and one's native soil']:
> Fine words! I wonder where you stole 'em.

Swift's early poetry consists of ambitious efforts in the 'Pindaric' manner of Cowley. These contain some interesting passages, which anticipate the later style of W.B. Yeats. But we can understand his kinsman Dryden's alleged remark: 'Cousin Swift, you will never be a poet'. Whether Dryden said this or not, Swift seems to have been hostile to Dryden in *The Battle of the Books*. After his early poems Swift confined himself to light verse. Here he showed himself a master of the octosyllabic couplet, which he handled more individually than any poet since Samuel Butler. His notorious poems 'On a Beautiful Young Nymph Going to Bed', and 'The Lady's Dressing Room', show a scatological interest, but they can also be seen as further aspects of his attack on Pride. In contrast the autobiographical 'Cadenus and Vanessa' is the most charming and graceful of Swift's poems. But his best poem is generally agreed to be 'Verses on the Death of Dr. Swift'. Nothing is more characteristic of him than the line in which he imagines how the news of his death will be received:

> The Dean is dead (and what is trumps?') . . .
> Poor Pope will grieve a month; and Gay
> A week; and Arbuthnot a day . . .
> The rest will give a shrug, and cry:
> 'I'm sorry, but we all must die'.

Swift's vigour and clarity will be acknowledged even by those whose taste is too romantic to enjoy his dry commonsense. 'Swift, as a rule, used his Pegasus for a cart-horse', said the poet T. Sturge Moore in 1910, 'but even when plodding in the ruts, its motion betrays the mettle in which it revels'. He avoided the formal satire so common in the poetry of his day, with the result that his verse is the least dated of the century, till Blake's. *The New Oxford Book of Eighteenth Century Verse* (edited by Roger Lonsdale, 1984) shows how great his influence was on the informal and occasional poetry of the time.

But by common consent the chief poet of the eighteenth century was Swift's friend Alexander Pope (1688–1744). In his early work Pope attempted a variety of literary kinds. The *Pastorals* (1709) are a precocious display of his gift for 'pure poetry'. *Windsor Forest* (1712) is a colourful example of local or topographical poetry. Pope, himself a child of the Forest, wrote one of the best poems of this kind. Its politics are now forgotten; its graphic descriptions of nature remain.

> The silver eel, in shining volumes roll'd,
> The yellow carp, in scales bedropp'd with gold.

Windsor Forest shows Pope as a very different poet from the indoor periwigged raconteur he was once supposed to be. The *Essay on Criticism* (1711) is a youthful success in the now little used genre of didactic verse, mixing ancient commonplaces and modern insights in a sustained flight of epigrammatic couplets. The 'heroic epistle' *Eloisa to Abelard* (before 1717) based on the true story of two unhappy medieval lovers, commands a kind of rhetoric rarely successful in English verse, combining declamatory eloquence with intimate matter; it is the nearest thing to Racine in our poetry. Another early poem, the *Elegy on an Unfortunate Lady* (before 1717) also employs the Racine-like tirade. It is a text which could be brought in evidence against the judgment of his younger contemporary Joseph Warton that he lacked 'sublimity' and 'pathos'. The most popular of Pope's early poems has proved to be the mock-heroic miniature epic *The Rape of the Lock* (1712). Here Pope is a verse-musician uniting light satire with sensuous beauty. It was a stroke of genius when he decided to introduce into the teasing little tale of 'Belinda' the sylphs and gnomes of Rosicrucian mythology.

> Some to the sun their insect-wings unfold,
> Waft on the breeze, or sink in clouds of gold;
> Transparent forms, too fine for mortal sight,
> Their fluid bodies half-dissolv'd in light,
> Loose to the wind their airy garments flew,
> Thin glitt'ring texture of the filmy dew,
> Dipt in the richest tincture of the skies,
> Where light disports in ever-mingling dyes,
> While'ev'ry beam new transient colours flings,
> Colours that change whene'er they wave their wings.

Pope delights in the ethereal and fantastic, but in the *Rape*, as in most of his poems, there is always a final stress on standards of reasonableness and good humour.

It was his translation of the *Iliad* (1720) that won Pope financial independence and the recognition of his supremacy among the poets of his time. The great scholar Richard Bentley (who was to be a butt of Pope's in the *Dunciad*) is said to have told him that it was 'a pretty poem, but you must not call it Homer'. No doubt according to the criteria of Bentley and his scholarly successors it leaves much to be desired in the way of learning and fidelity to the original, but the reader who approaches Homer by way of Pope will at least get the impression (which no modern translator will give him) that Homer was a mighty poet, ardent and noble. Pope always rises to the great occasions:

> Impetuous Hector thunders at the wall.

Pope had a passion for Homer's poetry. Few things ring truer in the *Essay on Criticism* than his aspiration to follow the master.

> O may some spark of your celestial fire
> The last, the meanest of your sons inspire,
> Who on weak wings, while he attempts your flights,
> Glows as he reads, but trembles as he writes.

Pope had been deprived of the conventional public-school and university education because he belonged to a Catholic family. His Classics were largely self-taught. This gives a freshness and a personal quality to his use of them, bringing him nearer than his birched and drilled contemporaries to modern poets who have had to find their own way to the Classics.

Among the other poets of antiquity, Pope cared most about Horace, the conversational Horace of the *Satires* and *Epistles*. His *Imitations of Horace* (1733–8) come late in his career, but long before that he had become one of the great talkers in verse, unequalled till Byron. His poetry, like Horace's, draws a portrait of the poet himself 'in the small circle of (his) foes and friends'. Pope carefully defines his moral and artistic point of view in autobiographical passages. The most moving are those in which he celebrates friendship. But for Pope 'the life of a wit is a warfare upon earth', and posterity has remembered best the terrible indictments of people whom (justifiably or not) he had come to see as enemies, such as 'Atticus' (Addison), in the *Epistle to Arbutnnot*, (1735) who can

> Damn with faint praise, assent with civil leer,
> And, without sneering, teach the rest to sneer

or 'Sporus' (Lord Hervey), in the same poem, who

> . . . at the ear of Eve, familiar toad,
> Half froth, half venom, spits himself abroad

The Dunciad (1728), originally in three books, is Pope's most ambitious creation in the field of satire. Through a sustained mockery of epic grandeur he sets in motion a grotesque world in which caricatured personalities of the age swarm and pullulate. The *Dunciad* is a concoction of farce, parody and surrealism, with now and then passages of poignant beauty. The fourth book, added later, is a *Paradise Lost* in reverse, ironically celebrating the triumph of the forces of unreason and chaos over the light. Its finale, when 'universal darkness buries all', is a magnificent demonstration of the compatibility of ironic satire with the grand style. But even Pope's admirers have had doubts about the *Dunciad*. Some, like Auden, have objected to its squalor (especially in Book II) and its obscurity. Others complain of its lack of proportion. Were Pope's targets too small for a great satirist? Most of the Dunces were merely the minor writers of the day, no better and no worse than the minor writers of any day. Why didn't he leave them alone? The controversy continues.

In the discursive poems now called *Moral Essays* Pope is often at his best. Some of their great set pieces – 'Timon's Villa', or the tale of 'Sir Balaam', indictments of *nouveaux riches* of the time – display dazzling poetic skill. We feel the poet's exultation over the fantastic incongruities of life. Pope's most ambitious enterprise as a moral poet is the *Essay on Man* (1733–4), in which he expounds the ancient philosophy of the Chain of Being. Some of the couplets of the *Essay* have become proverbial, part of the language: Pope is among the most quoted of English poets. But some readers, like Johnson, have found a superficiality in Pope's thought. 'Whatever is, is right', the keynote of the *Essay*, might have seemed profound coming as the final pronouncement from a poet like Dante or a mystic like Julian of Norwich, but it has a ring of shallowness here. The philosophy sounds at times too near that of Dr Pangloss in Voltaire's *Candide*, the complacent apologist of the 'best of all possible worlds'. The Pope who appeals to modern taste is not the Leibnizian reasoner but the mocking satirist and the prophet of virtue.

Pope's place in literature has always been a matter of controversy, and always will be. He tells us more about himself than any previous poet, and creates a literary personality which has been admired or disliked by good judges from his day to ours. Sometimes the dispute has turned on the question, not whether he was a great poet, but whether he was a poet at all. At any rate no one has ever denied that Pope was a powerful writer of some kind, a master of the art he had chosen. He brought fine technical skill to his favourite metre, the heroic couplet (two rhyming, regularly accented lines in iambic pentameter). So great was the effect of his consolidation of the metrical norms he inherited from his master Dryden that for many years English poetry was almost hypnotized by his example. A later eighteenth-century poet, William Cowper, while praising Pope's finesse in writing, his niceness of touch, and exactness of ear, complained that he had

> . . . made poetry a mere mechanic art,
> And every warbler has the tune by heart.

A reaction was inevitable. The Romantic poets dismissed Pope as too artificial, and in the Victorian age Matthew Arnold went so far as to call him 'a classic of our prose'. In the twentieth century Pope has been restored to favour through the agency of the poets Edith Sitwell, William Empson, and W.H. Auden, and the rhapsodist G. Wilson Knight. The Twickenham Edition paid him the honours due to a classic poet. He was favoured also by the most influential critic in Britain, F.R. Leavis, who saw his own role in our society as not unlike Pope's. To-day a scholarly industry, largely American, has gathered round Pope's work, some of which serves a useful purpose. In the Britain of our present discontents he is frequently quoted, though for his gibes against the political and social *status quo* rather than for his metaphysical defence of it. Tiny and crippled, he evokes personal sympathy for his gallant struggle against 'this long disease, my life'. And in a saturnine period like ours so great a master of ridicule and sarcasm cannot fail to find a hearing.

Pope, like Swift, belongs to a Tory literary circle, the Scriblerus Club, so called because it was dedicated to writing the memoirs of an imaginary pedant, Martinus Scriblerus. One of its minor members produced a unique masterpiece, *The Beggar's Opera* (1728). The story of the highwayman-hero Macheath held political implications at the time, which have been given a modern turn in Berthold Brecht's adaptation, *The Threepenny Opera*. The author, John Gay (1685–1732) was a charming poet. His *Tristia, or the Art of Walking the Streets of London* (1715) is in the mock-heroic style: Gay adopts the manner of Swift, but without his acidulousness. Another member of the Club, Thomas Parnell (1679– 1718), is remembered for his 'Night-piece on Death', which anticipates the poetry of 'sensibility' that was to become a popular alternative, as the century went on, to the 'rational' style of Pope and his followers. In the same milieu, although not actually a Scriblerian, we find Matthew Prior (1664–1721), who wrote in many forms. He is most remembered for his distinctive touch in familiar verse: his best poems are compatible to the anthology favourites of Praed, Hood, or Betjeman. 'Jinny the Just', only recovered in the twentieth century, has been much liked for its blend of affectionate feeling with good sense.

The best poets of Pope's school were very different from the master in temperament. They were Johnson, Goldsmith, and Crabbe. Samuel Johnson (1709–84) has many claims to fame besides his poetry, but he has a distinguished place in English verse. His *London* (1738) and *The Vanity of Human Wishes* (1749) stand in the same relation to poems of the Roman satirist Juvenal as Pope's 'imitations' stand to poems of Horace. Johnson's own formidable personality comes through the generalizing formality and abstraction of his style. Few passages of eighteenth-century poetry are as touching as the account of the 'young enthusiast' in *The Vanity of Human Wishes*:

Through all his veins the fever of renown
Burns from the strong contagion of the gown.

Goldsmith in *The Deserted Village* (1770) creates his own variant of Pope's manner – regular, antithetical, epigrammatic – by infusing into it his own nostalgia and pathos. Like Johnson, who contributed couplets to his poems, he can rise to heights of impressive declamation:

Ill fares the land, to hast'ning ills a prey,
Where wealth accumulates, and men decay.

The last master of this style, George Crabbe (1754–1832), produced some of his best work at a time when the Romantic school was well established. He drew astringent pictures of life among the poor and the respectable classes in *The Village* (1783) and *The Borough* (1810). The best known of his poems, thanks to Benjamin Britten's opera, is 'Peter Grimes', but the opera's libretto sentimentalizes the stern fierceness of Crabbe's portrait of the savage and tormented fisherman.

. . . and some on hearing piteous cries,
Said calmly, 'Grimes is at his exercise'.

Some of Crabbe's best work is to be found in the poems of his later years, the *Tales in Verse* (1812) and *Tales of the Hall* (1819). As a short story writer in verse he is surpassed only by Chaucer. After a long period of neglect he has found new admirers in the twentieth century. 'Crabbe', said one of them (E. M. Forster) 'is not easy to label', and a label would have been helpful. He has been called harsh, a realist, a Nature poet – none of these descriptions quite fits. As a satirist he has not the force of Pope. Nor was he a novelist who missed his vocation: he depicts character well within limits, but he makes no attempt to distinguish the varieties of speech; his gentry and his outcasts share the same diction. Crabbe's personality is not altogether attractive. Forster sees him as mainly disapproving. His picture of life is a grey one; human lives are wrecked, or made vacuous, by prudence or ennui. Mediocrity and failure loom larger in his stories than positive ideals. But Crabbe still has devoted readers. He wrote some beautiful descriptive passages, and he is one of the best of English topographical poets. He had a deep feeling for the scenes of his childhood, the coast of Suffolk. He hated Aldeburgh, 'where guilt and famine reign'; he associated it with his oppressive father and his miserable days as an unqualified surgeon and a disliked curate. But memories of Aldeburgh continued to appear in his poetry; in Forster's words, 'the sea, the flat coast, the local meannesses, and an odour of brine and dirt – tempered occasionally with the scent of flowers'.

There were other poetic currents in the eighteenth-century besides the tradition of Pope. Already in Pope's time a mode of reflective nature poetry was established by his friend the Scotsman James Thomson (1700–48), with

Winter (1726), later enlarged into *The Seasons* (1730), which enjoyed great popularity for at least a century. Thomson's renderings of weather and scenery create a style of poetry which has obvious affinities with English landscape painting. His blank verse, based on *Paradise Lost*, links him with many other eighteenth-century poets who in one way or another paid homage to the supremacy of Milton, ranging from the clever parody of John Phillips's *The Splendid Shilling* (1701) to the treatise poetry of Young, Akenside, and others, a genre culminating in Wordsworth's *The Prelude* (1850). Literary historians used to contrast the school of Milton (Whigs writing in blank verse) with the school of Pope (Tories writing in couplets). But this is over-simplified. Many eighteenth-century poets wrote in both styles, and the influence of Milton was not confined to his disciples and imitators. In Pope himself, as in his predecessor Dryden, Milton's work is used creatively; while in the poetry of Thomas Gray (1716–71) and his friends who cultivated Milton, there are many deep affinities with the tradition of Pope. Gray's most famous poem, usually called the *Elegy written in a Country Churchyard* (published 1751), is an accomplished personal adaptation of the rural, reflective, melancholy tradition to the epigrammatic style favoured by Pope and Goldsmith and Johnson. The 'divine truisms' (Tennyson's phrase) of the *Elegy* have made it the most popular poem in the English language.

> Full many a gem of purest ray serene
> The dark unfathom'd caves of ocean bear;
> Full many a flow'r is born to blush unseen,
> And waste its sweetness in the desert air.

It answers to Pope's description of 'true wit', as 'What oft was thought, but ne'er so well expressed'. Yet there are obscurities in the *Elegy*, and differences of mode; the first half of it is 'Augustan', the second 'Romantic'. Like all great poems it holds some secrets.

Gray's other major poems, *The Bard* and *The Progress of Poesy*, show a different aspect of his genuis. They belong to a genre which became extinct in English after the eighteenth-century, the Pindaric Ode. This is named after Pindarus, the ancient Theban poet born about 522 BC, called Pindar by English poets, and much admired and imitated by them. The most successful imitation is *Alexander's Feast* by Dryden, written in 1697 in honour of St Cecilia's Day. It tells the (historically impossible) story of how the music of Timotheos raised a series of different emotions in Alexander the Great at Persepolis. Dryden's poem may not seem like Pindar to modern scholars, but at least he has grasped that Pindar's odes had a definite structure, whereas Cowley, who was mainly responsible for the popularity of 'Pindarics' in the late seventeenth and eighteenth centuries, had regarded them as loose compositions allowing for a wide range of subject and metre. Gray's friend Mason says there was nothing Gray disliked more than 'that chain of irregular stanzas which Cowley introduced, and called Pindaric'. He went to much trouble to discover the form of the ancient compositions. But Gray's themes are not like those of the Greek choral lyricists, and he perhaps did not know that in Pindar's time the whole composition was not only sung but danced. In short, Gray's Odes are to be judged as English poems. They are ambitious and erudite exercises, rhetorically grand, and unlike anything else in English poetry. *The Progress of Poesy* is the more convincing of the two: in *The Bard* it is difficult to imagine Gray as a medieval druid about to commit suicide. Neither poem is as congenial to modern taste as Gray's light verse (such as the poem on Lord Holland's seat) in which he excelled. In his letters Gray speaks to us like a person of our own time, and charms us with his freedom of mind and independence of taste.

Gray is always linked in literary histories with the ill-fated William Collins (1721–59). Collins's Odes are to-day studied mainly for their place in the genealogy of the Romantic movement. The exception is the 'Ode to Evening'. Here the whole spirit of eighteenth-century reflective and descriptive poetry is captured in the most beautiful unrhymed lyric in the language: the poet in a hut on the mountainside views

> . . . hamlets brown, and dim-discover'd spires,
> And hears their simple bell, and marks o'er all
> Thy dewy fingers draw
> The gradual dusky veil.

The spiritual isolation we sense in Gray and Collins are seen in a more spectacular form in the poetry of Christopher Smart (1722–91). 'Kit' Smart, like Collins, was a victim of disappointed hopes, alcoholism, and mental disorder. His *Song to David* (1763) was too strange for his contemporaries, who attributed its religious 'enthusiasm' to the poet's insanity. The conclusion ('DETERMINED, DARED, AND DONE') suggests the triumphant finale of a great piece of orchestral music. In the extraordinary prose poetry of *Jubilate Agno*, not known till the twentieth century, the connexions and associations become even more private and esoteric.

William Cowper (1731–1800) was another poet of 'the age of reason' who had to endure religious mania, in which he was convinced that he was predestined to damnation (and sometimes that he was a unique victim of God's vengeance). The most powerful expression of this conviction in his poetry is the 'Sapphics' written after one or other of his attempts at suicide. The best known is 'The Castaway', written late in his life, in which he compares himself to a sailor washed overboard in an Atlantic storm. The same melancholy, though in a milder key, tinges the beautiful 'Lines on Receiving his Mother's Picture out of Norfolk'. In his long poem *The Task* (1785) the retired Cowper amiably invites us to share a world of rural domesticities and gentle pieties.

> I sing the Sofa . . .

The Task adapts the vocabulary and verse-movement of *Paradise Lost* to the purposes of an eighteenth century moralizing treatise poem, in the tradition of Thomson's *Seasons*. Cowper is the most distinguished poet between the time of Pope and the time of Blake. The appeal of his poetry will always be heightened by knowledge of the tragedy of his life and the liking many people have for the kindly and humorous personality revealed in his letters and his little poems about his pet hares. But William Hazlitt found Cowper's work too mild. 'If he makes a bolder experiment now and then, it is with an air of precaution, as if he were afraid of being caught in a shower of rain, or of not being able, in the case of any untoward accident, to make his retreat home'. (*Lectures on the English Poets*). Certainly the timorous, 'stricken deer' aspect of Cowper's personality is prominent in his poetry. But we also have glimpses of a rebellious Cowper, who enjoyed thunderstorms. After all, his own damnation, like thunderstorms, was one more revelation of the God who in Cowper's best known hymn

> . . . moves in a mysterious way
> His wonders to perform.

The hymns of the eighteenth century are an example of its superiority in public poetry to the centuries that followed. Isaac Watts (1674–1748) of 'Our God, our help in ages past', and John Wesley (1703–91) and his brother Charles (1707–88) are among the best hymn-writers in English. Charles Wesley's 'Wrestling Jacob' is not surpassed by Donne or Herbert for religious intensity. The finest of the eighteenth-century hymn writers were the true successors of the seventeenth-century devotional poets.

In secular poetry, as the century went on, dissatisfaction deepened with the standards established by Dryden and Pope, and there was a search for new models and a broadening of horizons. As a poet Edward Young (1683–1765), author of the Christian meditations called *Night Thoughts* (1742) – by no means always sepulchral, despite their reputation – may be no more than a period figure, but his *Conjectures on Original Composition* (1759), published anonymously when Young was 77, and emphasizing original genius rather than learning as the requisite of the poet, were to exercise influence throughout Europe and eventually to oust the Classicism of the eighteenth-century. Meanwhile Thomas Warton (1728–90) had become one of the first and best of literary historians in his *History of English Poetry* (1774–81), and this, together with his study (1754) of Spenser's *Faerie Queen*, was to bring home to readers and writers a new and wider vision of England's literary past. The renewal of interest in medieval and renaissance literature is reflected in Richard Hurd's *Letters on Chivalry and Romance* (1762).

The desire, characteristic of Romanticism, for a glamorous remote past is not always gratified by the actual early works that have survived. So it is understandable that writers were tempted to compose pseudo-antique pastiches which were more satisfying to eighteenth-century taste than the real thing. The most famous of these are the Ossianic poems (1762) alleged by James Macpherson (1736–96) to be translated from ancient Highland poetry (his true sources appear to have been Irish ballads). The success of these poems – or rather, prose rhapsodies – may have been partly due to a reaction of patriotic feeling in a Scotland which felt itself marginalized and provincialized in the years after the Jacobite rebellions (1708, 1715, 1719, 1745). At the same time the intellectual renaissance of eighteenth-century Scotland, flowering in splendid works of history, philosophy, and political economy, encouraged the need to feel that there were great Scottish creative writers too. Thus Macpherson became a poet to challenge Pope, just as Macpherson's friend Home (1722–88) became for a while a dramatist to challenge Shakespeare. Ossian had a European vogue, which lasted well into the nineteenth century. Napoleon loved it. And in the 1880s, largely because of the advocacy of Matthew Arnold, it was to be an important constituent in the movement known as the 'Celtic Twilight'. From Ossian onwards Celts had to be melancholy. Another exploiter, and victim, of the cult of the pseudo-antique was the boy Thomas Chatterton (1752–70). His suicide was to make him a symbol of the martyred poet for Wordsworth, Shelley, Keats, Alfred de Vigny and others. But his 'Rowley' poems were a less substantial contribution to the revival of medievalism than the researches of Bishop Thomas Percy (1729–1811), whose *Reliques of Ancient English Poetry* (1765) helped to establish the cult of the Ballads and prepare the way for modern ballad-poetry by Sir Walter Scott and Coleridge and their nineteenth and twentieth century successors. The work (1765) of the scholar Thomas Tyrwhitt on Chaucer's language and versification helped to dispel the mistaken belief that Chaucer was clumsy and naive. The growth of historical scholarship in the eighteenth century helped to bring about the consolidation of English Literature as it is now understood. It was in the same period that the foundations of textual scholarship on Shakespeare were laid by Lewis Theobald (so unjustly made a butt by Pope, a rival and inferior editor, in the *Dunciad*) in his *Shakespeare Restored* (1726), and his edition of the plays in 1733. Theobald was to have greater successors, such as Edmund Malone, but he was a pioneer.

The eighteenth-century idolatry of Shakespeare will always be associated with the name of the actor David Garrick (1717–79), who dominated the British theatre in his time. His death, said Johnson magnificently, 'eclipsed the gaiety of nations'. But the indigenous eighteenth century drama has not lasted well. The beginning of the century saw a reaction against the heartless comedy of the Restoration. It is common for public taste to swing between the cynical and sentimental: a *Portnoy's Complaint* is followed at the top of the bestseller list by a *Love Story*. The sentimental comedies of Steele and others had a long innings. In one form or another, melodramatic or lachrymose, sentimentality reigned in the eigtheenth-century theatre. A leading exponent was Richard Cumberland (1732–1811), now only remembered, if at all, as the original of 'Sir Fretful Plagiary' in Sheridan's *The Critic*. The reaction against sentimental affectation came with Goldsmith and Sheridan. In Goldsmith's *She Stoops to Conquer* (1773) the farce rests on something real: a man's repressed self often emerges into liveliness in an easy impersonal environment such as an inn. Richard Brinsley Sheridan (1751–1816), wit and orator, still holds the stage with three comedies: *The Rivals* (1775), *The School for Scandal* (1777), and *The Critic* (1779). They are full of stock figures and situations, but show a genius for the stage. The *School* is as polished as Congreve's *Way of the World*, and the plot is easier to follow. No eighteenth-century tragedy, by Sheridan or anyone else, is now remembered.

A new genre created by the eighteenth century now came to the fore, the novel. A novel is a feigned history, distinguishable from romance or epic by its realism of presentation, i.e. its incorporation – for the sake of verisimilitude – of details drawn from everyday life. Of realism in this sense the first English novelist, Daniel Defoe (1661–1731), was a master who has never been surpassed. Most of his writings belong to the world of popular journalism. His plain matter-of-fact prose establishes a sense of immediate contact between writer and reader. Defoe had an interesting and strange career as politician and secret agent. His novels belong to the later years of his life. They have something in common with the stories of rogues and adventurers told by Elizabethan writers like Nashe or Greene or Deloney, but Defoe goes far beyond these in creating the illusion of fact. It is hard to remember, as we read the imaginary memoirs of 'Moll Flanders' or 'Colonel Jack' or 'Captain Singleton', that they are not actual people telling their own story. Defoe achieved world fame with *Robinson Crusoe* (1719). Like other great works it has been interpreted in very different ways. As John Gross has pointed out, Leslie Stephen in the nineteenth century saw it as a book for 'boys, not men', but Albert Camus in the twentieth saw it as carrying a profound message for our time, about suffering and solitude. It has also been read as a parable of Economic Man. Defoe himself, in 'Robinson Crusoe's Preface', maintained that it was a religious allegory, but literary historians have seen this as a dodge to retain Bunyan's pious public. On the face of it there is a great difference between the symbolical world of *The Pilgrim's Progress*, in which imprisoned Christian suddenly finds a key about his person, and the island of Crusoe, where the interest centres on the struggle for physical survival, in a world which has to be subdued by unaided human effort. Allegorical or not, *Robinson Crusoe* remains the prototype, and the greatest, of desert island stories. Though a byword for 'realism', it is not probable, as may be seen by comparing it with the account of what really happened to Alexander Selkirk, the real-life original of Defoe's hero (Selkirk when rescued had forgotten how to talk). It has little drama or tension: the famous moment of the discovery of Friday's footprint is narrated very casually. Nor is the hero's psychology done with much inwardness. The most remarkable feature of this remarkable book is the way in which Defoe's obsession with material objects, evident in all his fiction, is here invested with almost a spiritual significance.

The novels of Samuel Richardson (1689–1761), like Defoe's, purport to be compiled from factual sources: the author's rôle is ostensibly no more than that of an editor. It was after composing a series of model letters that the idea occurred to Richardson of writing a novel by that means, and the result was *Pamela: or Virtue Rewarded* (1740), with which he won fame. The ability of this prim elderly printer to get inside the skin of a young serving-girl remains one of the marvels of literature. The implicit morality of the story, which tells how Pamela held off the immoral advances of her employer and finally secured his hand in marriage, has troubled readers from Henry Fielding onwards. (Is this *virtue* rewarded?) Richardson's masterpiece was another novel in letters, *Clarissa Harlowe* (1747–8); 'one of the great still books', said Tennyson. As in *Pamela*, though *Clarissa* is much longer, the story owes its power to its concentration on the sexual theme. The psychological inwardness of *Clarissa* gives readers an impression of verisimilitude which causes them to overlook the improbabilities of the story and the mythological and literary materials which underlie it. The very convincing villain Lovelace, tormentor and eventually rapist of the virtuous heroine, seems to derive from Restoration comedies in which the author, personally prudish though he may have been, was clearly well versed. *Clarissa* was regarded by Richardson himself and by many readers in his time as a Christian work, a saint's life. It has been seen in our own days as a contribution to liberationism. It repays moral, psychological, and sociological analysis as a memorable study of love, family oppression, and conscience. *Sir Charles Grandison* (1753–4) was meant as a companion piece to *Clarissa*: it was to be the portrait of a good man. But Richardson was not as gifted at drawing men as he was at drawing women, and the novel has been largely forgotten.

The third great pioneer of the eighteenth-century novel was Henry Fielding (1707–54). Fielding's path to the novel was in part through the periodical essay, but above all through the drama. Compelled by political opposition to give up writing plays, he turned to novels, which in their copious use of dialogue, as well as their plots and situations, owe much to stage comedy. Many of his scenes could be transferred directly to the stage. Fielding's impulse to the new form was further strengthened by his irritation with the false morality of *Pamela*. First, it seems, in the anonymous *Shamela* (1741), and then in *Joseph Andrews* (1742) he satirized the Pamela story. But after the opening pages of *Joseph Andrews* the parody becomes less important, and with the appearance of the great comic figure of Parson Adams Fielding opens out a world of his own, permeated with an aristocratic generosity of spirit, a richness of conscious humour, and a morality which spurned the pharisaism he detected in Richardson. Fielding's disagreement with his great predecessor was purely moral. He admired Richardson's work and wrote a fan letter to him about *Clarissa*. But he was a very different kind of literary artist. He evolved a theory of the novel as 'comic epic in prose' which looks back to Cervantes's *Don Quixote* for its model. He embellished his work with classical allusions and parodies, theoretical discussions of literary problems, and philosophic disquisition on moral questions, which link his novels with the polite literary-intellectual world of Addison and Swift and Pope rather than the unsophisticated imaginings of Defoe and Richardson. *Jonathan Wild* (1743) is a fierce satire on the Great Man – still salutary. In *Tom Jones* (1749) a masterly plot is brought to life with great energy and cheerfulness. *Amelia* (1752) separates the essayist and the novelist less rigorously than *Tom Jones*. It is a gentler, sadder book. And like all Fielding's novels it is an excellent story. With Fielding the English novel comes once and for all to literary self-consciousness. His most important technical contribution to its development was that he made the author part of the story. Some modern novelists (Joyce Cary, Mary McCarthy, J.D. Salinger) have from time to time returned to Defoe's method of complete mimicry. But Fielding's method has remained very typical of English fiction.

With the success of Defoe, Richardson and Fielding the English novel emerged from subliterature and became recognized as a major literary form; though strangely enough, despite Fielding's pioneering efforts (in the essays incorporated in *Tom Jones*) it was not until the late nineteenth century, in the time of Henry James, that a critical vocabulary was devised for discussing it.

After the 1740s the field of prose fiction was greatly widened, and many variations of both form and content were evolved. One of the most widely read eighteenth-century novels to-day is *Memoirs of a Woman of Pleasure* (?1749), usually known as *Fanny Hill*, by John Cleland (1709–89), which has been constantly, if surreptitiously, in circulation in Europe and America since the 1750s. It is frankly erotic, like *Lady Chatterley's Lover*, but unlike Lawrence's novel its manner is elegant: it is a sort of pastoral of the brothel.

The earlier novels of the Scotsman Tobias Smollett (1721–71) contain many technical experiments and have a flavour quite their own. *Roderick Random* (1748) and *Peregrine Pickle* (1751) represent the grafting onto English fiction of a foreign picaresque tradition (that of Le Sage) which the English novel has never quite assimilated. But in our time John Wain has found stimulus in them, and George Orwell called Smollett the greatest Scottish novelist. Smollett has a brutal farcicalness and a curious externality. But *Humphrey Clinker* (1771), unlike his earlier novels, has a quality which Dickens, who owed much to Smollett, called 'tenderness' (a modern critic might call it flexibility, or sensitiveness); a novel in letters, it is a ramble through English scenes. Much of the humour in it is of a simple kind, depending on comic mis-spellings, but it can still make readers laugh out loud.

Laurence Sterne (1713–68), who lampooned the grim Smollett as 'Smelfungus', was himself the master of a very different kind of humour. *Tristram Shandy* (published at intervals between 1760 and 1768) has never been surpassed for oddity. It is a fictional game with the reader which has attracted much twentieth-century interest, especially in France and the United States, for its deliberate mockery of the convention of the novel, its tricks with the relation between fictional and real time, its typographical peculiarities, and its fantasias on how the mind works. But *Tristram Shandy* is not an 'anti-novel'. Sterne's whimsies never result in an alteration of the lives of the characters in his book or of the events in which they are involved. Within the confines of the novel Sterne (or rather 'Tristram', the narrator) never suggests that his characters are fictitious. He says that Walter and Uncle Toby have fallen asleep and he now has a spare moment to write his preface, but he has to wait till they fall asleep of their own accord. In this way Sterne solved the problem of making his characters convincing. *Tristram Shandy* has been attacked ever since its own time for its mixture of glutinous sentimentality with prurience. It divides readers into two camps, those who see profundity in its affectations, and those who see nothing but silliness and indecency. But beyond the sniggerings of Shandyism it is possible to discern a credible picture of a family. It is as if we were looking for the first time at people we take for granted and seeing just how odd they are. No conventional novelist could have improved on the presentation of Tristram's father and Uncle Toby, bound together by deep affection, yet unable to communicate verbally. The much shorter *Sentimental Journey through France and Italy* (1768) lacks this dimension of emotion. It stands or falls by whether the reader enjoys the company of the narrator, 'Yorick'.

Sterne's cult of sentiment was part of a general trend in eighteenth-century society towards the softening of manners. The gentle humour of Goldsmith's novel *The Vicar of Wakefield* (1766) is an example. It is the early, idyllic part which is treasured, for the novel is faulty in construction and becomes more and more involved in improbable melodrama; and like *Pamela* it displays apparently uncriticized the immorality of conventional morality, in which nothing matters but a wedding-ring. What came to be known as the Gothic novel, where tender sentiment is less important than thrills and marvels, was invented by Horace Walpole (1717–97) in his *Castle of Otranto* (1765). It is not certain how serious Walpole was in his intention. The bizarre incidents of the *Castle* suggest an element of spoof. But it has had a long series of straight successors, down to Bram Stoker (of *Dracula*) in the nineteenth century, or John Dickson Carr in the twentieth. In the Gothic novel there is only enough realism of presentation to sustain and enforce an essentially dream-like content, and that is why it lends itself to the making of films. The short novel

Vathek (1786), originally written in French by the mysterious eccentric William Beckford (1760–1844), represents an unusual development. It involves the terrible but it is not a Tale of Terror: it is a philosophical romance in the manner of Voltaire's Oriental tales.

To the mainstream of feminine domestic fiction belong the novels of Fanny Burney (1752–1840), later Madame d'Arblay. Her novel in letters, *Evelina* (1778), retains something of the freshness and liveliness which delighted her earliest readers. It is the prototype of innumerable later novels about a young girl's first encounters with Society. Fanny Burney showed herself to have the two requisites for success in this type of novel: a sympathetic and convincing presentation of youthful ingenuousness, and the ability to mimic people. She wrote other novels after *Evelina*, notably *Cecilia* (1782), but she never showed again the swift, spontaneous movement and the convincing flow of incidents which keep *Evelina* still readable. Fanny Burney is chiefly remembered as a predecessor of Jane Austen. Like her, she is witty, in *Cecilia*, but far less accomplished as an artist. Jane Austen admired her and learned from her mistakes: for she submitted to influences that were not good for her, such as the brutality of Smollett, and (in her later work) the stately periods of Johnson. And the moralistic style of her novels deters modern readers. For this reason they may find her *Early Diary* (1768–78), where it does not appear, more enjoyable than her fiction. The characters in the *Diary* are more vivid than the characters in her novels.

Fanny Burney as a young woman knew Johnson and felt a deep affection for him, which has been shared by countless readers. Johnson is one of the few historical characters whom we seem to know as we know Falstaff or Micawber, yet he retains the unpredictability of real life, with the most copiously documented life-record of any English writer. Many have followed Macaulay in seeing him as a sort of lovably absurd John Bull, thundering out his antiquated prejudices. Bernard Shaw thought him an invention of Boswell. Certainly Johnson had many foibles and eccentricities, and at times he 'talked for victory' and was a tavern oracle, and this is an important aspect of him. But it is not the only one. We see him differently in his prayers and meditations, in the more personal passages in his letters and verse and in *Rasselas*, and in Mrs Thrale's portrait of him – less amusing than Boswell's, but more intimate. From these we have the impression of an imaginative nature, a poet, injured by melancholia; a deep thinker, victimized by irrational fears; a loving and compassionate spirit, held in check by lifelong disabilities of body and mind.

Johnson's value as a writer is a matter of controversy. Although he has a distinguished place in English poetry he cannot be regarded as one of the greatest English poets. His verse-tragedy, *Irene*, has less life in it than Addison's *Cato*. His chief literary medium was prose. His style is carefully balanced and solid. Every sentence carries a punch. There is no drivel;

language is used with the precision of a great lexicographer. He has been ridiculed from his time to ours for his excessive use of Latinate polysyllables, but this charge cannot be sustained; parodies of Johnson on that basis, though frequent, never catch his note. But it is true that in the *Rambler* (1750–2) his manner is at times excessively heavy and formal. Years later, in the *Lives of the Poets*, the style has grown easier and the sentences shorter. This is the prose of a man who had spend most of his life in conversation (the best recorded in English).

It was the *Dictionary of the English Language* (1755) that won Johnson his contemporary fame. In some ways of course it has been superseded, but Johnson's power of verbal definition has never been equalled (in the nineteenth century Henry Sweet came nearest). It is a pity that the *Dictionary* is now mostly quoted for the few deliberately satiric definitions which he allowed himself as relaxations from his tasks as 'harmless drudge' – one of his definitions of 'lexicographer'. The close of its great Preface is a fine example of Johnson's dignity of style, reticent but strongly felt in his brief allusion to the years of struggle and sorrow during which the *Dictionary* was composed.

Johnson's only novel, *Rasselas* (1759), is a short Oriental tale, with a surprising though quite coincidental resemblance to Voltaire's *Candide*, which appeared in the same year. The theme of both tales is the same: the futility of the search for happiness. But they are very different. *Candide* is a kind of surrealistic farce: *Rasselas* has Johnson's customary weight and gravity. But it has its moments of comedy also – the would-be aviator, the madman who thought he controlled the weather, the philosopher who taught that men should live according to the nature. *Rasselas* really belongs to wisdom literature. It is one of the great books of the world.

Johnson's edition of Shakespeare (1765), whatever its deficiencies by modern editorial standards, does not deserve the censure Macaulay heaps on it. Johnson's good sense steers us through many textual problems. As for the literary criticism in the edition, here he need fear no comparison with any scholar, old or new. The Preface is the most distinguished essay ever written on Shakespeare. It consolidates what had been said by Dryden and Pope, and reinforces it with Johnson's own inimitable stamp of finality. Bardolatry was already rampant, and Johnson's magisterial coolness was no doubt intentionally provocative. All the more impressive, then, is his ranking of Shakespeare among the supreme poets.

One of Johnson's most interesting publications was *A Journey to the Western Isles* (1775). His account of his journey, in Boswell's company, does not have the lively particularity of Boswell's account of his *Tour to the Hebrides* (1788), but Johnson goes deeper, making his little travel-book a study of the perennial problems of civilized man.

The most widely read of Johnson's writings is the last of his major works, usually called *The Lives of the Poets* (1781). These are in fact the prefaces to an edition of earlier English poets: Johnson neither chose the poets, nor edited the texts. The prefaces are both biographical and critical. They show Johnson's mastery in the art of brief biography. Taken together they make up one of the most delightful books in the language.

His scorn of the Great is repeated too often to be real; no man thinks much of that which he despises.

(from the *Life of Pope*).

The *Lives* are full of touches of this kind. The life of Milton was criticized in Johnson's time for its prejudice against Milton's personality. But then it is all the more to Johnson's credit that he was able to find unimprovable phrases with which to define the greatness of *Paradise Lost*, and to achieve formulations and ask questions which will come to mind as long as the poem is read. Johnson was similarly prejudiced against Swift, yet in his account of Swift's last years he came nearer than any other eighteenth-century writer to tragedy.

His madness was compounded of rage and fatuity. The last face that he knew was that of Mrs Whiteway; and her he ceased to know in a little time. His meat was brought him cut into mouthfuls: but he would never touch it while the servant stayed, and at last, after it had stood perhaps an hour, he would eat it walking; for he continued his old habit, and was on his feet ten hours a day . . . It is said that, after a year of total silence, when his housekeeper, on the 30th of November, told him that the usual bonfires and illuminations were preparing to celebrate his birthday, he answered, 'It is all folly; they had better let it alone'.

(from the *Life of Swift*)

Boswell perhaps did not fully comprehend Johnson's own tragic side, but his *Life of Johnson* (1791) remains a great and moving work. Unlike Johnson's own biographies Boswell's is very long: it is a vast rag-bag. It is unique in two respects: Boswell's ability to recreate actual dialogue, and his skill in setting the stage for his hero. He was so much an artist that he did not hesitate to cast himself, now and then, as Johnson's butt. Boswell is the chief source for the Johnson most people know – 'Dr Johnson'. But 'Dr Johnson' has been condemned as a travesty. A modern scholar, Donald Greene of the University of Southern California, sees Boswell as an undermining disciple, who condescended to Johnson both socially and intellectually. Johnson's 'Toryism', denounced by the Whig Macaulay, Professor Greene sees as something imposed on him by Boswell. This view abides our question. Other scholars who have studied the sources and methods of the *Life of Johnson* have been convinced of the essential truthfulness and good faith of Boswell's portrait. The *Life* may be best seen as a unique and happy accident of literature, bringing together two such different geniuses. Thanks to Boswell's amazingly frank Journals we have also a full portrait of him and can see the contrast all the more clearly. Johnson is a great representative of a world that is now dead:

Boswell is a modern man. There must have been many thoughts which Johnson, even if he had them, would have been unable or unwilling to record; in Boswell the scope and movement of his thoughts seem to have no 'period' limits. His Journals, not known until the twentieth century, are a testimony to the positive value of his obsession with himself. He records conduct that all moralists would condemn, yet as Ian Finlayson says in his life of Boswell (1984), what is surprising about him is his ability to 'attach himself to men of the sternest moral character and hold not only their attention but actively to inspire and retain their affection and concern, not as a licensed jester but as a sincere and good man with the impulse, if not the ability, to be a better man'.

Second only to Boswell's *Life of Johnson* among British biographies comes the life (1828) of the sculptor Joseph Nollekens (1737–1825) by John Thomas Smith (1766–1833). It takes us into a slightly later period: Johnson and Boswell put in lively appearances in its early pages. If Boswell was motivated by love, Smith was motivated by hatred, and his 'Nollekens' is a grotesque rather than a 'Dutch picture'. But the biography is a masterpiece of astringency.

Eighteenth-century prose was enriched by a tradition, happily not dead in Britain, of thinkers who write for the general literary public. Among the philosophers John Locke (1632–1704) is to be read mainly because of what he has to say, but the prose of George Berkeley (1685–1753) has a music in it which captivates us however unconvinced we are by Berkeley's arguments for the non-existence of matter, which as Hume said, 'admit of no answer and produce no conviction'. In the writings of David Hume (1711–76), now widely thought the greatest British philosopher, we have the pervasive sense of a personality sceptical and ironic, yet with a latent warmth and geniality. Hume cannot be technically classified among the philosophers of 'ordinary language', but no philosopher of any school, not even Bertrand Russell, has handled that wonderful instrument so elegantly as he. Hume's *Treatise of Human Nature* (1739–40), little regarded when it first came out, is an astonishing work of genius. His fundamental ideas came to him early in life, and we can still enjoy the thrill of youthful audacity in his speculations. From a literary point of view Hume's masterpiece is the *Dialogues concerning Natural Religion* (1779), published posthumously. Here the dialogue form immortalized by Plato receives its finest treatment in English. So effectively does Hume dramatize these conversations about ultimates that scholars still dispute which of the participants fully expresses Hume's thought; though no doubt the sceptical 'Philo' comes nearest to it.

Hume gave up writing philosophy to write the *History of Great Britain* (1754–61). His magnanimous cynicism makes it very readable. But the greatest eighteenth-century historian is now agreed to be Edward Gibbon (1737–94), Hume's younger contemporary. *The Decline and Fall of the Roman Empire* (1776–81) is still read by historians, and it is also read by many others who care little about the facts of Roman history. Gibbon's drafts of his autobiography, never consolidated by him into a single work, afford the surest entry to his singular and captivating personality. From them we learn of the days on which he conceived, and concluded, his greatest work:

It was in Rome, on the 15th of October 1764, as I sat musing amidst the ruins of the Capitol, while the bare-footed friars were singing vespers in the Temple of Jupiter, that the idea of writing the decline and fall of the City first started to my mind . . .

It was on the day, or rather night, of the 27th June 1787, between the hours of eleven and twelve, that I wrote the last lines of the last page in a summer house in my garden. After laying down my pen, I took several turns in a berceau or covered walk of acacias which commands a prospect of the country, the lake and the mountains. The air was temperate, the sky was serene, the silver orb of the moon was reflected from the water, and all nature was silent.

Gibbon's achievement in the *Decline and Fall* is a triumph of style. It is his Olympian manner alone that makes bearable the vast panorama of 'the crimes and follies of mankind' which he sets before us so magisterially. Now and then his tone is ironic, most obviously so in the innuendo which creeps into the historian's voice when he speaks of miracles:

But how shall we excuse the supine inattention of the Pagan and philosophic world to those evidences which were presented by the hand of Omnipotence, not to their reason, but to their senses? . . . Under the reign of Tiberius the whole earth, or at least a celebrated province of the Roman Empire, was involved in a preternatural darkness of three hours. Even this miraculous event, which ought to have excited the wonder, the curiosity, and the devotion of mankind, passed without notice in an age of science and history. It happened during the lifetime of Seneca and the elder Pliny, who must have experienced the immediate effects, or received the earliest intelligence, of the prodigy . . . Both the one and the other have omitted to mention the greatest phenomenon to which the mortal eye has been witness since the creation of the globe.

(from Chapter XV)

But Gibbon would not have lasted if his work had consisted of nothing but polished sneers. He is a master of organization and narrative. His great work is dominated by a sense of the significance of the past, the value of civilization, and – above all – its precariousness. Though he despised Voltaire as a historian, he was temperamentally of the school of Voltaire, not of Voltaire's enemy Jean-Jacques Rousseau. He believed in the civilized life; he had no belief in the rights or virtues of the Natural Man. The French Revolution broke out in Gibbon's lifetime, challenging and eventually overthrowing (it would seem permanently) the civilization Gibbon held dear. He saw in it the fanaticism which he had seen in the early Church, which he confessed made him feel about the early Church what Edmund Burke felt about the French Revolution. Gibbon's adequacy as a historian of Christianity will always be questioned. As with every great thinker his scope implies limits. For him the Rome of the Antonines was a crest of civilization, and so was the Paris of the

Enlightenment, but the period between them lay mostly in darkness and barbarism. Gibbon does not practise analytical history, the criticism of sources, which is the foundation of modern thought about the events and institutions of the past. Nor does he give us the local colour, the 'pictures and conversations' which were to be Scott's lasting legacy to writers on earlier times. But whatever Gibbon's limitations he remains the most entertaining of historians. No one has equalled the masterfulness and gaiety he brought to the stupendous drama of his subject.

Another great eighteenth-century prose writer, the Irishman Edmund Burke, (1729–97) is less read to-day, but he too is one of the most notable of stylists. The foundation of Burke's style is parliamentary oratory. There were many outstanding orators in those days, and as a matter of fact Burke himself was not especially effective as a speaker in the Commons; he was known as the Dinner Bell because the members poured out of the House when he rose. But his speeches read impressively, and are still occasionally quoted to give dignity to conservative pronouncements. *Reflections on the Revolution in France* (1790) is his most-read work to-day: the passage about Marie Antoinette ('But the age of chivalry is gone.') is the one that is most often quoted. (His opponent Paine's retort was memorable: 'He pities the plumage and forgets the dying bird'). Carlyle found Burke 'a resplendent far-sighted rhetorician, rather than a deep and earnest thinker'. The modern reader may not care about earnestness as much as Carlyle did; his objection is rather that Burke is tedious. A less orotund style is found in Thomas Paine (1737–1809), the famous radical and friend of William Blake. His straightforward hard-hitting prose in *The Rights of Man* (1791–2) is in a strong demotic English; no wonder the authorities denounced it. Paine's religious ideas in his *Age of Reason* (1794), in its day thought blasphemous, are now the commonplace of liberal-minded clergymen. But they do not write so well as he did. Brave, persecuted Paine ranks as a master of English with William Cobbett (1762–1835) of *Rural Rides* (1830), who first reviled and then acclaimed Paine; and he is less cranky than Cobbett.

A genre in which the eighteenth century excelled was familiar literature, such as letters. Jane Austen suggests its appeal in one of her letters when she says:

I have now attained the true art of letter-writing, which we are always told is to express on paper exactly what one would say to the same person by word of mouth; I have been talking to you almost as fast as I could the whole of this letter.

Jane Austen does not owe her place in literature to her letters. Horace Walpole does. Like his seventeenth-century French counterpart Madame de Sévigné, whom he greatly admired, his letters were his chief form of self-expression. They are as much a gazette as anything else, reporting to recipients abroad or in the provinces the doings of the great city. This form of writing has now been extinguished by newspapers and magazines, and by radio and television. The letter-writer/historian has disappeared. Meanwhile Walpole remains of inestimable value to the students of eighteenth-century politics and social history. The chief barrier to the enjoyment of his writings is his hauteur, his superiority complex. Macaulay, an ambivalent admirer, complains also of Walpole's gallicisms, but these do not seem all that frequent. Walpole's friend Gray continues an absorbing series of poet/letter-writers which began with Pope and was to continue with Cowper and Keats and Hopkins and D.H. Lawrence. Gray's love-letters to Charles Louis Victor de Bonstetten are particularly touching. Of more varied interest are the sincere, dignified, controlled letters of Johnson, and the delightful medley 'Thraliana', pertaining to his irrepressible Mistress. The bitter, censorious *Memoirs* of Pope's enemy Lord Hervey (1696–1745) are of primary importance to historians. Literary students should not miss the letters of the Earl of Chesterfield (1694–1773). His name has received a brand because of Johnson's scathing censure on him, both as a patron of literature and as a corrupting teacher of youth for whom manners replaced morals, but he too was a master of English and he can turn a graphic phrase, e.g. on Lord Lyttelton: '. . . his head, always hanging upon one or another of his shoulders, seems to have received the first stroke of the block'.

Finally, two works of miscellaneous interest may be mentioned as masterpieces in their kinds. The *Apology for his Life* (1740) by Colley Cibber (1671–1757) is the best autobiography of an actor in English, and Bernard Shaw thought it was the best book ever written about the Stage. *The Natural History and Antiquities of Selborne* (1789), by Gilbert White (1720–93), is better known. It will never be regarded as a major classic, because it does not deal with human beings; but to some readers that may be its chief attraction.

No simple formula can be found to cover the total achievement of eighteenth-century English literature. It did not excel in the kinds traditionally ranked highest by the European critical consensus – the epic, or the drama, or lyrical poetry. But it gave us our greatest philosopher, our greatest historian, our greatest biographer, and our greatest moralist and literary critic. It excelled also in satire and invective, in burlesque and controversy, and the lighter forms of poetry and prose fiction. It introduced the novel, which was to become eventually the chief form of creative writing in Europe and America. The combination of idiosyncrasy and good sense without which books are not re-readable is well preserved in the best work of this century. If one sentence had to be found to sum up the characteristic achievement of the period, the choice might fall on an often-quoted saying of the greatest eighteenth-century theologian, Joseph Butler (1692–1752), in his *Analogy of Religion* (1736):

Things and actions are what they are, and the consequences of them will be what they will be; why then should we wish to be deceived?

FIVE
From 1789 to 1832

The period designated by literary historians as 'Romantic' is associated with the political and social insurgencies which erupted first in America and then in France in the later years of the eighteenth century. But while the Romantic movement in France for a while seemed merely a matter of attitudinizing and red waistcoats, the corresponding development in Germany and Britain went much deeper, and involved important and lasting spiritual forces which seriously affected national taste and character. English Romanticism had its first and perhaps greatest representative in the poet and artist William Blake (1757–1827). When we come across a pronouncement of his, in whatever context, we know at once that here is a challenge we have to reckon with. Here is Blake:

Without Contraries is no progression. Attraction and Repulsion, Reason and Energy, Love and Hate, are necessary to Human existence.

Mental things are alone real, what is called corporeal is an Imposture.

Imagination is My World: this world of Dross is beneath my notice.

Those who restrain desire, do so because theirs is weak enough to be restrained.

Some of Blake's peremptory thrusts go to the heart of the implicit practical philosophy of the Western world by which most of us live:

Where any view of Money exists, Art cannot be carried on.

This is certain; if what Bacon says is true, what Christ says is false.

The last comment, a marginal note on Bacon's *Essays*, is difficult to answer. (Perhaps it is unanswerable?)

The known facts of Blake's life are few and unremarkable. He was a Londoner. He had a scanty education as an apprentice to the engraver James

Basire. He saw at first hand the rule of King Mob, the Gordon riots of 1780, with the burning down of Newgate prison. Two of his most important contacts with anti-Establishment thought were, first, the influence of the mysticism of the Swedish philosopher Emanuel Swedenborg (1688–1722), and, second, his relationship with Mary Wollstonecraft (1759–97), brave outspoken author of *A Vindication of the Rights of Woman* (1792). As the title of her book indicates, Mary was the feminine counterpart of Tom Paine, of *The Rights of Man*, and Blake was a friend of Paine also. On one occasion, unworldly dreamer though he may have been, he showed prompt commonsense when Paine did not, and saw to it that Paine escaped the authorities just in time. Blake himself was arrested on a charge of sedition, but acquitted. For a time he wore the red cap of the revolutionaries. In later years, however, Blake turned away from political activism and came to feel that 'Jesus should not have attacked the government'.

Blake's literary work is closely linked with his engraving and watercolouring. He illustrated his own poems and published them himself, and saw himself primarily as a visual artist rather than a poet. To-day his talents as both are recognized as outstanding, and if anything his poetry is more admired than his draughtmanship. Blake was utterly unrecognized in his lifetime. (The parallel with the Victorian poet G.M. Hopkins is striking.) His belated triumph is a striking example of the way tastes change and the passage of time affects contemporary reputations. The most popular poet of the 1780s was the amiable William Hayley (1745–1820), now remembered only because he had the misfortune to be Blake's benefactor. We may well wonder what unknown poet or artist of our own day will be adulated by the critics in 200 years' time.

In *Poetical Sketches* (1783) the youthful Blake already gives evidence of his unique genius, while showing himself able exquisitely to catch the note of earlier poets. 'To the Muses' laments the decline of eighteenth-century poetry in an eighteenth-century manner:

> The languid strings do scarcely move!
> The sound is forc'd, the notes are few!

Elsewhere in the volume he echoes other poets, the songs of Shakespeare, the stanza of Spenser, but always in his own way. He is already fully himself in lines like these, a touchstone for what is great in English poetry:

> O thou with dewy locks, who lookest down
> Through the clear windows of the morning, turn
> Thine angel eyes upon our western isle,
> Which in full choir hails thy approach, O Spring!
>   (from 'To Spring')

Blake's *Songs of Innocence* (1789) belong to a tradition of verses for children, such as those of Isaac Watts, but they sound the unique Blakean note of seemingly supernatural purity and simplicity. *The Book of Thel* (1789), which resembles the Songs in manner, is written in a 7-beat rhymeless line that was to become Blake's favourite in his *Prophetic Books*. The first series of these includes *Ahania*, *The Visions of the Daughters of Albion*, and *America* (1793). In these strange poems Blake alludes to the world in which the American and French Revolutions had already broken out, while the Industrial Revolution, pioneered by England, was already beginning to transform English social life. But Blake's ideas are presented in an abstract, visionary form, involved in complex mythologies and cosmogonies of his own making. In the first period of his mature work his message seems to be the need to liberate the human soul from the bondage of orthodox religious creeds and the repressive moral law. That which is conveyed to us by the ear and eye alone is rejected, along with the constrictions of the logical, rationalizing mind. Man must be free to enjoy the delights of the senses. The one instrument of truth is the poetic imagination. Blake's form and style are as revolutionary as his content. He was the first great English poet who never learned Latin, and he rejected the classical tradition – 'the Greek and Roman classics is the Antichrist', he declared – as completely as he rejected contemporary rationalism.

The prose work, *The Marriage of Heaven and Hell* (*c*. 1790) is the concentration, in aphoristic form, of Blake's campaign against religious and moral orthodoxy. *Visions of the Daughters of Albion* is a triumphant chant on the theme of sexual and spiritual liberation. But Blake is more compelling in the lyric, and some of his greatest work is to be found in the *Songs of Experience* (1794), in which the child-like vision of the poet of the *Songs of Innocence* is now turned on the world of cruelty and destruction within the human mind and heart. Of the Tiger, 'burning bright/In the forests of the night', supreme in strength and beauty, the poet asks the disturbing question: 'Did He who made the Lamb make thee?' Blake declaims against priestcraft, tyranny, social corruption. 'London' is a condensed statement unsurpassed for trenchancy in the whole of radical literature. This is the last verse:

> But most thro' midnight streets I hear
> How the youthful harlot's curse
> Blasts the new-born infant's tear,
> And blights with plagues the marriage-hearse.

In 'The Sick Rose' or 'Ah Sunflower' the doctrinal note is less explicit: they are self-sufficient poetic images. Other short poems invite explanation, while never quite yielding to it. 'The Mental Traveller' and 'The Crystal Cabinet', while powerful in suggestion, are so cryptic that the reader's emotions are troubled rather than assuaged. Blake is more lucid in the epigrams of 'Auguries of Innocence' and the hurrying rhymes of 'The Everlasting Gospel' (*c*. 1818), in which through terse maxims and fierce questions the fulminating anarch rewrites the gospel of Jesus in terms of his own defiant rejection of morality:

> If Moral Virtue was Christianity,
> Christ's Pretensions were all Vanity.

Blake's earlier series of prophecies was continued (1794–5) with *Europe*, *The Book of Urizen*, *The Book of Los*, and *The Song of Los*. The parables become more obscure and the intervals of lyrical relief fewer. The metre often becomes an abrupt four-beat staccato, perhaps suggested by the prose of Ossian. His four years' stay at Felpham, by the sea, inspired new visions, recorded in *Vala* (1797), rewritten as *The Four Zoas*, which Blake did not print. The Prophetic Books ended with *Milton* and *Jerusalem* (1804). By the time he reaches these poems the uninitiated reader comes to feel that he has lost contact with Blake's mind and purposes, and is at the mercy of crazy wilfulness. Yet some Blake scholars to-day see him as erudite rather than daemonic, and the poet Kathleen Raine (b. 1908) has unearthed a consistent neo-Platonic philosophy which for her clarifies and illuminates the Prophetic Books. But little in these bizarre poems has become current as English poetry, whatever their value as ideas. Fortunately Blake had not wholly abandoned the lyric. 'And did those feet in ancient time', the best known of his poems, comes from *Milton*. It has become, as F.W. Bateson said, 'a sort of unofficial national anthem'. Bateson, out of his knowledge of Blake's symbolic terminology, interprets the poem as an 'anti-clerical paean of free love'. But this does not mean that the good people who sing it as a Christian hymn are wrong. Blake's power as a poet was rooted not in any neo-Platonic system but in the English language and the ballad tradition and Protestant hymnography, and it is from these that the *feeling* of the poem comes.

In native genius for poetry Blake is surpassed by no writer in English, but his work is only intermittently readable, and then in small quantities. It presents the reader with immense formal and structural problems. Milton in *Paradise Lose* had renounced the 'troublesome bondage' of rhyme: Blake went further and gave up metre. Unlike Milton, and like Langland and Dryden, he had no gift for large-scale construction. But Langland and Dryden had the advantage of the majestic framework of Catholicism to hold their poems together, whereas Blake had invented his own religion (though he called it Christianity). And so his symbolism and mythology are hard to interpret, and attract more cranks than lovers of poetry. But lovers of poetry can find wonderful things in Blake. He can be simple and child-like without being falsely naive or mawkish:

> No, no, let us play, for it is yet day,
> And we cannot go to sleep;
> Besides, in the sky, the little birds fly,
> And the hills are all covered with sheep.

He can turn a cry of fear into poetry:

> The wild winds weep,
> And the night is acold . . .

or the pathos of 'this our exile':

> Ah Sun-flower, weary of time,
> Who countest the steps of the sun . . .

or the longing for another world:

> Father, O father, what do we here
> In this land of unbelief and fear?
> The Land of Dreams is better far
> Above the light of the morning star.

Admirers like A.E. Housman or Bertrand Russell, remote from Blake in their rationalistic outlook, have testified to the almost physical impact of Blake's lyric verse.

Blake wrote of the marriage of heaven and hell, and the whole labour of his life may be said to have been to bring it about. But perhaps he leaves out too much of what is neither heaven nor hell, but *this* world? – the men and women of Chaucer (whom he so much admired) or of Shakespeare?

Blake single-handed overthrew the poetic style of the eighteenth century, but his achievement passed unnoticed. His contemporary Robert Burns (1759–96) so potent an influence on the English Romantic poets who followed him, won fame, if not fortune, in his tragically short life. The Scottish poet who had been an Ayrshire farm labourer seemed at first to be the untutored peasant genius whom the polite eighteenth century had long looked for and never found, and this idea of him, together with an emphasis on his reckless wenching and drinking, still dominates his popular reputation. His real achievement as a poet is still not widely understood. Burns's work in Southern English is negligible; here he is little more than a minor follower of Gray and Thomson. Even the once famous 'Cotter's Saturday Night' does not represent him at his best. His best work is in Scottish dialect. It falls into two genres: colloquial poetry, and songs. In the volumes of 1786, 1787 and 1793 it is colloquial poetry that predominates. A masterpiece in this genre is 'Tam O'Shanter', blending ferocious humour with traditional Scots devilry. Outside Scotland Burns is mainly known for his songs. Here he is no wild genius, but a verbal mosaic-worker like Ben Jonson, a scholar-artist, blending different bits of old songs, adding his own perfecting touches. Sometimes he is in patriotic mood, as in 'Scots wha hae'; but most of his songs are love songs, sometimes suitable for the drawing-room, sometimes not ('Duncan Gray' has two versions, one for each category). The best of them, such as 'Auld lang syne', are perfect words for music; it is needless to add that they are simple in thought and direct in sentiment. Criticism to-day has nothing to say of poetry that just hits the nail on the head, once and for all, answering to Johnson's account of Gray's 'Elegy' as full of 'images that find a mirror in every mind, and sentiments to which every bosom returns an echo':

> I sighed and said amang them a',
> Ye arena Mary Morison.

or

> How can ye chant, ye little birds,
> And I sae fu' o' care?

This is the simplicity, not of artlessness, but of great art. It remains a perennial wonder that Scotland, so great in the prose of thought, so distinguished in prose fiction, so barren of poetry, could have given birth to this spring of inspiration: the only Scots poet whose name is known all over the world, the only one whose phrases, like Shakespeare's, have become household words, even, despite their dialect, among speakers of standard English.

Laughing or weeping, moralizing or law-defying, Burns is different in different poems. Matthew Arnold thought he had found 'the real Burns' in the cantata 'The Joly Beggars', but there is no 'real Burns'. His devil-may-care attitude, singled out by Arnold, is only one among many. But since Burns has become a national institution it is his attack on the smug and the 'unco guid' that should receive prominence. The satire of 'Holy Willie's Prayer', the dramatic monologue of a village hypocrite, has lost none of its bite with time: it ranks with Chaucer's Pardoner and Browning's Duke (in 'My Last Duchess') as a masterly study in self-betrayal.

William Wordsworth (1770–1850) has traditionally been regarded as the chief poet of the new age, though it may be that his poetry had more to say to the nineteenth century than it does to the twentieth. Do many moderns spontaneously assent to Wordsworth's central and endlessly reiterated message?

> One impulse from a vernal wood
> Will teach you more of man,
> Of moral evil and of good,
> Than all the sages can.
>
> Enough of science and of art,
> Close up those barren leaves . . .
>   (from 'The Tables Turned')

Many of us fail to perceive any necessary connexion between mountain scenery and moral uplift. But those who are prepared to suspend disbelief in Wordsworth's doctrine that Nature is benevolent will find him impressive. As a poet he rediscovered the value of simplicity.

The memory of what has been,
And never more shall be.
(from 'Three years she grew')

Men are we, and must grieve when even the shade
Of that which once was great has passed away.
(from 'On the Extinction of the Venetian Republic)

In his early verse, *An Evening Walk* and *Descriptive Sketches* (both 1793), Wordsworth still uses conventional eighteenth-century language, and describes nature with a literalness and minuteness he was later to reject. There is more emotional power, and more sense of personal conflict, in 'Guilt and Sorrow' and the closet drama *The Borderers* (1795–6). The decisive moment in Wordsworth's development is the *Lyrical Ballads*, first published in 1798, the product of his close relationship at that time with Samuel Taylor Coleridge (1772–1834), whose chief contribution to it was 'The Ancient Mariner'. The Wordsworth/Coleridge relationship, famous in literary history, is not easy to summarize, and even the briefest account of it cannot omit the background presence of Wordsworth's sister Dorothy (1775–1855), to some a more sympathetic character than her brother, though she confined herself to the role of uncomplaining drudge, and made her contribution to literature not as a 'writer' but as a woman with great sensibility to natural things, who kept journals. Wordsworth's ballads were experiments in what he claimed to be 'the real language of men', provocatively identified by him with the alleged language of rustics, children etc. He was determined to make poetry about simple people and simple life. But 'The Idiot Boy' and 'The Thorn' don't really come off. ('The Affliction of Margaret', written in 1804, is perhaps his best poem in this kind.) The best poem by Wordsworth in *Lyrical Ballads* is neither lyrical nor a ballad, but the blank-verse meditation 'Tintern Abbey'. Here Wordsworth inaugurates the kind of word–music which was to dominate the poetry of the nineteenth century.

Five years have passed, five summers, with the length
Of five long winters . . .

More *Lyrical Ballads* were published in 1800, and many new poems appeared in the volumes of 1807. It is generally agreed that most of Wordsworth's best poetry was written during this decade (1797–1807). It was in those years that he worked out the first versions of his poetic autobiography, *The Prelude* (published posthumously in 1850, in its finally revised form).

After the great decade Wordsworth produced a large body of work, much of which can only be enjoyed by devoted admirers. *The Excursion* (1814), the largest-scale poem of his published in his lifetime, disappointed even friendly contemporaries. And only rarely does inspiration visit the poet of those innumerable sonnets and calm moralizing meditations.

Even Wordsworth's best poems rarely make the overwhelming immediate impact that Donne's or Blake's do. For the most part they answer to his own account of the origin of poetry in 'emotion recollected in tranquillity'. Of his lyrical poems the most attractive are the little elegies on the mysterious 'Lucy'. In these short and apparently pellucid lyrics Wordsworth expresses, what too often he seems to be only groping for in *The Excursion* and *The Prelude*, the crucial emotions of his life. They hint at a profound upheaval, connected in some way with his feeling for his sister, and 'rocks and stones and trees', and a sense of irrecoverable loss. Many twentieth century readers have been more convinced by these cryptic poems than by the more fully orchestrated treatment of the theme in the great Ode on 'Intimations of Immortality in Early Childhood'. Here with grand oratory Wordsworth celebrates and laments the transfiguration of the earth which he had once known for a brief period, the light which had once irradiated his vision, and for which the 'years that bring the philosophic mind' were to prove no substitute.

Although Wordsworth never repudiated his cult of simplicity he was in fact an extraordinarily powerful rhetorical poet, the strongest since Milton. This appears not only in the great Ode but in the large collection of sonnets which he produced. The sonnet had fallen into neglect in the eighteenth century. Gray wrote one, but only one. Towards the end of the century the form was revived by versifiers such as Thomas Russell, Thomas Warton, and William Lisle Bowles, the last of whom greatly impressed the youthful Coleridge. But with Wordsworth the English sonnet made a comeback as major poetry. Wordsworth's sonnets were inspired by Milton's, which Dorothy read to him. By the time he wrote them he had abandoned his belief in the French Revolution and become a patriotic Englishman, and some of them are spirited outbursts against Napoleon. Of these 'public' sonnets perhaps the best is the tribute to the defeated Negro rebel leader Toussaint L'Ouverture:

> There's not a breathing of the common wind
> That can forget thee; thou has great allies,
> Thy friends are exultations, agonies,
> And loves, and man's unconquerable mind.

Of the more intimately personal sonnets the best are perhaps that on 'Westminster Bridge' (1802), and the later 'Surprised by joy', unusual in Wordsworth for its impulsive opening, at once followed by a poignant recoil as the poet suddenly recollects his sorrow. The sonnet became Wordsworth's normal choice for the record of a single thought or observation. One of the finest things among his rather dreary later works is the sonnet sequence on the River Duddon.

Apart from the sonnet Wordsworth's favourite medium was blank verse, and some of his best as well as some of his dullest work is written in that form. His blank verse is usually slow, measured, reflective. Simple narratives like

'Michael' and 'The Brothers' show him using it to create a poetry of retrospect, suffused with a feeling of consolation and reconciliation, as agents and sufferers alike fade away into the past.

The Prelude is to-day the most admired of Wordsworth's long poems. It tells the story of the poet's childhood and youth in the Lake District, his days at the university of Cambridge, his travels on the Continent, his visit to France at the time of the Revolution, his original enthusiasm for the France of Revolution and his later revulsion as it turned into the France of the Terror and tyranny. The whole of the poem is of great historical and biographical interest, but the finest poetry is probably to be found in the earlier books, especially I, II and IV. Wordsworth would have deserved our gratitude if he had done no more than record, as only he could record them, a few glowing moments in a man's life. But Wordsworth had intended *The Prelude* as merely the first part of a great philosophic poem to be called *The Recluse*, and so a good deal of it consists of high-sounding but rather woolly verbiage which a good many readers have come to associate with the 'Victorian' Wordsworth.

Modern scholars have done much to 'de-Victorianize' him. The first impulse to do this came early in this century, with the discovery of Wordsworth's affair with the French girl Annette Vallon, which resulted in the birth of their child. Then it became a commonplace of 'radical chic' to explain Wordworth's poetic decline as due to guilt over his desertion of Annette, which was associated with his abandonment of the revolutionary cause. (The fact that Annette was a royalist, who was decorated by the French government for services to royalism, did not fit in with the story and so went unmentioned.) Present-day de-Victorianization of Wordsworth has taken a better course, bringing to our notice the sharper earlier versions of *The Prelude*, and extracting new poems, christened 'The Pedlar' and 'The Ruined Cottage', out of the material that eventually was worked by him into the inert *Excursion*.

Wordsworth's personality and the true story of his emotional and imaginative development must always remain problematic. But there is no doubt about the subject of his poetry: human beings' search for happiness. That in some of his most deeply felt work this is associated with the suffering of women is no doubt biographically significant, but it is hard to say more than that with confidence. Wordsworth is the great spiritual visionary of English literature. His affinities are with Blake and Traherne, who evoke a world beyond the one accessible to the senses, but unlike them Wordsworth locates his spiritual world firmly in actual places, Snowdon or the Simplon Pass, or the landscape of 'visionary dreariness' in which he saw the scene he could never forget of the Girl with the Pitcher. His greatness, what he called 'the hiding-places of my power', lay in his capacity to perceive 'unknown modes of being' at work amidst the known modes, the homely and the familiar. A word that had a special meaning for him was 'inland' (cf. the 'soft inland murmur' in *Tintern Abbey*.) It occurs in this passage from the 'Immortality' Ode, where Wordsworth speaks as the man who had a glimpse of heaven, and could tell us what it was like. It was like being with your children at the seaside:

> Hence in a season of calm weather,
> Though inland far we be,
> Our souls have sight of that immortal sea
> Which brought us hither,
> Can in a moment travel thither,
> And see the children sport upon the shore,
> And hear the mighty waters rolling evermore.

Wordsworth's high place in poetry, according to Matthew Arnold, is secured by the 'ample body of powerful work' he has left us. No one could say that of Coleridge. His reputation as a poet rests on four or five poems, of which the greatest is 'The Ancient Mariner', written in the year of his close association with Wordsworth, which bore fruit in the *Lyrical Ballads* volume. According to the account later given by Coleridge the two poets agreed on a division of labour whereby Wordsworth was to take his matter from ordinary life and throw over it a 'colouring of imagination', while Coleridge was to take a supernatural subject and so treat it as to make it seem real, by bringing about that 'willing suspension of disbelief for the moment, which constitutes poetic faith'. In other words, the reader of 'The Ancient Mariner' is asked to join the poet in make-believe. The poem is based on the metre and diction of popular ballads, as in the abrupt opening. In the first version there is a good deal of mock-archaism, much reduced in the final version. It was a great improvement when Coleridge changed this:

> Since then at an uncertain hour,
> Now oft times and now fewer,
> That anguish comes and makes me tell
> My ghastly aventure.

to this

> Since then, at an uncertain hour,
> That agony returns:
> And till my ghastly tale is told
> This heart within me burns.

J.L. Lowes in his famous *Road to Xanadu* (1927) showed in great detail how many memories of Coleridge's reading went into the making of the poem. But it can be enjoyed without thought of its sources, whether literary or biographical. It is a fairytale, into which is woven the imaginative development of a moral theme: the story of a mysterious crime and its punishment, the torture of spiritual isolation:

> Alone, alone, all, all alone,
> Alone on a wide, wide sea.

The Mariner obtains release from his oppression by the rewakening of his sense of beauty, accompanied by feelings of pity and sympathy, when he sees the water-snakes. But the remission is only temporary. The Mariner is given absolution by the Hermit, but at the end 'that agony returns'. Yet this is what gives him the power to compel the Wedding Guest to hear his weird tale. Readers who feel the need for allegory can see the whole poem as a parable about the neurosis of the Romantic poet, but the 'Mariner' can be enjoyed without reference to this. It was stronger than anything he had written before, because of his use of the plain, hard-hitting, matter-of-fact language of the early English Voyagers, of whose yarns Coleridge was a devotee.

'Christabel' appears to be aiming at a similar effect, but it is less successful. For one thing, it is incomplete, consisting of three fragments. The first two succeed in evoking the right atmosphere for the story of a spell of silence imposed by a witch's evil power of fascination on an innocent girl. But unlike 'The Ancient Mariner' the poem does not create its own coherent world; there is no reason, not even of a dream kind, for what Geraldine does. The third part changes to the key of chivalrous romance, and is agreed to be inferior. And Coleridge found himself unable to devise a conclusion to pull the whole poem together, though he always hoped to do that. The most secure contribution of 'Christabel' to English poetry is its metre, a four-beat line with a free allowance of unstressed syllables:

> Is the night chilly and dark?
> The night is chilly, but not dark . . .
> And the spring comes slowly up this way . . .

It was with that tune in his head that Walter Scott embarked on his series of verse romances, beginning with *The Lay of the Last Minstrel* (1805). Later, poets like Byron and Rossetti were to adopt it also.

'Kubla Khan' purports to be unfinished, inspired by a dream brought on by opium, which Coleridge took for his many ailments; its composition was allegedly interrupted by the notorious 'person from Porlock'. The story, told by Coleridge in a note on the poem, is untrue, but it is so charming that, like much else in Coleridge, it makes it easy for the reader to suspend his disbelief. Many opinions have been expressed about the meaning and method of 'Kubla Khan'. For some, like Yvor Winters, it is no more than a tissue of romantic clichés; poets, said Winters, are important for their intelligence, not for their 'flashing eyes' and 'floating hair'. For others it is a marvellous example of pure poetry, poetic magic. For others, again, it is an intricate allegory which they think they can decipher: most plausibly as an allegory of the creative process itself. Meanwhile the poem stands apart, curiously unaffected by anything anyone says about it:

In Xanadu did Kubla Khan
A stately pleasure dome decree,
Where Alph, the sacred river, ran
Through caverns measureless to man,
Down to a sunless sea . . .

Coleridge's best poems are like music, in that they have to be taken on their own terms or not at all. Apart from the great three his other poems are disappointing. His distinction comes out most in 'Frost at Midnight' and 'Dejection'. While these lack the hallucinated quality of the great three, they have the compensating advantage of bringing us nearer to the intimate personal voice of the poet. 'Frost at Midnight' is a domestic meditation, the same kind of poem as 'Tintern Abbey'; but the sensibility at work in it is less chilly, more feminine and tender, than Wordsworth's:

Therefore all seasons shall be sweet to thee . . .

(Wordsworth is never 'sweet'.) 'Frost at Midnight' is a poem of tranquillity and hope. 'Dejection', after a quiet opening, swells into a lament: it is a poem of anguish and frustration. In its original, longer version, Coleridge spoke frankly about the chief cause of his personal unhappiness, the failure of his marriage. The final version, less complete as a confession, is more satisfactory as a poem, since it now centres on a single theme, the poet's sense of the failure of his imaginative powers.

Coleridge also wrote much prose, the best known of which is the autobiographical farrago *Biographia Literaria* (1817), together with remarkable lecture-notes on Shakespeare and miscellaneous literary topics, and the records of his talk. He is one of the three great talkers of English literature, the others being Johnson and Oscar Wilde. Coleridge never recaptured the inspiration of 'The Ancient Mariner', and none of his large-scale prose projects came to fruition, but he did create a second career for himself as critic, journalist, lecturer, political thinker, and high-level middleman of German Idealism. Twentieth-century Coleridgeans like Kathleen Coburn acclaim him as the founder of modern thought. Unfortunately this is also true in a bad sense; for to Coleridge must be assigned some of the ultimate responsibility for the disordered garbage that passes to-day for 'thought'. He was the first recognizable Intellectual in English literature, and both Carlyle and Peacock (in the character of 'Mr Flosky' in *Nightmare Abbey*) have left amusing caricatures of Coleridge as half-exploiter, half-dupe of his own cloudy verbiage. His prestige helped to sanction the bad notion that a great thinker must be obscure and use jargon which the common herd cannot understand; unlike Bacon, Hooker, Hobbes, or Hume, who wrote for the general reader. And if Norman Fruman's *The Damaged Archangel* (1972) is correct Coleridge's character must appear in still darker colours. But it would be unfair to see Coleridge as only the symbol of the Intellectual. He is better seen as the symbol of the Imagination, the writer who found the best phrase ever coined to describe it: the 'shaping spirit'. Even if 'damaged', he was still an 'archangel'.

John Stuart Mill in a famous essay contrasted Coleridge with Jeremy Bentham (1748–1832) as the two rival master-spirits of the time. Bentham has a bad reputation in literary circles to-day, not because of his works, which are not read, but because F.R. Leavis summed up everything Leavis hated in the modern world as 'technologico-Benthamism'. This is a libel on Bentham, who (though the founder of Utilitarianism) was no philistine. His personality in later life is wonderfully sketched by Hazlitt in *The Spirit of the Age* (1825). But Bentham was hardly a 'writer', and among the authors of that time a better foil to Coleridge is William Cobbett (1763–1814). Cobbett's life consisted of quarrels and provocations. His point of view was a curious mixture of the radical and the reactionary. In many ways he anticipated the positions taken by G.K. Chesterton, who wrote an excellent book on him (1925). For instance, like Chesterton he saw Henry VIII's dissolution of the monasteries as an act of robbery committed against the English people. Cobbett's prose style is the antithesis of Coleridge's. It suggests a clear sky and fresh air, while Coleridge is smoky and indoors, and it moves vigorously forward, whereas Coleridge seems usually to be waddling slowly from one side of the road to the other. The best word-picture of ferocious old 'Peter Porcupine' appears in Cobbett's own *Rural Rides* (1830).

We return from unpoetic Bentham and Cobbett to poets of the time – Southey, Scott, Byron, Shelley, and Keats. In his own time Robert Southey (1774–1843), Coleridge's brother-in-law, was linked by reviewers with Coleridge and Wordsworth as one of the 'Lake Poets' (they all lived in that region of northwest England). Few read his large output to-day, and he is mostly remembered for his sardonic poem 'After Blenheim' and his children's story 'The Three Bears', the only literary fairystory that sounds like a genuine folktale. (It has not so far been suggested that it is an allegory of the three Lake Poets.) Like Coleridge and Wordsworth Southey began as a political radical, and like them he turned conservative. He was appointed poet laureate in 1813, and his commemoration of the death of George III in 1820 provoked the derision of the radical Byron in his *Vision of Judgment* (which had been Southey's own title.) Southey has a special interest for the literary historian, as he was the first fulltime non-bohemian man of letters.

Another popular versifier of the day was Walter Scott (1771–1832). Scott had much to do with the great outburst of narrative poetry which occurred at this time. If this genre ever comes back into favour Scott's verse-tales – *Marmion* (1808) is the best – should again stand high. Scott, like Johnson, whom he greatly admired, was only a real poet at times, but he had his moments, as in the lines in *Marmion* on the death of Pitt, beginning

Now is the stately column broke,

> The beacon-light is quench'd in smoke,
> The trumpet's silver sound is still,
> The warder silent on the hill!

The song 'Proud Maisie' is Scott's greatest poem. It must remain doubtful whether the power of this poem springs solely from his love and knowledge of the ballad mode, of which it is the quintessence, or from the personal depths of feeling which Scott, the most enigmatic of the great popular artists, usually withheld from the view of the world.

Scott abandoned the verse tale for prose fiction. His reason was simple: 'Byron beat me.' George Gordon, Lord Byron (1788–1824) had the kind of fame in his own day that is now only enjoyed by footballers and pop stars. He began very mildly as a poet with *Hours of Idleness* (1807). When this was savaged by the *Edinburgh Review* he hit back with *English Bards and Scotch Reviewers* (1809), which shows that the spirit of Pope, Byron's favourite poet, was not dead in poetry, though Byron has nothing of Pope's neatness and deadly elegance. Byron's European travels produced the first cantos of *Childe Harold's Pilgrimage* (1812). He uses the Spenserian stanza in a most un-Spenserian manner, fast-moving and declamatory. With *Harold* Byron 'awoke and found himself famous'. He was identified with a figure which for a while fascinated Europe, 'the Byronic hero', guilt-haunted, misanthropic, caught (in the limelight) in a posture of gloomy disdain:

> I have not loved the world, nor the world me.

The Byronic hero is in fact Milton's Satan, and his descendants appear in *Jane Eyre*, in *Wuthering Heights*, in Daphne du Maurier's *Rebecca*, and innumerable other romances. Byron continued the series himself with *The Giaour*, *The Bride of Abydos*, *The Corsair*, *Lara* etc. The turning-point in his life came in 1816, when his marriage broke up, for reasons that have never been clearly explained, and he left England for ever. Some of his post-exilic verse continued to be in his serious Romantic style, like the third and fourth cantos of *Childe Harold* (1816), or *The Dream* (1816), or *The Prophecy of Dante* (1821). To this style also belong *Manfred* (1817) and *Cain* (1821), the only plays of Byron – they are better called dramatic poems – that are still remembered.

But the verse of Byron that is popular to-day is the serio-comic verse which he wrote in his exile. His years in Italy brought sunshine and humour into his poetry. And he found the technique that was right for him in the octave stanza of *Beppo* (1818). It has been said that he was like someone trained to play the violin who discovers that his true talent is for the brass band. Byron adopted the manner of *Beppo* for another amusing poem, *The Vision of Judgement* (1821). Southey, the poet laureate, had deferentially ushered George III (d. 1820), old, mad, and blind, into Heaven in solemn English hexameters. Byron seized the opportunity to imagine instead a debate at the gate of heaven between the Archangel Michael and Satan:

> The spirits were in neutral space, before
> The gate of heaven: like eastern thresholds is
> The place where Death's grand cause is argued o'er,
> And souls despatch'd to that world or to this:
> And therefore Michael and the other wore
> A civil aspect: though they did not kiss,
> Yet still between his Darkness and his Brightness
> There pass'd a mutual glance of great politeness.

With carefree patrician mockery Byron scores off all his opponents, symbolic figures of the Tory régime. In the hilarious climax of the poem St Peter strikes down the still reciting laureate with his keys, and in the resulting confusion George III slips into Heaven.

The faster-moving stanza used in *Beppo* and *The Vision of Judgement*, known as *ottava rima*, suited the rapid movement of Byron much better than the Spenserian stanza, slow-moving and self-retarding, which he had used for *Childe Harold*. Scholars dispute over the origin of this new manner, but it seems probable that Byron picked it up from the mock romance *Whistlecraft* (1817–18), by John Hookham Frere (1769–1846), which made a hit at the time, though it is now forgotten. But Byron made this manner so completely his own that it is always now associated with him. He used it for his masterpiece, *Don Juan* (1819–24), which he had already begun in 1819. It consists of 16 cantos and a fragment of the seventeenth. Southey, Coleridge, Wordsworth, the Duke of Wellington, and other reactionaries are ridiculed in frequent digressions from the narrative of this long, rambling novel in verse. But Byron shows considerable skill in returning to the story from his digressions, and the poem is to-day the most widely read and enjoyed of all his works.

To ask what *Don Juan* is about is like asking what T.E. Lawrence's *Seven Pillars of Wisdom* (1926) is about. At one level the answer is easy: the *Seven Pillars* is about Arabs, the desert, camels, etc. Similarly Byron's poem is about the adventures of a Spanish youth who had many affairs with women, and took part in a number of heroic (and unheroic) exploits. But readers expecting a character like Mozart's Don Giovanni will be disappointed, for Byron's Don Juan is a colourless character. He can be brave and resourceful in action and tight spots, but in his relations with women he is completely passive. We do not have to read very far in *Don Juan* to discover that the plot is not the point; the poem is a quasi-autobiographical extravaganza in which Byron reveals some of the facets of his strange personality.

The early Cantos have more of a champagne flavour than the later ones. Don Juan at the age of 16 is sent abroad in disgrace, after a love-intrigue, by his severe mother (in whom we see some traits of Byron's wife, with whom he had quarrelled). His ship is wrecked – opportunity for poetry about the sea, the 'black comedy' of cannibalism, etc. – and he is cast ashore on a Greek island and made love to by Haidée, daughter of a pirate (opportunity for idyllic love-poetry). The pirate, supposed dead, reappears and breaks up the idyll, and Juan is chained up as a prisoner in one of the pirate's ships. Then he is sold as a slave in Constantinople to a Turkish princess. The jealousy he arouses in her causes him to be threatened with execution, but he succeeds in escaping to the Russian army, which is besieging Ismail. Here the gaiety of the poem disappears; Byron takes the opportunity to denounce romantic nonsense about war and emphasize its savagery and bloodshed. Juan's bravery results in his being honoured with the task of taking dispatches to St Petersburg, where he wins the interest of the Empress Catherine II, notorious for her love-affairs. (Opportunity here, probably, for Byron to use what he had learned from his relationship with Lady Oxford.) In the last part of the poem he is sent on a mission to England. The closing cantos vigorously satirize English high life from the point of view of the puzzled foreigner Juan. The mysterious character 'Aurora Raby' appears in these 'English' cantos. Her real-life original (if she had one) is not known, but a suggestion that might repay exploration is that she is another aspect of Byron's wife (who obsessed him).

The Byron of *Don Juan* is the chief exponent in English poetry of the serio-comic. The poem is the half-sincere, half-attudinising expression of some of the many things that Byron had been – the Venetian libertine, the semi-paternal companion of Countess Guiccioli, the apostle of freedom who was to die for the cause of Greek independence. His characteristic mood is caught in this stanza, written on the back of his manuscript of Canto I:

> I would to heaven that I were so much clay,
> As I am blood, bone, marrow, passion, feeling –
> Because at least the past were pass'd away –
> And for the future – (but I write this reeling,
> Having got drunk exceedingly to-day,
> So that I seem to stand upon the ceiling)
> I say – the future is a serious matter –
> And so – for God's sake – hock and soda-water!

(– which was much used to cure hangovers at that time.)

Byron was long taken to typify the Romantic movement in poetry, but he did not care for these poets, and was himself in many ways unromantic and even anti-romantic. The colloquial, jocular manner of the Byron of *Beppo* and *Don Juan* and *The Vision of Judgment* is well imitated by W.H. Auden in his 'Letter to Lord Byron'. In this style, as in his immensely enjoyable letters, Byron seems completely a man of the twentieth century. Byron's character puzzled his contemporaries. To-day he appears to have been the same sort of man as Colonel T.E. Lawrence (1888–1935). In both, the riddle may be partly explained by their homosexual tendencies. And both have the curious quality of appearing to be at the same time heroic figures and anti-heroes; in part creators, and in part victims, of their own legends.

One of the things to be said in favour of Byron is that he won the friendship of really good men like Walter Scott and Percy Bysshe Shelley (1792–1822). But Shelley was a very strange person, an eccentric of a kind that English aristocratic families are apt to produce from time to time. Most people who have heard of him know that he was an idealistic theoretical revolutionary; that he was sent down from Oxford for publishing a pamphlet on *The Necessity of Atheism*, that he married very young and left his first wife Harriet (who committed suicide) for Mary, daughter of the ideologue William Godwin and his wife Mary Wollstonecraft of the *Rights of Women*; that he spent the last years of his short life in Italy, and was drowned in a small boat while crossing the gulf of Spezia. His poetry, indeed the whole of his writing, conveys the sense of a very distinctive personality, which has been idolized or scorned by different readers at different times. The best-balanced memoir of him is by T.L. Peacock, who knew him well and put a good-humoured caricature of him into his novel *Nightmare Abbey* (1817) – which amused Shelley. Peacock depicts Shelley, both in real life and as 'Scythrop', as a man of real genius and noble character, but out of touch – calamitously so – with people and things as they are, a victim of delusions, and now and then extremely absurd. Students of Shelley's life and work have to feel that there is some truth in this, even if Peacock over-states it.

The Necessity of Atheism must arouse curiousity as apparently the first open advocacy of atheism in English. (Paine was a Deist). Shelley relies much on Hume's arguments, but these if valid seem to show the non-necessity of theism, rather than the necessity of atheism. Shelley was helped in this pamphlet by T.J. Hogg (1792–1862), who was later to play a somewhat grubby part in his private life. In Hogg's description of Shelley and himself at Oxford they figure as the first recognizable undergraduates in English literature. *Queen Mab* (1813), a poem that has been read a good deal by revolutionaries and radicals, is chiefly remarkable for its prose Notes, in which Shelley documents his belief that Christianity has been overthrown by the discoveries of modern science. Shelley's first really good poem is the lyric beginning 'Away! the moor is dark beneath the moon' (1814). The rhythm and movement of this poem announce the arrival of a major poet. For the next few years the poetry of Shelley is self-absorbed; he seems a lonely unhappy man trying to forget his personal problems by contemplating the beauty of nature. The blank verse of *Alastor* (1816) suggests Wordsworth's, but the theme, a young hero dying in pursuit of an ideal woman, is thoroughly Shelleyan. 'Laon and Cythna', later revised as *The Revolt of Islam* (1818) is in Spenserian stanzas. This poem, Shelley's longest, is like Spenser's in being dream-like, but not in Spenser's way. It throbs with febrile optimism: Shelley dreams of the liberation of the whole human race. The unfinished *Prince*

Athanase reintroduces the brooding self-absorbed figure of the Shelleyan solitary. 'Mont Blanc' shows the poet seeking to lose his self-preoccupation in recognizing a grandeur outside and beyond him. The 'Stanzas written in Dejection near Naples' are pervaded by despair and a longing for death.

In the personal lyric of melancholy Shelley is supreme. 'Rarely, rarely comest thou,/Spirit of delight' is characteristic. In the 'Lines written among the Euganean Hills' he seeks for a 'green isle' in the sea of misery. In the lyrical drama *Prometheus Unbound* (1820) Shelley soars beyond personal disillusionment to a kind of transcendental politics: a vision of a redeemed society, ruled by love. Whatever it may owe to Godwin's thought, it is nearer in spirit to Isaiah. The vision embraces not only renewed humanity, but the transformation of nature and the earth into a realm of beauty and peace. The Prometheus legend might have been invented for Shelley, just as the Samson legend might have been invented for Milton. *Prometheus Unbound* has no dramatic tension. The overthrow of Jupiter by Demogorgon is almost an anti-climax. What is most remembered is the fourth act, added as an afterthought, which has the effect of a series of hymns of apocalyptic humanism. Here are some of the closing lines:

> To suffer wrongs which Hope thinks infinite;
> To forgive wrongs darker than death or night;
> To defy power, which seems omnipotent;
> To love, and bear; to hope till hope creates
> From its own wreck the thing it contemplates . . .
> This is alone Life, Joy, Empire, and Victory.

Here Shelley anticipates the Polish saying that 'to be vanquished and not to surrender is victory'.

Shelley's powers as a dramatist are more evident in *The Cenci* (1819). All the Romantics wrote plays, but this is the only one that merits serious consideration. For long the theme (father–daughter incest) barred it from the stage, but it has been successfully produced in modern times. It may be the best poetic tragedy since Otway. But that is not a high claim; and the dramatic effects, as well as the poetry, too obviously, if innocently, derive from Shakespeare.

The fantastic narrative of 'The Witch of Atlas' (1820) laughingly resists the efforts of critics to find its allegory and moral. *Epipsychidion* (1821) is even more esoteric: it is a mystical plea for free love, addressed to Emilia Viviani, imprisoned in a convent. *Adonais* (1821), a lament for the dead Keats, contains the most famous lines that Shelley wrote:

> Life, like a dome of many-coloured glass,
> Stains the white radiance of Eternity.
> Until Death tramples it to fragments . . .

It has been held against Shelley that *Adonais* is more about himself than about Keats, but that is apt to happen in the great English elegies: *Lycidas* is about Milton, *In Memoriam* is about Tennyson, 'Thyrsis' is about Arnold, rather than about Edward King, Hallam and Clough respectively.

A different Shelley is seen in the impish *Peter Bell the Third* (1819) which contains the best criticism ever written on Wordsworth, better than Coleridge's in *Biographia Literaria*; and in *The Mask of Anarchy* (written 1819) a Blake-like satire, with lines like

> I met Murder on the way:
> He had a mask like Castlereagh

– Castlereagh being one of the pillars of the Tory government hated by Shelley and Byron. *The Mask of Anarchy* was inspired by the incident known in English history as the 'Peterloo Massacre'. Although the poem loses grip at its climax – or non-climax – it is probably the best introduction to Shelley's poetry for a modern reader. His prose work, *The Defence of Poetry* (1821), a sort of answer to Peacock's clever 'Three Ages of Poetry', should also not be missed. *Hellas* (1822), written to celebrate the independence of Greece, is mainly remembered for its last chorus, beginning

> The world's great age begins anew,
> The golden years return

with its pathetic final recoil, typical of Shelley:

> O cease! Must hate and death return?
> Cease! must men kill and die?
> Cease! drain not to its dregs the urn
> Of bitter prophecy.
> The world is weary of the past:
> O might it die and rest at last!

Shelley is most admired for his short poems and for the wealth of lovely fragments which Mary published after his death. In the later nineteenth century his attacks on Christianity were forgiven and he was rated the greatest of English lyrical poets, but in the twentieth century the tradition of hostile criticism inaugurated by Matthew Arnold, intensified by T.S. Eliot, and brought to final definition by F.R. Leavis, has prevailed. These critics all find Shelley 'embarrassing', but they all hasten to explain that this is not because of his ideas, but because of his bad writing, confused imagery etc. Well-known pieces like 'To a Skylark' and 'The Cloud' are clearly vulnerable. But Leavis's depreciation of the 'Ode to the West Wind' begs the question by criticizing Shelley for his 'weak grasp upon the actual.' Eliot and Leavis concurred, however, in praise of the unfinished *Triumph of Life*, published posthumously, in which Shelley recreates in English the style of the Dante of the *Inferno*. This is the place to remark on the excellence of Shelley as a translator, of the Homeric Hymns, Euripides, Plato, Calderón, and Goethe (he is the only translator of *Faust* to write great poetry). Shelley was the most learned English poet since Gray, and he wore his learning more lightly. He was steeped in ancient Greek poetry, and Grecisms constantly appear in his syntax and vocabulary. He splendidly initiated the love-affair between English poetry and Greek which lasted till the time of Swinburne and Gilbert Murray. Shelley died at 29; how much had Shakespeare achieved by that age? His range is much wider than is sometimes supposed, and for linguistic excitement his verse has no equal.

John Keats (1795–1821) died even younger. He was temperamentally different from Shelley. Where Shelley's movement is rapid, airy, stormy, in his hectic pursuit of the flux of existence, Keats is slow-moving, pictorial, lingering over what he says:

> And many a chapel bell the hour is knelling,
> Paining me through . . .
> > (from 'Isabella')

> Ay, in the very temple of Delight
> Veiled Melancholy hath her sovereign shrine.
> > (from the 'Ode to Melancholy')

Often he is like his Saturn in *Hyperion*, 'quiet as a stone', brooding and withdrawn. Life to him was not 'a dome of many-coloured glass', but 'a vale of soul-making'. Keats's senses were alert. 'Nothing seemed to escape him', wrote his friend Severn, 'the song of a bird and the undernote of response from covert or hedge, the rustle of some animal, the changing of the green and brown lights and furtive shadows'. Keats's early work suffers from both structural and stylistic defects. Its vulgarity is usually blamed on Leigh Hunt (1784–1859), whose *Story of Rimini* is full of it, but this seems hard on Hunt. Keats did not *have* to write like Leigh Hunt: it was optional. *Endymion* (1818), a poem in four books, begins with the poet's best known line:

> A thing of beauty is a joy for ever;

but it is loosely knit and stylistically too eclectic. Spenser and other Elizabethan and Jacobean poets stimulated Keats's love of 'fine phrases'; they did not teach him how to organize poems. *Endymion* was roughly handled by reviewers, and Byron believed that Keats was 'killed off by an article', but this is not true: he was killed by tuberculosis. He understood better than the reviewers the real fault of *Endymion*, when he wrote: 'The imagination of a boy is healthy, and the mature imagination of a man is healthy; but there is a space of life between, in which the soul is in a ferment, and the character undecided, the way of life uncertain, the ambition thick-sighted: thence proceeds mawkishness.'

The three tales in the 1820 volume are artistically superior to *Endymion*.

The verse of 'Lamia' shows Keats reacting against the sprawling movement of *Endymion*: its tightened couplets show the effect of his study of Dryden. The fault of 'Lamia' is that our sympathies are pulled in different directions, and not finally harmonized. The 'Lamia' theme, taken from a story of Burton's in the *Anatomy*, is a tale of the deceit and illusion of the serpent-woman, yet the poet hates the 'cold philosophy' which exposes her, destroying the hero Lycius in the process. *Isabella*, taken from Boccaccio's *Decameron*, has lovely lines and stanzas, but Keats is a poor story-teller, and half-way through he seems to recoil from the 'wormy circumstance' in which the subject involves him. And there is also some mawkishness, as Keats admitted. The best of these tales is 'The Eve of St Agnes'. The icy weather and the constant encroachment of old age and death, personified in the Beadsman and Angela, make an effective contrast to the warmth and luxury of Madeline's 'poppied nest'. The poem owes something to *Romeo and Juliet*, but only at the end is there a really dramatic moment, when the glowing present is suddenly thrust into the remote past of romance;

> . . . ages long ago
> Those lovers fled away into the storm.

Keats's delight in the visible and tangible world embraced man-made beauty as eagerly as nature; he responded with the same immediacy to a Claude or a Titian or the Elgin Marbles, Sandys's Ovid and Chapman's Homer, the mythology of Greece which appealed as strongly to him as it did to Milton, though Keats knew no Greek and had to depend on paraphrases like Lemprière's.

The poems of Keats that are now most admired express the impulse to escape from actual life and personal problems into the contemplation of something beautiful and permanent. This longing underlies the 'Ode to a Nightingale' and the 'Ode on a Grecian Urn'. In these Odes Keats is like Shakespeare, not in dramatic power, of which he had little, but in the sensuousness of his writing and the ability to express common thoughts and feelings with the greatest felicity. Of the other Odes 'Psyche' is the most delicate in symbolism. In 'To Autumn' (not entitled an Ode) the poet is wholly absorbed in the picture; there is no moral, no allegory, only the essence of an English autumn, when

> . . . gathering swallows twitter in the skies.

The ballad 'La Belle Dame Sans Merci' is the most haunting of Keats's poems. Luxuriousness of phrase is wholly absent; the effect is obtained by the simplest of words:

> And no birds sing.

In the unfinished 'Eve of St Mark' again there is no moral, only, in Keats's words, 'the sensation of walking about an old country town in a coolish evening'. 'La Belle Dame' and the 'Eve of St Mark' anticipate, and furnish, the whole mode of writing that came to be called 'Pre-Raphaelite'.

No better short poems have ever been written than 'To Autumn' and 'La Belle Dame Sans Merci'. But Keats could not be satisfied with short poems. For him the drama and the epic were the supreme forms, and these demanded, as he knew, not only powers of large-scale construction (which like all the Romantics he lacked) but depth of insight into the problems of human life. His attempts at drama are failures. Opinion is divided about *Hyperion*, the most ambitious of his poems since *Endymion*. It is like the earlier work in having a mythical story embodying a parable, and superior to it in clarity of outline. But Keats was dissatisfied with *Hyperion*, finding too many 'Miltonic inversions' in the style, and abandoned it. (It is hard to see how he could have continued the story after Apollo has dethroned Hyperion.) The philosophy of the poem, epitomized in Oceanus's speech, is an evolutionary one: the assertion of the 'eternal law', that 'first in beauty shall be first in might'. At some stage in the poem's composition Keats wrote a prelude to it with new symbolic figures, in verse suggesting the study of Dante's *Purgatorio*. (The debt to Dante is not the only similarity between it and Shelley's *Triumph of Life*.) The theme seems to be a conception of spiritual progress from passive self-centred sensuality to union with the joys and sufferings of all human beings. But this union can only be reached through personal agony. This is what the poet sees when Moneta lifts her veil. Here the founder of the Aesthetic Movement seems to be saying that aestheticism is not enough, and saying so in lines that could have been Shelley's:

> 'None can usurp this height,' returned that shade,
> 'But those to whom the miseries of the world
> Are misery, and will not let them rest.'

Keats may be unique among poets in one respect: the standing of his letters. Poets' letters can be uninteresting, like Wordsworth's; or delightful, like Hopkins's; or detrimental to their authors, like Rilke's and D.H. Lawrence's. But perhaps it is only Keats whose letters are often more admired than his poems. In his serious poetry there is a feeling of remoteness. It does not, as the letters do, show Keats's attractive personality, the affectionate friend and brother, open-hearted, humorous and generous. Of course it is for their insights into poetry that the letters are prized above all other letters. But the sense of direct contact with a living human being is also important. Only towards the end does this appear in the poetry: the appeal as of an individual to an individual, across the frontiers of time and art. In this haunting fragment the dead man seems to be asking the reader – perhaps originally imagined as the girl Keats loved, Fanny Brawne – to give him life again:

> This living hand, now warm and capable
> Of earnest grasping, would, if it were cold
> And in the icy silence of the tomb,
> So haunt thy days and chill thy dreaming nights
> That thou would'st wish thine own heart dry of blood
> So in my veins red life might stream again,
> And thou be conscience-calm'd – see, here it is –
> I hold it towards you.

The life of the peasant-poet John Clare (1793–1864) was less abruptly tragic than Keats's, but even more painful: it was a story of long drawn out poverty and neglect, years of solitude and the madhouse. Clare is usually called a nature poet, and this description will suffice if it is understood that, like the twentieth century poet Edward Thomas, Clare knew nature not only from books, as most poets do, but from his own loving and accurate observation.

> To note on hedgerow baulks, in moisture sprent,
> The jetty snail creep from the mossy thorn,
> With earnest heed, and tremulous intent,
> Frail brother of the morn,
> That from the tiny bent's dim-misted leaves
> Withdraws his timid horn,
> And fearful vision weaves.
>   (from 'Summer Images')

Clare knew Keats's poetry and thought it too literary and artificial. This could also be said of George Darley (1795–1846), who, talented as he is, sounds too like his Elizabethan and seventeenth-century masters, and of Thomas Lovell Beddoes (1803–49). But Beddoes seems less a derivative than a reincarnation of Jacobean drama. He had many of the qualities of a great poet, but he lacked the power of construction; he is a poet of fragments:

> Thou art so silent, lady; and I utter
> Shadows of words, like to an ancient ghost
> Arisen out of hoary centuries
> Where none can speak his language.

or

> Ay, ay, *good man*, *kind father*, *best of friends*.
> These are the words that grow, both grass and nettles,
> Out of dead men, and speckled hatreds hide
> Like toads among them.

Thomas Hood (1799–1845) was influenced by Keats in his serious poems; he is less passive in sensibility, but also less compelling in diction; he offers variations on Keatsian themes, rather than radically new poems. He also wrote light humorous verse which now raises groans rather than laughs, with its compulsive punning (a taste he shared with Lamb). 'Ben Battle' is a particularly grisly piece, which unfortunate small boys were once made to recite. 'The Haunted House' shows Hood at his best, and he is a master of what Orwell called 'the good bad poem' – poems which no one would call great poetry, but which have been retained in the national heritage, such as 'I remember, I remember', 'The Bridge of Sighs', and 'The Song of the Shirt'. Walter Savage Landor (1775–1864) is for the most part the kind of writer who is excessively disparaged to-day, the Stylist. (Logan Pearsall Smith (1865–1946), the American expatriate, was perhaps the last of this kind.) Landor's prose *Imaginary Conversations* (1824–9; 1853) are probably retained more in scattered beautiful sentences, single thoughts, than in bulk. In poetry also he is remembered most for his short pieces. Sometimes these are poignant, as in 'Rose Aylmer', or magnificent, as in 'Stand close about, ye Stygian set'. But some of his best epigrams are comic:

> Clap, clap the double nightcap on!
> Gifford will tell you his amours,
> Lazy as Scheldt, and cold as Don;
> Kneel, and thank heaven they are not yours.

The early nineteenth century was chiefly an age of poetry. The drama was dead. The philosophers, historians and other non-fiction prose writers are mostly second-rate (Godwin, Bentham etc.). The chief rival to poetry at this time was already prose fiction. The main authors here are Scott and Jane Austen, but some minor novelists are still read. William Godwin, (1756–1836), father-in-law of Shelley, was once famous, and infamous, for his *Political Justice* (1793), but is now read only in his novel *Caleb Williams* (1794), a powerful thriller. It is also a novel of ideas – Godwin's ideas – and none the worse for it. His daughter, Shelley's second wife Mary (1797–1851), has her place in literature with *Frankenstein* (1818), the pioneer example of what is now called Science Fiction. The traditions about the circumstances in which it was written are 'almost totally false', says James Rieger; those curious to know the facts should read Rieger's *The Mutiny Within* (New York 1967). Mary Shelley is now getting much attention from the Women's Movement; her output of both fiction and non-fiction was large, and her letters will fill three volumes. She was not just the widow of a great poet, but a woman of determination and character, if not herself a great writer. Of the other 'advanced' writers of the day Robert Bage (1728–1801) still finds some readers for his curious *Hermsprong, or Man as he is Not* (1796).

The Gothic novel flourished at this time. Ann Radcliffe (1764–1823), of *The Mysteries of Udolpho* (1794), was an object of satire to Jane Austen in *Northanger Abbey* (1817); but Jane Austen read her, and so did Keats, and many others, and she still has readers. The curious 'semantic gap' between the terrors and marvels she relates and her own sedate style does not spoil the reader's pleasure, but enhances it. *The Monk* (1796) by Matthew Gregory Lewis (1775–1818) is pornographic – of the 'soft' variety – and very sensational, but far from unreadable. Charles Maturin's *Melmoth the Wanderer* (1820), which on one occasion gave his fellow-Irishman Oscar Wilde a pseudonym, has more genuine literary quality than *The Monk*, but at times it is not clear whether or not the author is covertly parodying the genre.

A more modern manner is seen in Susan Ferrier's *Marriage* (1818), with its crisp opening. But the history of the novel would have been the same if Susan Ferrier had never lived. This is not true of the Irish writer Maria Edgeworth (1767–1849). She did something momentous in fiction when she introduced the regional novel with *Castle Rackrent* (1800), complete with footnotes and glossary of dialect words. Jane Austen knew her work, and Scott acknowledged his debt to it. Maria Edgeworth's place in literary history (though not her place in literature) is that she was the forerunner of Scott. Another Scottish contemporary, John Galt (1779–1839) has a similar claim to attention, while *The Confessions of a Justified Sinner* (1824) by James Hogg (1770–1835) is probably the most remarkable work of fiction written by a Scot.

The most famous novelist of the day, a writer of European reputation, was Sir Walter Scott. His novels, beginning with *Waverley* (1814), appeared anonymously; he did not avow their authorship till 1827, though by then it was well known. Scott put Scotland on the map for persons of romantic sensibility. And he created the historical novel – two lasting achievements. The differences between Gibbon, who sees people of the past as if they were contemporaries, and Macaulay, who is always insisting to his Victorian readers that people from the past were different, is due to Scott, as G.M. Trevelyan pointed out. Famous European novelists, like Balzac in France, or Manzoni in Italy, acclaimed him. But to-day the Great Unknown has become the Great Unread. This is understandable. *The Waverley Novels* are too slow for modern taste, especially in the opening pages. The style is stilted. There is no sex interest, no psychological analysis. Furthermore Scott only rises to great literary heights when writing in the Scottish vernacular, as in 'Wandering Willie's Tale', or in the dialogue of the short tragic story 'The Two Drovers'.

Scott was a man of conscience when it came to paying off (at the expense of his health and eventually his life) the debts of his bankrupt publishers. But he did not have the literary conscience of a Flaubert or a Henry James. Not for him the agonized struggle for the *mot juste*! But his novels are full of life if you can once get into them. The more realistic ones, like *Old Mortality* (1816) and *The Heart of Mid-Lothian* (1818), tend to be most praised to-day. Scott's touch is heavy when he deals with the aristocracy and high-flown sentiment, but it is sure when he brings to life on the page the common people whom he loved. The later novels of Scott are fantasies, which should not be judged too realistically. They are the daydreams of the lame man of great physical strength, who longed for action. In *Ivanhoe* (1819) Scott is equally present in the assault on Front de Boeuf's castle, in Ivanhoe lying wounded in the turret chamber, and in Rebecca reporting to him the progress of the action. Finally he is the Black Knight, Scott freed from his infirmity and frustration, invulnerable, exulting, triumphant. *Redgauntlet* (1824), another late novel, is no fantasy, but is set in a credible eighteenth-century Scotland. It is one of his best books, showing Scott's complex attitude towards the history of his country (in this instance, the failure of Jacobitism). Scott was a great man and a great writer. His *Journals*, begun late in his life, are as great as the best of his novels.

But the only novelist of this period widely read to-day is Jane Austen (1775–1817). She is now the most accessible classic of English literature, the only writer who is read as if she were a contemporary. Scott himself, a shrewd as well as a generous critic, recognized in this young lady a master in a very different manner from his own 'big bow-wow'. Jane Austen has always been greatly admired. Some of her admirers resemble her Mr Collins in *Pride and Prejudice* when he contemplated the goodness of Lady Catherine de Bourgh: 'Words were insufficient for the elevation of his feelings; and he was obliged to walk about the room'. Extravagant tributes can be quoted from Macaulay (who called her the prose Shakespeare), or George Eliot ('the greatest artist that has ever written'). Tennyson and Kipling were devotees. But there has always been an opposition too. This is Charlotte Brontë on *Pride and Prejudice*:

. . . an accurate daguerreotyped portrait of a commonplace face; a carefully tended, hightly cultivated garden with neat borders and delicate flowers; but no glance of a bright, vivid physiognomy, no open country, no blue hill, no bonny beck.

Charlotte Brontë thought the French novelist George Sand 'sagacious and profound', but Jane Austen only shrewd and observant. To Mrs Browning Jane Austen's people seem 'wanting souls'. Mark Twain would rather have been condemned to John Bunyan's heaven than read her work. Joseph Conrad asked H.G. Wells in bewilderment 'What is all this about Jane Austen?' D.H. Lawrence called her 'The mean Jane Austen'. We see the same divergence among professional critics, between the love of A.C. Bradley, R.W. Chapman, or George Sampson, and the hatred of Oliver Elton, H.W. Garrod, or Herbert Read. Jane Austen, then, may be 'the prose Shakespeare', but about her work (unlike Shakespeare's) there is no agreement whether she is good or bad, major or minor.

The Janeite/anti-Janeite dichotomy cuts across other divisions – highbrows and lowbrows, conservatives and radicals, men and women. Her novels need no explication: readers will make up their own minds. For those unfamiliar with her work, a few straightforward observations may be in order. Jane

Austen's subject-matter was domestic life in English country villages. Her novels all turn on the question who is going to marry whom. Jane Austen, unlike Fanny Burney, and many rash women novelists since her time, leaves out the distinctively masculine world except in so far as it impinges on the women characters. Her youthful writing consists largely of burlesques of the conventional fiction of her day, whether lachrymose or Gothic. Similarly in her mature work she avoids strongly dramatic situations, and is sparing of tender sentiment and pathos. The sufferings of real life, the cruel blows of fate, neurotic conflicts, violent passions, are kept at a distance: 'Let other pens dwell on guilt and misery'. She ignores politics, and rarely touches on the problems which agitated the radicals and reformers of her time. In this respect she is like Chaucer and unlike Milton.

Jane Austen is primarily a comic writer. The characteristic tone of her novels, as of her letters, is ironical. We cannot miss her lemon flavour. But there are things she is not ironical about. She sets a high value on good manners and personal agreeableness, but more important still are openness, rationality, a capacity to see things as they are, and genuine warm-heartedness (not effusion). At her most serious moments Christian principles are invoked: Edmund Bertram in Mansfield Park, in his hour of disillusionment, saw in Mary Crawford 'a mind darkened, but fancying itself light'. Individual clergymen are ridiculed, but never the Church.

Her admirers do not agree about which is her best novel. Few would give the palm to the posthumous *Northanger Abbey* (probably an early work revised). It is in part a skit on the Gothic novel. Of all her mature novels it is the one most like her schoolgirl writings. *Sense and Sensibility* contains fine things. The opening scene, displaying the selfishness of Mr and Mrs Dashwood, already proclaims the master. But the machinery of the novel sometimes creaks, and there are relapses upon melodramatic literary conventions. Of the other completed novels any could reasonably be thought the best. *Pride and Prejudice* is the most sparkling, and most of it rings true; we seem to have lived in that family of girls. With the skill of a great master the novelist sets in relief the story of Darcy's 'pride' and Elizabeth's 'prejudice' by contrasting it with two other love stories, one idyllic (Jane) the other frivolous (Lydia). *Mansfield Park* explores more difficult and painful territory: unhappy marriages, poverty, the 'generation gap'. There is also the 'Milton's Satan' problem: critics endlessly differ about whether the 'villains', the Crawfords, are more attractive than the author meant them to be. *Emma* contains nothing really painful. It is a comedy of errors, largely presented through the character of Emma Woodhouse, a masterpiece of characterization. Every fresh reading reveals new fine points of irony. In *Persuasion*, which Jane Austen did not live to revise, there is a new warmth and a note of tenderness, where the heroine Anne is concerned. The novelist's reserve, usually guarded either by irony or by conventionality, seems less impenetrable in this book. Yet some of the comedy is more astringent than in the earlier books, and a little of it is rather ill-natured. (There is reason to think that this blemish would have been removed in revision.) The fact that the moral of *Persuasion* appears to be the opposite of the moral of *Sense and Sensibility* tempts us to believe in some personal development in Jane Austen, as well as in her art as a fictionist; but of course we do not know.

The disagreement about Jane Austen cannot be resolved. The pro's and con's on both sides are obvious, and have been rehearsed again and again. To the Janeites it must surely be granted that she writes excellent comedy and gives us people we can still recognize. A modern African writer has told us how he recognized 'Lady Catherine de Bourgh' in a woman of his village. To the anti-Janeites it should be conceded that talk of Shakespeare, and other 'big' authors, is out of place. Jane Austen's world (as she knew) was a tiny one, and it could reasonably be judged that she was unable, or reluctant, to see even all of that world with full clarity. But it is irrelevant to condemn her for not writing about the Napoleonic wars (and many other things). Jane Austen had intuitively grasped the sound principle that writers can only write interestingly of what they know about, and which interests them.

The search for 'another Jane Austen' is vain, but one writer of the time comes near it. Compare this, the opening of *Mansfield Park* (1814):

About thirty years ago, Miss Maria Ward, of Huntingdon, with only seven thousand pounds, had the good luck to captivate Sir Thomas Bertram, of Mansfield Park, in the county of Northampton, and to be thereby raised to the rank of a baronet's lady, with all the comforts and consequences of a handsome house and large income.

with this, the opening of Peacock's *Melincourt* (1817):

Anthelia Melincourt, at the age of twenty-one, was mistress of herself and of ten thousand a year, and a very ancient and venerable castle in one of the wildest valleys of Westmorland. If follows of course, without reference to her personal qualifications, that she had a very numerous list of admirers, and equally of course that there were both Irishmen and clergymen among them. The young lady nevertheless possessed sufficient attractions to kindle the flames of disinterested passion . . .

Surely the tone and point of view are very similar? Thomas Love Peacock (1785–1866) is usually described as a satirist. But he is unlike many satirists in the warmth and passion of his writing. In fact his novels are a blend of satire and romance, not really like anything else. Peacock's novels would have seemed odd at any period. They have obvious defects, but as 'Seithenyn' says of his embankment in *The Misfortunes of Elphin* 'the parts that are rotten give elasticity to those that are sound'. Peacock's novels are full of 'elasticity'. He is in the first class of English comic writers.

Finally the essayists of the period should be mentioned. Sydney Smith (1771–1845), a witty clergyman, is more remembered as a person than a writer; in his jokes he was a forerunner of Disraeli and Wilde. With Jeffrey and Brougham he founded the *Edinburgh Review* (1802), which opened the epoch of the Great Reviewers. The best known of these is Francis Jeffrey (1773–1850), famous because he began his review of Wordsworth's *Excursion* with 'This will never do!' (Posterity has agreed.) The Reviewers have many virtues. They have a fund of good commonsense, and they never drivel. But they are rarely very penetrating, and none of them is capable of Wordsworth's insight that a great writer creates the taste by which he is enjoyed. To-day we have more to learn from the prophetic-poet critics of the day – Wordsworth, Coleridge, De Quincey – than from the Reviewers.

Probably the most widely read nowadays of the critics of this period is William Hazlitt (1778–1830). He is in the line of the great English essayists that stretches from Addison to Max Beerbohm and Virginia Woolf. Hazlitt is more like George Orwell than any of these, incisive, hard-hitting, obsessed with politics; but his work is much richer in interest. Orwell is sour, self-conscious, afraid to let himself go. Hazlitt's literary personality is much more secure; he has confidence in his own pleasures. His work is full of gusto. Hazlitt belonged to what was called the Cockney School, which included his best friend, Charles Lamb; Keats, whose genius Hazlitt perceived, and who owed much to Hazlitt the critic and aesthetic theorist; and Leigh Hunt, who was imprisoned for his principles, but managed to keep his paper the *Examiner* going all the same. Hazlitt is one of the top four or five English critics. His doctrine was a sound one: 'The seat of knowledge is in the head; of wisdom, in the heart. We are sure to judge wrong, if we do not feel right'.

Charles Lamb (1775–1834) was a great but entirely intuitive critic. In his *Essays of Elia* (1823, 1833) he lived in the memories of his childhood; he writes as one who resents adult life. But his letters show that he had a keen sense of reality. The world of 'Elia' was a deliberate excursion into fantasy. Thomas De Quincey (1785–1859) is best known for the *Confessions of an English Opium Eater* (1822, enlarged edition 1856) in which the relative proportions of fact and fantasy are not known. His published reminiscences of the Lake poets ensure him the equivocal distinction of being the first modern journalist; he used his knowledge of the private lives of his friends for copy. De Quincey resembles Poe in his mixture of literary genius with bogusness. One of his best known essays is 'On Murder Considered as one of the Fine Arts', which anticipates Wilde's point of view, and some of Wilde's affectations also. Another is 'On the Knocking on the Gate in Macbeth', the subtlest analysis in existence of a Shakespearean scene. One of the problems with De Quincey is the difficulty we have in distinguishing in his own work what he himself called 'literature of knowledge' from 'literature of power'. If he is instructing us about (say) Kant, we wonder about the quality of the instruction. There is no such problem with Lamb. He did not write to inform us about chimney-sweeps, or Quakers. These things were only his pretext for writing. What he wanted to convey was not facts but his own way of viewing facts; he was a composer of fantasies. His work cannot be defended against the kind of malignant crosspatch who uses 'escapism' as an adverse comment. Lamb performed a service to literature by renewing interest in Elizabethan and Jacobean dramatists other than Shakespeare. His own creative work is not so much admired as it was by the Victorians and Edwardians. He is one of those writers, like Cowper, whose work is not powerful enough to be fully appreciated without reference to its biographical context. Lamb's life had been darkened by the 'day of horrors' in 1796, when his sister Mary killed their mother in a fit of insanity, and he looked after her for the rest of her life. His deliberately old-fashioned prose ('Hang the age', he said, 'I will write for antiquity') is based on his connoisseuring of sixteenth- and seventeenth-century writers, and it can be tiresome reading at first; but after a while it becomes soothing, and leads us into a world free from fear and grief and pain.

Lamb and De Quincey introduced a new development in Romantic literature: the prose poem. Lamb's 'Dream Children', De Quincey's 'Levana and Our Ladies of Sorrow', deliberately exploit the memory of dreams, and make dream logic an organizing principle. Historically they stand midway between Sir Thomas Browne, whom they both admired, and a late-Victorian stylist like Walter Pater. But their most important successor was the Frenchman Charles Baudelaire (1821–67). In his prose poems French and English Romanticism finally join hands.

From 1832 to 1914

The long reign of Queen Victoria (1837–1901) gave her name to the Victorian age. When people speak of 'the Victorians' as confident, full-blooded, marvellously energetic writers, 'an age of giants', there could be no better symbol of this age than Macaulay. Thomas Babington Macaulay (1800–59) was one of the Great Reviewers, and it was with his essay on Milton in the *Edinburgh Review* of August 1825 that a new star was born. Macaulay was once much more read than he is now. By the 1840s and 50s he had become one of the most famous writers in the English-speaking world. His point of view was of course partly responsible for this; he represented the glad confident morning of Victorian imperialism. Macaulay as a civil servant was responsible for the educational system of India, basing it on the language, literature and history of Great Britain. He believed in Utility and Progress (see his essay on Bacon) and laughed at the foreboding of Southey about possibly negative aspects of Britain's commercial and industrial expansion. He loved Johnson as the hero of Boswell, but thought Johnson's views absurd. Macaulay was a Whig in a much stronger sense than the sense in which Johnson may be called a Tory (if he can be called one at all). Indeed to define a Whig it is sufficient to point to Macaulay. And so the early Victorians found him a congenial spokesman. But his hold over them was not based on these views, which many of them would have taken for granted. It was based on Macaulay's command of literary art. His *Essays* illustrate the traditional conception of literature: instruction with delight. Macaulay imposed his version of history on his countless readers largely because he tells a story so well and has a firm sense of direction. He knew what he thought was right or wrong, good or bad, beautiful or ugly, delightful or boring. Macaulay was determined never to be boring. He wanted to secure the public of novel-addicts for his *Essays* and his *History* and he succeeded. He was a rhetorician, but he was an honest one according to his lights. Nor was he at all naive, as John Clive shows in his authoritative study of Macaulay (1973). If he practised what Herbert Butterfield (1932) attacking Lord Acton called the Whig interpretation of history, he did it well knowing what he was doing. And is it not just as well for the historian to have a bias, if this makes the reader feel that he is 'getting somewhere?'

Macaulay won his fame as a writer with his *Essays*. Here are a few sentences to give their flavour:

Every schoolboy knows who imprisoned Montezuma, and who strangled Atahualpa.
(from the essay on Lord Clive, 1840)

We know no spectacle so ridiculous as the British public in one of its periodical fits of morality.
(from the essay on Byron, 1831)

We have no enmity to Mr Robert Montgomery. We know nothing whatever about him, except what we have learned from his books, and from the portrait prefixed on one of them, in which he appears to be doing his very best to look like a man of genius and sensibility, though with less success than his strenuous exertions deserve.
(from the essay on Montgomery's poems, 1830)

In spite of oceans and deserts, of hunger and pestilence, of spies and penal laws, of dungeons and racks, of gibbets and quartering blocks, Jesuits were to be found under every disguise, and in every country; scholars, physicians, merchants, serving-men; in the hostile court of Sweden, in the old manor houses of Cheshire, among the hovels of Connaught; arguing, instructing, consoling, stealing away the hearts of the young, animating the courage of the timid, holding up the crucifix before the eyes of the dying.
(from the essay on Ranke, 1840)

The sentence on the Jesuits suggests the quality of Macaulay when he is writing on a subject which captures his imagination. No one could have disapproved more of the Society of Jesus and its aims than he did, but where there is any great historic occasion to rise to he always does rise to it.

The *Lays of Ancient Rome* (1842) show the same qualities transposed into swift-moving, Scott-like narrative verse:

Lars Porsena of Clusium,
By the Nine Gods he swore
That the great house of Tarquin
Should suffer wrong no more.
(from 'Horatius')

Now read on! the verse seems to say; and we do. 'Horatius' is a transparent celebration of the ideals of Victorian imperialism. But it gains effect immeasurably from the use of Livy and Roman legend; the feeling that these were indeed the 'brave days of old' colours every sympathetic reading of this great poem.

The *History of England* (first two volumes 1848, third and fourth 1856, fifth 1861, posthumous), beginning with the accession of James II, was not completed; it stops at the death of William III. But it achieves the effect of a finished epic on the triumph of a culture-hero. Macaulay's narrative power and gift for exposition, and his power of evoking local colour and period atmosphere, are all here at their best. The hero (William) is wooden and the villain (James) a grimacing marionette, but there are plenty of colourful minor characters and exciting episodes (such as the Massacre of Glencoe) to ensure that we read on. Macaulay was the Philistine as Artist. Even Matthew Arnold, who hated his style and rejected his point of view, had to admit the tremendous force of Macaulay's rhetoric and the spell he casts over unsophisticated readers.

Macaulay's style is over-emphatic, and there are those who prefer James Anthony Froude (1818–94) as a writer. His point of view in his *History of England* (1856–70), which covers the period 1529–88, is similar to Macaulay's – Whig, Protestant, patriotic – but his movement is more varied than Macaulay's, and his colourful passages are more sensuous. Macaulay suggests poster-colours; Froude, painting in oils. Froude is most remembered now, however, for his memoirs of Carlyle and his wife (1881–4), a notorious example of the genre that came to be called 'destructive hagiography'. (Middleton Murry's *Son of Woman*, on D.H. Lawrence, and Norman Malcolm's memoir of Wittgenstein, are modern examples). It is possible that Carlyle's reputation has never recovered from the exposure of his character which his faithful friend felt compelled to make. But there was bound to be a reaction against Carlyle, even if he had been as lucky in his biographer as Macaulay was with his (his nephew G.O. Trevelyan's *Life*, published in 1876, is delightful).

Thomas Carlyle (1795–1881) had a much harder struggle to achieve super-stardom. He was born in Dumfriesshire, in Scotland, of peasant stock, and he had none of the social advantages of Macaulay. 'The Rembrandt of English prose', as he came to be called, was a much more troubled, introspective, complex character than Macaulay. His emotional and religious problems, his difficult (though deeply rooted) marriage to his wife Jane Welsh (1801–66), one of his few rivals as a brilliant letter-writer, and even his digestive troubles, became part of the strong personal image which he projected on to the Victorian scene. Carlyle is the chief representative of the impact of German thought and literature on Victorian Britain. In this capacity he was the successor of Coleridge. (He left a corrosively funny account of the old Coleridge in the *Life of John Sterling* (1851).) But Carlyle's response to the great spiritual movement of German Romanticism was a limited one. That movement included Kant and Beethoven, for example; but Carlyle was as incapable of realizing the importance of *The Critique of Pure Reason* as he was of appreciating the Ninth Symphony. No wonder Nietzsche, a man of

European culture, dismissed Carlyle as a British boor. There remained a good deal of the Scottish peasant in Carlyle. But that was not altogether unattractive to the larger Victorian social and intellectual world into which Carlyle's literary gifts, and his personality, soon brought him. Outlandish vocables like 'Ecclefechan' and 'Craigenputtock' began to be heard from the lips of Victorian intellectuals, and the Carlyles moved to London, where he was known as the 'Sage of Chelsea'.

The German writer for whom Carlyle became the chief publicist in Britain was Johann Wolfgang von Goethe (1749–1832), once reckoned as the peer of Shakespeare and Dante, but now little read outside Germany (and perhaps not much read there either?). But Goethe appealed very greatly to the Victorians, and Carlyle must be given a good deal of credit for his translations and expositions which made Goethe available to them. Modern readers are likely to feel less gratitude for the extraordinary mannerisms of Carlyle's style in his own writings, whether or not these are ascribed to German influence. Still, his portentous tone does convey a sense of mighty forces at work.

The mad primeval Discord is hushed; the rudely-jumbled conflicting elements bind themselves into separate Firmaments: deep silent rock-foundations are *built* beneath, and the skyey vault with its everlasting Luminaries above; instead of a dark wasteful Chaos, we have a blooming, fertile, heaven-encompassed world.

(from *Sartor Resartus*)

Sartor Resartus (first published in New York 1836, in London 1838) is an indescribable book, standing beside the great oddities of literature, Sterne's *Tristram Shandy*, James's *The Golden Bowl*, Joyce's *Ulysses*. Its driving-force comes from Carlyle's passionate rejection of the mechanical philosophy of the eighteenth century and the new industrial and commercial civilization which had sprung from it. Unable to believe in the Christianity of his childhood, he struggled through lurid vaticination and cloudy symbolism to supply an emotional equivalent for his many readers who were in a similar position. *The French Revolution* (1837), hectic, ejaculatory, all in the present tense, may be Carlyle's most powerful single work. Modern archival historians may be more accurate, but they convey no such sense of how it must have felt to live through a revolutionary period. This strange book, conceived in the 'blackness, whirlwind and storm' of Carlyle's soul, is still unequalled in its power to do that. Apart from being a sage and a prose-poet Carlyle was a considerable historian of a more orthodox kind, and his later gigantic labours on Cromwell and Frederick II of Prussia cannot be dismissed as mere vapouring. But the change from the early radical Carlyle to the Carlyle of *Latter Day Pamphlets* (1850), the snarling reactionary, caused a break with the liberal intelligentsia, such as Mill, who had formerly admired him. It would not be correct to brand the later Carlyle as a Nazi; but there are too many resemblances between some of his attitudes and those of Nazism to make his revival as a thinker likely or desirable. It is Carlyle the literary artist, the sardonic character-sketcher and word-painter, the witty old grumbler, whom time will pardon. Those who have never sampled Carlyle are advised to start with *Past and Present* (1843), a study in what would now be called 'comparative history' which remains an extraordinarily original undertaking. Its influence in its time was considerable, and it is still the most readily accessible of Carlyle's historical writings.

The poets of the early Victorian age were all impressed by Carlyle, even Arnold, who came to feel great distrust about his influence. The reason is no doubt in part the fire and storminess of Carlyle's personality, but it must also be remembered that like him they all were aware of the religious problem, and aware of it in the same way – as also were novelists like George Eliot and, later, Thomas Hardy. In old-fashioned language, it was a matter of the conflict between the head and the heart. This can be amply illustrated from the work of the chief Victorian poet, Tennyson.

Alfred Tennyson (1809–92) made his decisive impact with his *Poems* of 1842, though these were selected, and some improved and recast, from earlier volumes of 1830 and 1833. They show the uneasy relation between the aesthete and the preacher in him. In some poems, such as 'Mariana' and 'The Lady of Shalott' he is the poetic heir of Keats and Coleridge, creating little worlds of pure beauty – a word-painter, a master of the emotional suggestiveness of rhythms and sounds. 'The Lotos-Eaters' consists of variations on themes of Homer and Spenser; its sweeping finale, added in 1842, counterbalances the mood of languor, but this comes back at the close:

> O rest ye, brother mariners, we will not wander more.

A didactic note is heard in 'Oenone', which decoratively re-tells the old story of the Judgment of Paris, drawing the moral that

> Self-reverence, self-knowledge, self-control;
> These three alone lead man to sovereign power.

Similarly in 'The Palace of Art', while the poet lavishes his skill on descriptions of the beauty of the Palace, in the end his soul cannot live there. A self-absorbed art is rejected. These poems are sincere, but seem to come from the head rather than the heart. A deeper, inconsolable note is heard in the lyrics 'Break, break, break' and 'Come not when I am dead'. Melancholy and activism are more balanced in 'Ulysses', one of Tennyson's best poems. This ends on a note of positive resolution:

> To strive, to seek, to find, and not to yield.

But Christopher Ricks may be right in suggesting that we cannot help catching an undertone which tempts us to read this line as

> To strive, to seek, to yield, and not to find.

In any case, no one would dispute that Tennyson's elegiac accent is often his most convincing.

Tennyson's four most ambitious poems were *The Princess* (1847), *In Memoriam A.H.H.* (1850), *Maud* (1855) and *The Idylls of the King* (1842–88). *The Princess* is a fantasia on the then topical theme of female education: a rather unpalatable mixture of the beautiful and the tiresome. It is now most enjoyable for the songs added in 1850, together with the blank verse stanzas 'Now sleeps the crimson petal, now the white' and 'Tears, idle tears' – a new kind of lyric, and quintessential Tennyson. In 'Tears, idle tears' he gives perfect expression to the 'passion of the past' which lay at the heart of his profoundest poetry, the song of transience he heard in 'The splendour falls', with its bugle echoes 'dying, dying, dying'.

The masterpiece of the elegiac Tennyson is *In Memoriam*, a sequence of poems all in that closed octosyllabic quatrain to which, though it had been used before, e.g. by Ben Jonson and Lord Herbert, Tennyson gave his own unmistakable ring:

> He is not here; but far away
> The noise of life begins again,
> And ghastly thro' the drizzling rain
> On the bald street breaks the blank day.
> (from the 7th poem)

The sequence is a long self-communing, as the poet broods over the loss of his beloved friend Arthur Hallam, looks back at their student days, or takes loving note of English scenery and the progress of the seasons. His meditations are set in a philosophical framework, which is of interest to students of Victorian thought, but not directly adaptable to modern preoccupations. The blind ruthlessness of nature, 'red in tooth and claw', and the emptiness of a life from which the hope of personal immortality has been banished, are things which moderns have learned to live with, though they may be depressed at times by the thought of them. The more philosophical poems of the sequence are now probably less popular than those that start from some finely delicate observation of nature:

> To-night the winds begin to rise
> (15)
> When rosy plumelets tuft the larch
> (91)
> Now fades the last long streak of snow.
> (115)

Tennyson had in life a closer relation to the man lamented than the mourners of 'Lycidas' or 'Adonais', but the sections which extol Hallam's virtues perhaps move us less deeply than those in which the poet cries out in bewilderment at the incomprehensible universe:

So runs my dream: but what am I?
An infant crying in the night,
An infant crying for the light,
And with no language but a cry.
        (from the 54th poem)

In the splendid finale of *In Memoriam* the poet attempts to unify the nineteenth-century conception of ethically significant evolution (change for the better) with the Christian hope:

. . . that far-off divine event
To which the whole creation moves.

But it seems widely agreed that Tennyson moves us more when he is the poet of doubt than when he is the poet of faith.

The savagery of nature and the cruelty of the man-made, capitalist world are brought closer together in *Maud* (1855). It is often said that Darwin's *Origin of Species* broke the hold of Christianity in the Victorian age. But this book was not published till 1859. The earlier speculations of astronomers and geologists, together with the Higher Criticism of the Bible, were the intellectual correlatives for Tennyson's melancholy, not Darwin, and the assumption that some kind of evolution occurs in nature was widespread long before the *Origin of Species*. In *Maud* the turbulent, Carlyle-like side of Tennyson's personality gets full expression. It had already appeared in 'Locksley Hall': Tennyson is so often taken as the epitome of Victorian conformism that it comes as a surprise to realize that in much of his early work his political and social outlook was very like that of the poets of the 1930s (he even went to Spain to take part in a civil war). In *Maud* the hero is a half-deranged figure, and the poem has to be seen as a dramatic monologue. How far his views were Tennyson's — especially at that moment of national crisis, the war with Tsarist Russia, later called the Crimean War — it is hard to say. The skill with which Tennyson uses different metres and verse-forms to convey the changing moods of his hero was something new in poetry, and has never been rivalled. The poem is like a Romantic song cycle, such as Schubert set to music. 'O that 'twere possible', 'O let the solid ground', 'Go not, happy day' are among Tennyson's finest lyrics. But the story of *Maud* is not clearly told, and it is oppressively melodramatic. Tennyson's gift for the dramatic monologue is seen to better advantage in an earlier poem, 'St Simon Stylites', and a later poem, 'Lucretius' (1868).

The crowning work of Tennyson's life, the *Idylls*, was spread over many years. They are based on Malory. Tennyson had earlier versified the story of the death of King Arthur in 'Morte d' Arthur' (later entitled 'The Passing of Arthur') in 1842. Despite over-decoration in places it comes nearer than the later *Idylls* to the heroic plainness of the original. Tennyson wishes to do two things in the *Idylls*: to create a modern equivalent for the style of epic, and to write a great poem of ethical instruction for his age. He was convinced that sexual immorality was responsible for a great many things that had gone wrong in modern life, and he therefore focused on the sin of Guinevere with Lancelot, the betrayal of Arthur, perfect king, perfect husband, perfect man (with overtones of the lost Arthur Hallam and of the lost Prince Consort, unceasingly mourned by Victoria since his death in 1861). But allegory is a very awkward form, and the 'blameless king' is more impressive in his death than in his life. To get us to accept the voice of a cuckolded husband as the voice of God is a difficult undertaking, and it has usually been felt that Tennyson did not succed. The *Idylls* are most admired to-day for individual fine passages, and interesting Victoriana, rather than as the moral epic intended by the poet.

At the beginning of his career Tennyson was roughly handled by the same reviewers who had told Keats to go back to his galley-pots. By 1850, when he was appointed poet laureate, he was already recognized as the leading poet of the day, and by the later nineteenth century he had reached a pinnacle of acclaim. The Victorians delighted in the Tennysonian miracles of expression, wondering how writing of such quality could ever have come into being, and if it could ever be surpassed; as here, when Tennyson in Edinburgh is thinking of Italy:

> How faintly-flush'd, how phantom-fair
> Was Monte Rosa, hanging there
> A thousand shadowy-pencill'd valleys
> And snowy dells in a golden air . . .

> And I forgot the clouded Forth,
> The gloom that saddens heaven and earth,
> The bitter east, the misty summer
> The grey metropolis of the north.
>   (from 'The Daisy')

Inevitably there was a reaction against Tennyson. He was ridiculed as the pre-eminent Victorian in the bad sense, shallow and parochial in his moral outlook, old-fashioned or silly in his social attitudes. His genteelisms of style earned him the nickname of 'Lawn' Tennyson. But this anti-Victorianism has become outmoded in its turn. The dated has turned into the historical, and poems like 'Enoch Arden' (1864) can now again be read with interest, while the most resolute opponent of Victorian imperialism can delight in lines like these from 'The Revenge' (1878):

> So Lord Howard past away with five ships of war that day,
> Till he melted like a cloud in the silent summer heaven . . .

To some of Tennyson's greatest poems his opinions are entirely irrelevant. 'Flower in the crannied wall', 'To Virgil', 'Crossing the Bar', do not distract us with them. Tennyson was capable of much pettiness, but at its best his poetry takes us far away from it, as when he evokes for us

> . . . such a tide as moving seems asleep,
> Too still for sound and foam,
> When that which drew from out the boundless deep
> Turns again home.

(from 'Crossing the Bar')

Robert Browning (1812–89) had much longer to wait for recognition than Tennyson, and he never achieved anything like the same popularity. Tennyson started from Keats; Browning started from Shelley. His early long poems, *Pauline* (1833), *Paracelsus* (1835), and *Sordello* (1840) are Victorian Shelley, wrestling with Shelleyan problems of the relation between 'love' and 'knowledge', 'poetry' and 'life'. They make heavy demands on the reader, and the obscurity of *Sordello* became a byword. Browning tried to reach out to a wider public in the theatre, but he is not now admired as a dramatist. The best of his plays, *Pippa Passes* (1841), is chiefly remembered for Pippa's little song, which ends

> God's in his heaven –
> All's right with the World!

– lines which were widely quoted as giving the essence of Browning's optimistic philosophy, but which have a terrible irony in their context, where they are overheard by two murderers (a guilty wife and her paramour).

Browning found his proper form not in stage plays but in the dramatic monologue. A single speaker tells his story and reveals his personality, sometimes intentionally, like the Duke in 'My Last Duchess' –

> . . . Oh, Sir, she smiled, no doubt,
> When'er I passed her; but who passed without
> Much the same smile? This grew; I gave commands;
> And all smiles stopped . . .

– sometimes unwittingly, like the Italian Renaissance bishop 'ordering his tomb'. Some of the monologues show Browning's interest in visual art and artists: Andrea del Sarto muses self-indulgently over his own weaknesses of character; Fra Lippo Lippi jovially defends his zestful naturalism as a painter. Some are concerned with the religious problem, characteristically seen from an unusual angle. An Arab physician of the first century AD examines the case of the risen Lazarus. Caliban on his island tries to work out a natural theology, using his own symbols, 'the Quiet', and 'Setebos':

> His dam held that the Quiet made all things
> Which Setebos vexed only; 'holds not so.

In lengthier discourses the worldly Bishop Blougram, the cheating spiritualist Mr Sludge, deliver paradoxical apologias for their own hypocrisy. Browning has something of a cultural anthropologist's kind of interest in his people. They are taken from a wide variety of times and places. Renaissance Italy is a favourite source, but there are many others, French and Spanish and Jewish, ancient and medieval and modern.

Yet Browning is not a great creator of character. He does not leave us with the memory of people who seem to live independently of the author, whether historical figures like Plato's Socrates and Boswell's Johnson, or fictitious ones like Falstaff and Trollope's Mrs Proudie. His characters are the poet himself in disguise. But the disguise can be thorough, and modern readers tend to prefer those poems where it is so to those in which the speakers are more obviously the poet's mouthpieces, such as 'A Grammarian's Funeral', or 'Saul', or 'Rabbi Ben Ezra'. They are more interested in the ambiguous and oblique aspect of Browning, the poet of the 'dangerous edge of things', fascinated by the seedy and the seamy aspects of life, who attracted the interest of Graham Greene.

Browning's most extended use of the dramatic monologue is found in his largest-scale work, *The Ring and the Book* (1868). Here he recreates the people involved in a murder case in seventeenth-century Rome. The poem is in twelve books. In the first book the poet describes how he found his subject, sets the scene, and sketches the outline of the story (Browning thus deliberately eliminates the element of suspense). Later books look at the events from different points of view. Some are put into the mouths of the three principals: the murderous husband (allowed two monologues, one hypocritical, one candid), his dying wife, the priest who helped her. Others are given to spokesmen representing different shades of Roman opinion, and the lawyers on both sides. The good Pope, Innocent XII, finally sums up and pronounces his verdict on the rights and wrongs of the matter. In the last book the poet provides a brief epilogue.

In *The Ring and the Book* Browning anticipates the technique of Kurosawa's film *Rashomon*, or Lawrence Durrell's *Alexandria Quartet*, and it has been argued by Robert Langbaum in *The Poetry of Experience* (1957) that his purpose, like theirs, was to bring out the relativity of truth and its total dependence on human subjectivity. This seems doubtful. The poet in his own voice, as well as that of the Pope, declares the total innocence of the wife and the priest and the guilt of the husband, whereas Browning's source, 'the Old Yellow Book', could be interpreted quite differently, as Carlyle pointed out. (Carlyle thought the wife and the priest probably *were* adulterers). Apart from this lack of real tension the poem is much too long and garrulous, and at least half of it seems unnecessary. C.S. Calverley's parody in 'The Cock and the Bull' is to the point:

> Such, sir, are all the facts, succinctly put,
> The basis or substratum, what you will,
> Of the impending eighty thousand lines.

Some have thought Browning should have written novels. But we cannot wish his best things, such as 'Instans Tyrannus', or 'Child Roland', to be other than they are. Moreover, Browning was not really a story-teller, except in such charming light poems as 'The Pied Piper of Hamelin'. Nor was he much concerned with dramatic situation. What interested him was the conflicts and contrasts within a single personality.

Browning came into his own only in the later nineteenth century. After the First World War his stock fell again, because he was thought to be a hearty insensitive optimist, 'bouncing Browning', as Aldous Huxley called him. To-day his readership is mainly an academic one, and much thought is given to the early and especially the late poetry, when Browning returned in the years after *The Ring and the Book* to the writing of long obscure philosophical poems, such as *Fifine at the Fair* (1872). The common reader, if he likes Browning, generally prefers the poems of the middle period, such as those in *Men and Women* (1855). There is also something attractive to our taste in Browning's quick light touch in his lyrics of modern life. Here a dying man speaks:

> That lane sloped, such as the bottles do,
> From a house you could descry
> O'er the garden wall; is the curtain blue
> Or green to a healthy eye?
>
> To mine, it serves for the old June weather
> Blue above lane and wall . . .
>
> (from 'Confessions')

His genius lay in his perception of discords and incongruities. As with Donne, a reader who can learn to tolerate his oddities – his grotesque rhymes, his cacophonies and corrugation – will be richly rewarded. But it may be that in the end Browning returns to the memory not so much in complete poems as in short snatches:

> What's become of Waring,
> Since he gave us all the slip . . .
>
> I would we were boys of old
> In the field, by the fold . . .
>
> Never the time and the place
> And the loved one all together!
>
> Escape me?
> Never –
> Beloved!
>
> Infinite passion, and the pain
> Of finite hearts that yearn.

During her lifetime the poetry of Elizabeth Barrett Browning (1806–61) far exceeded her husband's in popularity. Everyone knows the story of his rescue of her from her autocratic father and her life of psychosomatic invalidism. Edward Moulton-Barrett may have been over-melodramatized by the popular play and film as a Victorian tyrant with incestuous motives, but it is a historical fact that he never had anything to do with her again after her elopement to Italy with Browning. Mrs. Browning was a woman of real independence of mind and force of character, and she could write with vigour, but her versification is rather rough-and-ready. The *Sonnets from the Portuguese* (first printed in *Poems* 1850) represent her main claim to a high place in poetry. It seems, however, as if (with the great exception of Drayton's 'Since there's no help . . .') the intimate kind of sonnet does not really work in English: a greater formality and distancing, whether in Shakespeare's way, or Milton's, or Wordsworth's, is more effective in this form. *Aurora Leigh* (1857), a novel in verse, is being re-read a good deal to-day. Here Elizabeth Browning made a spirited attempt to challenge the predominance of prose fiction as the medium for treating modern life. But she seems to owe much to her prose rivals, such as Charlotte Brontë. Among her other poems 'The Cry of the Children' still retains some of its edge, even if it has to be classed with 'good bad' poems, such as Hood's.

The eighteen-thirties and forties were a good time for comic verse. *The Ingoldsby Legends* (first collected 1840) of Richard Harris Barham (1788–1845) are still remembered. Barham, an Anglican clergyman, made affectionate fun of the Old Religion and the neo-medievalism inspired by Walter Scott and the Oxford Movement and the Gothic Revival. The best known of the Legends is 'The Jackdaw of Rheims', but Barham shows more of his powers when he is macabre, as in 'Bloudie Jacke'. He is as fond of rhyming ingenuities as Browning:

> . . . I vow they'd have called me a blockhead if
> At school I had ventured to use such a vocative . . .

But unlike Browning he does not use them in serious poetry. Winthrop Mackworth Praed (1802–39) had a gift for the kind of light society verse which Johnson called 'easy poetry'. His charming poem 'The Vicar' is a good example. He was a friend of Macaulay at Cambridge and wrote historical ballads that are rather like Macaulay's. In the history of English social verse Praed comes midway in the line that links Matthew Prior with John Betjeman.

Tennyson, the Brownings, Christina Rossetti, Swinburne, and other leading Victorian poets, all seem to have written too much. They are what a French critic has called *langoustes* (lobsters); the delicious morsels have to be picked out from a large mass of inedibility. Their over-production was probably due to the fact that they did nothing but write poetry. The more continuously readable Victorian poets, such as Arnold, Clough, or Hopkins, had other things to do, and wrote less, and so they have left us less dead wood in their collected works. Matthew Arnold (1822–88) began as a poet, but when poetry gave him up he wisely turned to prose, instead of continuing to write uninspired verse, and he became the leading literary and social critic of the Victorian age. As a literary critic Arnold was a firm classicist. He thought the Romantic poets 'did not know enough', and criticized them severely for defects of form and style. His masters were the Greeks, and among the more recent poets he most admired Goethe and Wordsworth. He found fault with his predecessors, especially Keats, for neglecting the primacy of subject in favour of local and incidental beauties of style. Arnold came nearest to putting his critical ideas into effective practice in *Sohrab and Rustum*, an old Persian story which he handles in a manner deliberately reminiscent of Homer. But even here it is the décor that we remember rather than the story and characters, and the passage most quoted from the poem is the conclusion, which carries us away from human beings to the River Oxus journeying homeward to the sea.

In fact Arnold was not gifted as an epic or dramatic poet, nor was he good at large-scale construction, much as he valued it as a critic. He was essentially a personal and lyrical poet. The songs of Callicles in *Empedocles in Etna* stand out as intervals of poetic relief amid Empedocles's rugged ponderings. In his best poems Arnold is free from artifice. The Grand Style and the great subject are forgotten: all is pathos and longing. 'The Forsaken Merman' belongs in spirit essentially with the lamenting poems about the mysterious 'Marguerite'. Often Arnold is slow-moving and reflective, as in 'Stanzas from the Grande Chartreuse'. He is close here to being an essayist in verse. For many modern readers he is above all the poet of 'Dover Beach', recoiling from the confusion of the world we have made, 'where ignorant armies clash by night'.

Arnold was a busy, active man, an inspector of schools, a wit, a lively journalist and pundit, and in his later work a publicist for de-supernaturalized religion. But his best poetry is quiet and unpolemical. He was repelled by the industrial and commercial civilization in which he had to live, and for consolation he turned to dreams of Greece, and to nature in its reassuring aspects – calm waters on a summer night, English streams and meadows, mountains in the distance. The landscape of the Oxford countryside dominates his two most beautiful poems, 'The Scholar Gipsy' and 'Thyrsis', which both in theme and style owe much to Keats's Odes. Most characteristically he is a sad poet.

> . . . from time to time, vague and forlorn,
> From the soul's subterranean depth upborne
> As from an infinitely distant land,
> Come airs, and floating echoes, and convey
> A melancholy into all our day.
>   (from 'The Buried Life')

Arnold's friend Arthur Hugh Clough (1819–61) is the poet mourned in Arnold's 'Thyrsis', but he was a more robust character than he appears in that poem. He was, though, a troubled soul, and at times he appears almost the type of the Victorian wistful agnostic. He can be very earnest, as in the much-anthologized 'Say not the struggle naught availeth'. But Clough can be much sunnier and livelier than that. He was the Victorians' Louis MacNeice. His world is the world of social life, manners, and the novel. He caught the accent of colloquial English better than Browning, who so often attempted it. His 'long vacation pastoral', *The Bothie* (1848) is witty and high-spirited. It is written in accentual hexameters, like Longfellow's *Evangeline*. The American poet wryly observed that in this metre 'the motions of the English Muse are not unlike those of a prisoner dancing to the music of his chains'. Clough put this metre to its best use in English, i.e. for serio-comic verse. In *Amours de Voyage* (1858) he used hexameters for a novel in letters, set in Rome during the war between the French and Garibaldi in 1849.

> So, I have seen a man killed! An experience that, among others!
> Yes, I suppose I have; although I can hardly be certain,
> And in a court of justice could never declare I had seen it.
> But a man was killed, I am told, in a place where I saw
> Something; a man was killed, I am told, and I saw something.
>
> (from Canto II)

This has a modern ring to it. Clough introduced into English the sophisticated, introspective, self-mocking anti-hero who was often to occur in literature between 1890 and 1940.

Edward FitzGerald (1809–83) was another doubter, but if we are to take the quatrains he freely translated from the Persian poet Omar Khayyam as expressing his own views he was more angry than wistful about the Christian God:

> O thou who Man of baser earth didst make,
> And didst with Paradise devise the snake,
> For all the sin wherewith the face of Man
> Is blacken'd, – Man's forgiveness give, – and take!
>
> (from *The Rubáiyát of Omar Khayyam*)

FitzGerald belongs to the same literary type as Thomas Gray, a lonely, homosexually-oriented scholar-poet. He expressed his alienation in a witty and ironic style. Edward Lear (1812–88) expressed his indirectly, through humour and nonsense. His poetry is often bracketed with 'The Hunting of the Snark', by 'Lewis Carroll', i.e. Charles Lutwidge Dodgson (1832–98), famous also for *Alice in Wonderland* (1865) and *Through the Looking Glass* (1871). But Carroll's nonsense is the nonsense of a logician; Lear's is the nonsense of a romantic poet. In Poe (e.g. 'Ulalume') there is a kind of poetry always trembling on the edge of unintentional nonsense. By taking it over the edge into intentional nonsense, as in 'The Dong with a Luminous Nose', Lear heightened the pathos by heightening the absurdity. He entered the world of the child without sentimentality, and, as Auden said, 'Children flocked to him like settlers. He became a land'.

In Clough, FitzGerald, Lear, and Carroll – in very different ways – we sense the presence of divided natures. A contrast here is the Dorset poet William Barnes (1801–86); *his* strength lies in his clarity of mind and purity of emotion. His poems can be very sad, as in 'Woak Hill'. But they accept life as it is, and see joys in it as well as sorrows. Barnes was a scholar-poet, who deliberately wrote in a stylized form of the Dorset dialect. He regretted that the English of King Alfred had gone the way it had; he tried to restore it on his own, and so placed himself outside the main stream of modern English poetry. But greater poets, Hardy and Hopkins, admired his work, and learned from it.

A new fashion in English poetry arrived in the 1860s, called the Pre-Raphaelite movement. The leading figure was Dante Gabriel Rossetti (1828–98), son of an Italian patriot émigré who settled in England. He became first known as a painter, with Holman Hunt, Millais and others, who founded the Pre-Raphaelite Brotherhood. They rejected the tradition of Renaissance painting exemplified by Raphael, and sought to return to earlier Italian styles. Rossetti's poem 'The Blessed Damozel' suggests the qualities of Primitive painting, but without its religious fervour. Rossetti's poetry owed much to the dreamy archaizing poems of Keats and Coleridge, and to the Tennyson of 'Mariana' and 'The Lady of Shalott'. He was indifferent to Tennyson's moralizing and social concerns. There is a flavour of decay in Rossetti's work. It seems gruesomely appropriate that his *Poems* of 1870 were disinterred from his wife's grave, where he had buried them in a fit of passionate remorse.

Rossetti was attacked for the 'fleshly' element in his poetry by one Robert Buchanan, under a pseudonym, in 1871, but this would now be rather a recommendation than otherwise: so much Victorian poetry seems strangely sexless. The sonnet sequence *The House of Life* (1870–81) shows him as one of the few masters of sonnet form.

> And now that I have climbed and won this height,
> I must tread downward through the sloping shade
> And travel the bewildered tracks till night.
> Yet for this hour I still may here be stayed,
> And see the gold air and the silver fade,
> And the last bird fly into the last night.

Rossetti held that the sonnet should be 'a moment's monument'. Many English sonnets have good lines, but usually supported by inferior ones. A poem on so small a scale cannot afford flaws, and Rossetti's best sonnets are flawless. His other superiority to his Romantic predecessors is that, unlike them, he wrote narrative poems which are well-told stories, like 'The Bride's Prelude' and 'The King's Tragedy'.

Christina Rossetti (1830–94), his sister, has the Pre-Raphaelite decoration in her poems:

> Raise me a dais of silk and down;
> Hang it with vair and purple dyes,
> Carve it in doves and pomegranates,
> And peacocks with a hundred eyes . . .
>   (from 'A Birthday')

But her poetry is predominantly the expression of an austere devotional religion. Her playful side is revealed in her most famous poem, 'Goblin Market', when she conjures up the goblin people:

> One had a cat's face,
> One whisked a tail,
> One tramped at a rat's pace,
> One crawled like a snail,
> One like a ratel tumbled hurry skurry.

Often she is quiet and intimate:

> Yet come to me in dreams, that I may live
> My very life again though cold in death:
> Come back to me in dreams, that I may give
> Pulse for pulse, breath for breath:
> Speak low, lean low,
> As long ago, my love, how long ago!
>   (from 'Echo')

Christina Rossetti wrote an immense number of poems, and her work in bulk is rather monotonous. She is narrowly pietistic, and some of her poems have a sharp, old-maidish quality which is off-putting; she rebukes the hypocritical reader as if she were a spinster Baudelaire. But much can be forgiven her for poems like 'Twilight Calm', or 'Remember', which begins

> Remember me when I have gone away . . .

and ends

> Better by far you should forget and smile
> Than that you should remember and be sad.

Another poet of the Pre-Raphaelite group was William Morris (1834–96). Morris wrote some fine incantatory poetry in the volume called *The Defence of Guinevere* (1858). His later narrative poems invite the reader to 'Forget six counties overhung with smoke', in *The Life and Death of Jason* (1867) and *The Earthly Paradise* (1868–70). The weakness of his narrative poems is that they are, as Morris himself said, 'too long and flabby, damn it!' But some of his poetry is tough and hard-hitting. In 'The Haystack in the Floods' he does not flinch from the violence and cruelty of medieval life. *Sigurd the Volsung* (1876) is perhaps his most considerable work in poetry, and a high proportion of it is strong, muscular writing. In later years Morris turned more to prose. The *Dream of John Ball* (1889) mingles prose and verse. *News from Nowhere* (1891) brings a poet's vision to imagining what a classless society might be like, though as Americans often suppose they have one already the book may leave them cold. Morris's work for socialism was not only done through direct propaganda and campaigns against bad workmanship and for the return of art to the people. His own art caught the youthful imaginations of future socialist and social-democratic leaders, through late prose romances like *The Well at the World's End* (1896), in which he anticipates Dunsany and Tolkien in the creation of a new genre, the romance completely of an imaginary and self-sufficient poetic world.

Algernon Charles Swinburne (1837–1909) belonged in his younger days to the Rossetti circle, and he wrote poems in the manner of the Pre-Raphaelites, but their imaginary Middle Ages was not his favourite dream country. He preferred an equally imaginary Ancient Greece. Swinburne made his first, violent impact on readers, especially the young, with *Atalanta in Calydon* (1865), frankly celebrating the erotic in his leaping rhythms:

> And Pan by noon and Bacchus by night
> Fleeter of foot than the fleetfoot kid,
> Follows with a dancing and fills with delight
> The Maenad and the Bassarid;
> And swift as lips that laugh and hide
> The laughing leaves of the trees divide,
> And screen from seeing and leave in sight
> The god pursuing, the maiden hid.

Poems and Ballads (1866) reinforced the impression of exultant neo-paganism, with hints of sado-masochism and sexual deviance. Swinburne was in some ways another Shelley, an eccentric aristocrat with radical views, a torrential flood of words, and a seemingly inexhaustible lyricism. He sings of Revolution and Liberty. But his excitement seems to derive from words, not things, or people. 'I never could sympathize with Swinburne's work', wrote Morris, to whom it seemed to be founded on 'literature, not on nature'. The history of Swinburne's creativity does not fit the usual pattern of growth, flowering, and decline. 'By the North Sea' or 'A Nympholept' are just as powerful as his early work. All his work suffers from the same defect:

> Miles and miles and miles of desolation!
> Leagues on leagues on leagues without a change.

His description of the Dunwich coast fits his own poetry. The last thirty years of his life were spent in the unvarying daily routine of his home at Putney, under the watchful guardianship of Theodore Watts-Dunton. Much of his best work of those years is in his excellent, if over-exuberant, literary criticism, and his letters, which (apart from his dreary fixation on flogging) are delightfully funny and witty. Swinburne is the un-Victorian Victorian, so much so as to invite the parodist. But he was a great writer, in some ways. At present his reputation stands lowest among the major Victorian poets, and re-assessment would be an arduous matter: Swinburne is voluminous. But it would be worth while.

Two other poets, George Meredith (1828–1901) and Thomas Hardy (1840–1928), bring us decisively into the late Victorian period, in which both of them were to win fame as novelists. For the same writer to be both a major poet and a major novelist must be unusual, since the two arts require such different gifts, but in the next century Joyce and Lawrence were to continue this twofold tradition. Meredith's novels are to-day out of fashion, but poets still read his *Modern Love* (1862), which is a sort of novel in the form of a sonnet sequence. It tells, somewhat obliquely, the story of the tragic breakdown of a marriage. Meredith is usually thought to have his own marriage in mind (his wife, Peacock's daughter, left him), but Rossetti's marriage has also been suggested. Could it be that Meredith used his imagination and invented things? (Not every author is a Christopher Isherwood.) The reader who wants to be clear who did what to whom, and when and where, is going to be rather baffled by *Modern Love*, which is often very cryptic. But much of it is powerful. Meredith devised a new form for the sonnet, extending it to sixteen lines. His openings are sometimes as good as Shakespeare's, and he usually ends more strongly:

> In desperate hints here see what evermore
> Moves dark as yonder midnight ocean's force,
> Thundering in rampant hosts of warrior horse
> To throw that faint thin line upon the shore!

Most of Hardy's best poems did not appear till the twentieth century, long after he had won fame as a novelist. He did not begin publishing poetry until he abandoned prose fiction in the 1890s, but he had beeen writing it throughout his long life: 'Neutral Tones', one of his best and most characteristic poems, is dated by him as from 1867. To-day he is one of the most loved and admired poets of the whole nineteenth century. Some of Hardy's poems are obviously the poems of a novelist. He likes to tell stories in verse, gloomy or grotesque or piquant little anecdotes. But often his poems are songs; his starting-point is a tune, or a new metre invented for the occasion. The titles of two of his volumes suggest his perpetual subjects, 'Satires of Circumstance', 'Time's Laughingstocks'; the cruelty of time, the blind blows of fate, the helplessness of human beings in a world bereft of any lasting consolations. Hardy, like most thoughtful men and women of his time, was much preoccupied with Christianity. At times (as in his little poem 'The

Oxen') he writes of it wistfully. At times he envies those who are capable of faith in it:

> I am like a gazer who should mark
> An inland company,
> Standing upfingered, with, 'Hark! hark!
> The glorious distant sea!'
> And feel, 'Alas, 'tis but yon dark
> And wind-swept pine to me!'
> (from 'The Impercipient (At a Cathedral Service)')

At other times he is sarcastic about orthodox ideas, associating them with the respectability and social conformity that arouse his scorn as a poet (though in real life he frequented the company of the 'best' people). Now and then he has a bout of the hatred of God that breaks out also in Shelley, Swinburne, FitzGerald, A.E. Housman, and Empson. Hardy was as obsessed as some modern thinkers, the Existentialists, with the absurdity, irrationality, and gratuitousness of the world. The Victorian science that had appalled Tennyson was equally an implacable reality for him. Yet it is as if he could not help affirming in poetry values which for science are irrelevant, and assigning them an alternative and higher order of existence:

> . . . was there ever
> A time of such quality, since or before,
> In that hill's story? . . .
>
> Primeval rocks form the road's steep border,
> And much have they faced there, first and last,
> Of the transitory in Earth's long order,
> But what they record in colour and cast
> Is – that we two passed.
> (from 'At Castle Boterel')

At the end of 'After a Journey' he insists that though now an old man, he is 'still the same as when' he was the happy young husband on his honeymoon.

By the later years of the nineteenth century it was becoming widely felt that Matthew Arnold's attempted compromise would not do, and the choice for a Victorian intellectual lay between T.H. Huxley (1825–95), 'Darwin's bulldog', symbol of Victorian science, and J.H. Newman (1801–90), whose conversion to the Roman Church in 1846 had set going a numerous movement of the élite in that direction. Hardy, as we have seen, had regretfully chosen the way of Huxley. But another major poet of that time, Gerard Manley Hopkins (1844–89), took whole-heartedly the way of Newman, becoming a Roman Catholic, and then a Jesuit priest. Now, for the first time since Crashaw, the accent of Roman Catholic piety was heard in English poetry. Coventry Patmore (1823–96) had already had a popular success with a novel in verse, *The Angel in the House* (1854–64), celebrating the Victorian notion of an ideal marriage. He became a Catholic in the 1860s and his mystical-erotic poems of *The Unknown Eros* (1877) had a less general appeal. The touching poem 'The Toys' is the only one of the series that is widely known. Patmore with his three marriages, his monogamic mysticism, and his outbursts of anger, provoked by a civilization he hated, was bound to seem eccentric. He was a Catholic of a type more often seen among 'cradle' Catholics than converts: he constantly denounced the priesthood, and even the Pope. Alice Meynell (1847–1922), a woman poet and essayist whom Patmore loved, and his disciple Francis Thompson (1859–1907), are other figures of this late-Victorian movement who are still not altogether forgotten. But Hopkins is now by far the best known and most studied of them. Hopkins's poetry was unknown to the public during his lifetime. A collection of it did not appear till 1918, when it was edited by his fellow-poet and confidant Bridges (poet laureate since 1913). Robert Bridges (1844–1930), a graceful traditionalist, has been accused of inadequate sympathy with Hopkins's work, but at least (unlike Patmore, who could make nothing of it) he recognized its troubling originality.

Hopkins's early work is comparatively conventional, but by the 1870s he had come to 'doubt Tennyson' and see something Parnassian and artificial in the master's work. And he worked out a new rhythm and diction, discarding traditional poetic diction and archaism, and doing everything he could to ensure that every word in his verse worked for its living. (He was positively Herodian in his massacre of innocent English particles). The new manner which burst upon English poetry with the 'Wreck of the Deutschland' (1876) bewildered Hopkins's friends, and it can still be a stunning experience to come upon it for the first time. 'The wreck he describes', said F.R. Leavis, 'is both occasion and symbol. He realizes it so vividly that he is in it; and it is at the same time in him'.

> I did say yes
> O at lightning and lashed rod;
> Thou heardst me truer than tongue confess
> Thy terror, O Christ, O God;
> Thou knowest the walls, altar and hour and night:
> The swoon of a heart that the sweep and the hurl of thee trod
> Hard down with a horror of height:
> And the midriff astrain with leaning of, laced with fire of stress.

Hopkins's innovations were welcomed in the twentieth century, and he was granted an honoured place among the moderns. Obscurity was no disadvantage in the epoch of Yeats and Eliot. Congenial too was Hopkins's bitter indictment of capitalist civilization, the filth and pollution of the late Victorian 'inner city' in which he spent his life as working priest, and which at one moment provoked him, in a letter to Bridges, to call himself 'a Communist'. Understandably, the Left poets of the nineteen-thirties took him up, and his

Yes. Why do we all, seeing of a soldier, bless him? bless
Our redcoats, our tars . . .?

(from 'The Soldier')

became Day Lewis's

Yes. Why do we all, seeing a communist, feel small?

But Day Lewis's adaptation loses the stamping feet and beating drums of Hopkins's poem, as well as its ingenuousness. It soon come to be realized that in many ways Hopkins was a typical Victorian poet in his themes and attitudes, his old-fashioned patriotism and love of the redcoats and the jolly jack tars, his passion for nature, his cult of sensuous beauty.

Hopkins's packed style can be very effective. He gets Oxford into a single line:

Towery city and branchy between towers.
(from 'Duns Scotus's Oxford')

But sometimes his distortions of the English language leave his poems muscle-bound:

. . . This to hoard unheard,
Heard unheeded, leaves me a lonely began.
(From 'To seem the stranger')

Surely 'began' as a noun is not English? Yet in a poignant way the words 'a lonely began' suggest Hopkins's strange tortured personality, and the place of his style in English poetry – a dead end?

Hopkins had a sense of humour (see his letters to Bridges) but his personality was austere, intense, self-denying. He felt misgivings about writing poetry at all. And some obscure crisis, possibly to do with his homosexual orientation, is felt to lie behind his most desolate poems, the so-called 'terrible' sonnets written at the end of his life. Reminders of the sensuousness of his earlier poems only enhance the effect of aridity and self-disgust, as in 'I wake and feel the fell of dark, not day'. In the best known of these poems he arraigns God, beginning with words taken from the book of Jeremiah:

Thou art indeed just, Lord, if I contend
With thee; but, sir, so what I plead is just.
Why do sinners' ways prosper, and why must
Disappointment all I endeavour end?
Wert thou my enemy, O thou my friend,
How wouldst thou worse, I wonder, than thou dost
Defeat, thwart me? . . .
Mine, O thou lord of life, send my roots rain.

Hopkins died in 1889. The leading poets of the decade after his death lived on and wrote on in the twentieth century, and the greatest of them, W.B.

Yeats, will be considered in the next chapter. Yeats was the historian and elegist of 'the tragic generation', the short-lived new poets of the nineties, in some of his poems and in his *Autobiographies*. Otherwise the best memorials to the *fin de siécle* are Max Beerbohm's story 'Enoch Soames' (in *Seven Men*, 1919) and Ezra Pound's poem 'Hugh Selwyn Mauberley' (1920). The tone of Nineties poetry is chiefly melancholy. That was by no means a new tone in Victorian poetry, but its associations with city life – preparing the way for further depressed urban poetry in the twentieth century – gave it a special flavour, though even this had been anticipated by James Thomson (1834–82) in his *City of Dreadful Night* (1874). Thomson's long poem was inspired by the pessimistic Italian poet Leopardi; the Nineties poets took their cue from Baudelaire and the French poets who followed him, and the period became very much a French one – another link with the early work of Eliot and Pound. The most influential French poet at this time was Paul Verlaine (1844–96), sad, languid, vague. But there were very different voices also. Rudyard Kipling (1865–1936) offered the banjo and the bugle as alternatives to Verlaine's 'sanglots longs/Des violons'. In *Barrack Room Ballads* (1892), often to the tune of music-hall songs, he brought the Cockney vernacular of the British private soldier into poetry. Kipling was an artist in verse in many other styles, too. He can be hortatory and stern, as in 'Recessional', one of the few English hymns since the eighteenth century that can be called great. He can be gentle and nostalgic, as in 'The Way Through the Woods'. But his most original contribution to poetry was that, more compellingly than Swinburne or the Pre-Raphaelites, he brought up to date the bleak simplicity of the traditional ballads: his 'Danny Deever' is almost intolerably painful. Another masterpiece which gets it effect from its modernization of the ancient form is Oscar Wilde's *The Ballad of Reading Gaol* (1898), perhaps the best known poem of the Nineties. The style of popular verse was also favoured by Alfred Edward Housman (1859–1936) in his volume *A Shropshire Lad* (1896). This and its successors *Last Poems* (1922) and the posthumous *More Poems* (1936), both indistinguishable from it in style, have made Housman one of the most popular of English poets. Housman was a lyric poet: his accent, which is unmistakable, is one of melancholy seasoned with irony. Occasionally a felicitously chosen learned word reminds us that the poet in real life was not a Shropshire rustic but a professor of Latin, but usually Housman's vocabulary is plain and colloquial, even slangy. Housman gave epigrammatic, lapidary form to the pessimistic strain of Victorian verse which runs from Tennyson to Thomson. His sentiment is closest of all to FitzGerald of the *Rubáiyát*, as in this four line poem which uses its stanza-form and rhyme scheme:

> To stand up straight and tread the turning mill,
> To lie flat and know nothing and be still,
> Are the two trades of man; and which is worse
> I know not, but I know that both are ill.

The 'Edwardian' and 'Georgian' poetry that was to follow in the years up to 1914 was much influenced by Housman, and later the work of Hardy began to be a potent presence also. The preoccupation with English country life shared by Housman and Hardy was an important agent in the reaction against the French Nineties which now became dominant. But few of those poets are much read now. The most original of them was Walter de la Mare (1873–1956), whose *Songs of Childhood* (1902), published under the name of 'Walter Ramal', introduced the special de la Mare magic, mystery and visionary quality. De la Mare's work, highly individual in prose as well as verse, was to continue under, and survive, the 'Modernist' movement, by which it was untouched.

Victorian Romantic poetry went out of favour in the new century, though it is now being re-read with more interest and respect. But it is still usual to judge that the Victorian novelists surpass the poets. Certainly the Victorian novel is one of the great 'chapters' of English literature, like the Elizabethan drama. And as in Shakespeare's time, there now appears to be one star figure, at the centre of a number of other writers of great talent. Charles Dickens (1812–70) is now widely regarded as the greatest Victorian novelist – perhaps the greatest English novelist of any period. His first novel *The Pickwick Papers* (1836–7) at once won him popularity on an enormous scale that has never been approached by any English writer before or since. Dickens was the first novelist of the modern city, the creator of a sort of urban folklore. Many of his characters and sayings have become part of the language. We need only mention the Wellers, father and son, in *Pickwick*, Oliver Twist asking for more, Little Nell of *The Old Curiosity Shop*, Tiny Tim of 'A Christmas Carol', the sacrifice of Sidney Carton in *A Tale of Two Cities*. Also typical of Dickens are those larger-than-life characters who give a special meaning to Wittgenstein's saying that 'to imagine a language is to imagine a form of life': Pecksniff and Mrs Gamp in *Martin Chuzzlewit*, Micawber in *David Copperfield*.

Dickens's novels are mainly remembered for their characters rather than their plots. Their episodic nature may be due in part to his usual practice, like that of other Victorian novelists, of publishing his novels in serial instalments. Dickens never wholly abandoned the old loose-knit rambling tradition of the English novel, with its alternation of comic, sentimental and melodramatic incidents. But from *Dombey and Son* (1846–48) onward he showed an increasing tendency to organize his novels more closely. In his mature work the plots cease to be a mere device to hold heterogeneous material together and become themselves expressive of the main themes and interests of the novels. The plot of *Great Expectations* (1860–1), not to be disclosed here in case the reader does not yet know it, is not only a magnificent story in itself; it is what *Great Expectations* is actually 'about', as much as if it were a fable of Aesop. Dickens was a master of all the resources of the novelist's art. Already in the joyous adventures of Mr Pickwick he was displaying his intense interest and delight in the social minutiae of English life. Says Alfred Jingle at the charity ball:

'Fun presently – nobs not come yet – queer place – dockyard people of upper rank don't know dockyard people of lower rank – dockyard people of lower rank don't know small gentry – small gentry don't know tradespeople – commissioner don't know anybody'.

But he has other strings to his bow – psychological inwardness, ability to conduct an action over long stretches of time, a keen sense of place and atmosphere. He earns his unique status by his power to combine the methods and materials of the immemorial craft of fiction with the characteristically modern art of the Novel.

Dickens's genius was bound up with his gift for recapturing the world of childhood, its joys and terrors, its misapprehensions and fancies, its vulnerability and poignancy. No writer has surpassed his insight into that world in the earlier part of *David Copperfield* (1849–50). Though told in the first person, this novel is not mainly autobiographical, but it vibrates, in the blacking factory episode, with Dickens's memories of his own early sufferings. It was these that inspired his passionate sympathy with the underdog and made him the foremost 'crusading' writer of the world. Dickens's radicalism was, however, not intellectually coherent, and he was criticized by Carlyle for his warm-hearted sentimentality and rose-coloured idealizations of human nature. He launched tirades against social injustice, but he had no positive programme. Any kind of collective action at once suggested bureaucracy to him. He hated 'machinery' of every kind, the Law and all its trappings, for example – as in *Bleak House* (1852–3) – and all the flinty inhumanities and social falsities which alienate man from man and freeze the genial current of the soul. Dickens's antipathy to the creed of 'Facts' (as in *Hard Times*, 1854) or to the Victorian Civil Service, ridiculed by him as 'the Circumlocution Office' in *Little Dorrit* (1856–7), sprang from the same source: the repugnance he felt towards the mentality which deals with human beings only in the aggregate, and so denies the individual's God-given right to respect as a person.

Dickens casts a spell over the readers who care for his works. But there have always been other readers, from his own time to the present, who resist it. He has been accused of vulgarity, sentimentality, crudity of effect. His characters have been dismissed as one-dimensional 'humours', their individuality merely a matter of odd external peculiarities and mannerisms, of reiterated catchphrases ('Barkis is willin', etc.) Dickensian benevolence has been criticized as patronizing and unreal, and unfavourable conclusions have been drawn about the relationship between his celebration of the happy hearth and the novelist's own troubled domestic life. Then there is the darker side of Dickens – his obsession with prisons, and murder, and (not always so often remarked) people watching people: his last, unfinished novel, *The Mystery of Edwin Drood* (1870) breaks off after one of these 'watching' scenes. Personal obsessions have been detected here, and the quality of their imaginative appeal has been questioned.

Dickens's Victorian critics were also apt to dwell on the alleged limitations of his creative range. They said he could not draw a gentleman, and was ill at ease in depicting educated people; that his literary and artistic culture was slight, and he had no interest in ideas, or in the kind of person to whom ideas matter; that he was in many ways a typical Victorian householder, insular, complacent, *bourgeois*. These objections are less heard to-day, but other traditional criticisms are still often made, e.g. that many of his heroes are sticks, mere 'walking gentlemen'. And many modern readers, especially women, find it hard to share his fondness for one particular type of 'angel in the house', the small girl who combines child-like with maternal qualities.

How fair are all these criticisms? There can be no doubt that some, at least, of Dickens's novels are full of faults. They were written hastily. And sometimes Dickens was too aware of his public, and made concessions which an austerer artist would not have made. But surely his achievement was very great? His novels glow with life. They have an almost hallucinatory effect; we remember them as we remember our own dreams. It is hard sometimes to realize that his characters were not actually part of our own lives. Also it should be understood that there are many Dickenses. He can be as broad in his effects as a music-hall entertainer, but he can also be a subtle and profound psychologist. Twentieth century criticism has had no difficulty in assimilating his work to that of Dostoevsky, or Kafka, both of whom owed much to him. Dickens's style is very varied. He can write with the suggestive economy of a great poet (see the description of 'Chesney Wold' in *Bleak House*, for example). He can reiterate his points loudly and tediously; he can be at other times as terse as La Rochefoucauld. He can preach, denounce, storm; he can also fill the reader with a sense of well-being, and irradiate the dreary commonplaces of existence with the sunshine of his humour and geniality. Was Dickens a fantasist or a realist? He himself often insisted that he was a realist. But many critics see him as the creator of a unique Dickensian universe. Perhaps the peculiarity of Dickens is that he unites a fairytale unrealism with an extraordinarily minute observation of the details of actual life.

Dickens's chief rival for the affections of the literary public was William Makepeace Thackeray (1811–63). There were Dickensians and Thackerayans. But to-day there are few Thackerayans. Thackeray lacked Dickens's vitality and ruthless driving power. And he seems miscast as the merciless ironical satirist that he was supposed to be (by Ruskin, for example). In real life, it seems, much more than Dickens, who was a hard man, Thackeray was soft-hearted to the point of sentimentality, and easily moved to sympathy. Some of his best work is scattered among a mass of journalism, ephemera, and *jeux d'esprit*. As a familiar essayist, in *The Roundabout Papers* (1863), he is at his best, a lively inquisitive man. There is an air of careless largesse about them, and about all Thackeray's work. Two of his novels, *Vanity Fair* (1847–8) and *Henry Esmond* (1852), rank with the best of Dickens's, but no others. The trouble with Thackeray is that he pulls his punches, and nothing lowers the reader's vitality more than a halfhearted satirist. His best drawn character, Becky Sharp in *Vanity Fair*, appeals to us because she accepts that society is a jungle and fights back, but Thackeray tones down her revolt and blackens her character by hinting, at the end, that she murdered her husband. Thackeray introduced a useful concept into English with the word 'snobbery' (see his *Book of Snobs*, 1848). Like 'Lifemanship' introduced in 1950 by Stephen Potter (1900–69), it has become so familiar that people use it without a thought of its originator. Those for whom the ramifications of snobbery are of absorbing interest will find an ample field for comment in Thackeray's work. Thackeray, unlike Dickens or Tennyson, was not fully at one with his own age, but was not able to find another one with which to identify himself. He has many resemblances to Lytton Strachey. Strachey mocked the Victorians but his heart was really with them; Thackeray condemned the eighteenth century in his *Four Georges* (1860), but was really more at home there than he was in Victoria's middle years.

Now only of historical interest are a number of novels which dealt directly with what was then called 'the Condition of England' question: the effects of early industrialism on social life, the political stir of Chartism, etc. The three most often mentioned are *Sybil* (1845), by Benjamin Disraeli (1804–81), *Mary Barton* (1848), by Elizabeth Gaskell (1810–65), and *Alton Locke* (1850), by Charles Kingsley (1819–75). To read them, as some people do, for 'straight' social history is a mistake, but they do have some interest as anticipating themes that are treated in profounder ways by later novelists such as George Eliot and D.H. Lawrence. Disraeli is credited with great insight for having pointed out in *Sybil* that England was two nations, the rich and the poor. Mrs Gaskell tried to combine a murder mystery with a concern about the cotton-spinners. (You have to be Zola to do this sort of thing effectively). Kingsley's novel is a social document about the sufferings of exploited apprentices in tailors' workshops. All three novelists meant well and tried to keep up to date, but from the literary point of view these novels rank with soap operas. They all wrote better elsewhere. Disraeli is very witty in *Coningsby* (1844), with his political experts Tadpole and Taper ('I am all for a religious cry,' said Taper. 'It means nothing, and will not interfere with buisness when we are in.'). Mrs Gaskell gave us what is usually, and aptly, termed 'a minor classic' with *Cranford* (1853), and in her best novel, *Wives and Daughters* (1865–6), she wrote one of the finest of the more realistic books that were coming into favour at that time, about people in a small town managing to survive and endure and make the best of ordinary life. As for Kingsley, proponent of muscular Christianity, Protestant romancer, vigorous hunting clergyman who hailed the 'wild North-Easter' as the 'wind of God', he is at his best in the astonishing fantasia *The Water Babies* (1863). Commonly classified as 'children's literature', it uses the story of Tom the little chimney sweep (one is reminded of Blake) as an occasion for virtuoso performances in several of the major modes of literature: the didactic allegory of Langland and Bunyan, the satirical extravaganza of Swift and Rabelais (see the passage about the 'backstairs'), the high symbolic vision-poetry of the Spenser of the Garden of Adonis; all this in a re-creation, in an Early Victorian setting, of the theme of Christian baptism.

Meanwhile the spirit of the Romantic movement in poetry had at last made itself felt, in full power, in novels written by women. Charlotte Brontë (1816–55) startled the whole literary world with *Jane Eyre* (1847). It is a rewrite of Richardson's *Pamela*, but by an author who had been influenced by Scott and the Gothic novelists and by Byron (the main influence on all the verse written by the Brontë sisters). Everyone knows the story of the brilliant, tragic sisters in the remote Yorkshire parsonage. Even to-day *Jane Eyre* retains its hold on readers. The heroine has two aspects. She longs for passion and its consummation; but she, is also drawn to a life of hardship and self-denial and spiritual struggle. At the beginning we sense an intuitive symbolism in the description of Jane behind red curtains, reading about the Arctic. These are extremes that are later to be expressed in personal terms by her two suitors, Mr Rochester and the clergyman St John Rivers. The late 1840s were a revolutionary period in Europe, and Charlotte's passionate questioning of what is expected of, and what is possible for, a woman, disturbed even her more liberal-minded contemporaries. *Villette* (1853), her name for Brussels, where she had been a student, reintroduces her as 'Lucy Snowe' (originally called 'Lucy Frost' – Charlotte Brontë's names usually have symbolic significance) another study in that dialectic of puritanism and romanticism for which her books are remarkable. She wrote other novels, but *Jane Eyre* and *Villette* are the best. *Jane Eyre* is more gripping, because of its strong plot; *Villette* is perhaps subtler.

Charlotte's sister Emily (1818–48) with her one novel, *Wuthering Heights* (1847), was even more shocking to her contemporaries. Her Yorkshire background may account for the complete absence of prudishness and genteelism from her novel. Otherwise the book is problematic. The critics agree that it is one of the most powerful works of fiction in English, but they cannot agree on what it says. It can be read as a story of social conflict, with the mysterious Heathcliff, of unexplained origin, breaking up the ordered existence of the farming Earnshaws and the Lintons, who are country gentry. But there is much dispute as to what attitude the reader is expected to take towards him and towards the strange events of the story, the overwhelming but oddly non-physical passions, the brutality, the fierce acquisitiveness. Socialists have seen Heathcliff as the revolutionary whose cruelty and tyranny can be partly justified as revenge on his oppressors. At present the usual reading of the novel is ultra-romantic, its message being that intense love justifies everything. *Wuthering Heights* is one of the most popular English novels. It has been adapted for the stage, and for film and television, Heathcliff and Cathy figure in a pop song. But it is doubtful whether Emily Brontë meant the story to be read in quite this way. The book is too complex for so simple a reading. What makes *Wuthering Heights* unusual is that, while some critics argue that Emily Brontë does have a moral attitude towards her characters, all agree that this is not explicit, as it tends to be in most Victorian novels.

Few critics (except George Moore) have put Anne Brontë (1820–49) top of the Brontë novelists, but *Agnes Grey* (1847) and *The Tenant of Wildfell Hall* (1848) have not been forgotten. Charlotte in her 'Biographical Notice' (1850) suggested that the character of the drunkard Huntingdon in the latter novel was based on their brother Branwell, and discussion of the *Tenant* has often been drawn into the Brontëan biographical orbit.

In the middle years of the century the major novelists are now often thought to be Anthony Trollope (1815–82) and George Eliot (pen name of Mary Ann Evans) (1819–80). Trollope's 'Barchester' novels deal with County people, the country gentry, the higher clergy, the respectable poor. 'Barchester', a Cathedral city, is at the centre, with frequent excursions into surrounding villages. Trollope's character-drawing is at its best in autocratic Mrs Proudie, the Bishop's wife, and the tragi-comic figure of the wrongly accused clergyman Mr Crawley. *The Last Chronicle of Barset* (1867), in which they both figure prominently, is perhaps Trollope's masterpiece. Trollope's dialogue is (to use a phrase of Johnson's) 'level with life'. He is preeminently the novelist for those who like long and leisurely exploration of people's dilemmas, and motives, and errors of judgment, against a background of still recognizable English country life. In his later novels Trollope entered the world of politics and high society, and sometimes chose challengingly 'unpleasant' and disturbing themes, such as pathological jealousy in *He Knew He Was Right* (1869), and moral sordidness and greed and financial fraud in *The Way We Live Now* (1874–5). To judge from the London newspapers this is still to a large extent 'the way we live now'.

George Eliot was unusual among novelists in being an intellectual, grounded in the study of philosophical and ethical problems, and contemporary scientific thought, before she came to the writing of fiction. Mrs Gaskell brings a clergyman's 'doubt' into a story as a plot-motif, but she does not tell us what his doubts were. In George Eliot we would have been told. She had first become known as the translator (1846) of the *Life of Jesus* by D.F. Strauss, a German pastor who had won great notoriety as the chief popularizing, self-publicizing, unbelieving preacher of his day. (Nietzsche was later to write scathingly about him.) Mary Ann Evans took his work very seriously, and toiled to translate it, gazing up for relief at a statue of the Risen Christ. She also (1854) translated a much greater work, Feuerbach's *Essence of*

Christianity, which Karl Marx admired. George Eliot thus brought a knowledge of the advanced contemporary thought of her day to her novels. But she was in many ways a moralist in the evangelical tradition. Even if she no longer believed in heaven and hell, she believed in Victorian ideals of duty and self-denial and honesty. What all these moral commands were supposed to be based on was not clear, as Nietzsche pointed out in his excessively severe remarks about George Eliot (whom he saw as a type of English hypocrisy). For her, God, Immortality, and Duty were the important things; but it was difficult to see why the kind of reasoning which compelled her to dismiss the first two should not have disposed of the third also. However, George Eliot's position was at least emotionally satisfactory to her large and devoted public, which will have included many people like the Dodson family in *The Mill on the Floss* (1860). George Eliot sympathized with them, though she saw that their culture and morality were narrow. Her best novel is agreed to be ' *Middlemarch* (1871–2). Virginia Woolf's description of it as 'one of the few English novels for grown-up people', though irritating, has some truth in it. *Middlemarch* does deal in a mature way with the credible problems of people in marriage, in their careers, in their attempts to realize their ideals, in their moral muddles and failures. But it is impossible not to have sympathy with young students in the twentieth century who have to struggle through it. The reassurance that 'one day' they will see how good it is, though soundly based, is not sufficient. George Eliot's reputation for heaviness is not altogether unwarranted. It cannot be irrelevant to use her novels as documents of social and intellectual history, since this is what, in part, they are intended to be. When Herbert Spencer founded the London Library he excluded fiction, but made an exception for George Eliot's novels. All this obscures the fact that, besides being a sociologist and a moral teacher, George Eliot was also an excellent Victorian novelist, i.e. a popular entertainer, and in her best work a great artist.

The right way to read George Eliot is to forget about the light her novels throw on Victorian problems, and read them as we read other stories: to find out what happened to the heroine. *Middlemarch* is set in the years before the Reform Bill (1832), but its 'feel' is mid-Victorian. The two most fully drawn people in 'Middlemarch' (George Eliot's name for an imaginary town in the Midlands) are Dorothea Brooke and Tertius Lydgate. Dorothea vaguely yearns to become a great saint, a modern Teresa of Avila, and her story turns on her marriage with Mr Casaubon. She at first sees him as another Milton or Locke, whom it will be her mission to serve adoringly, only to discover that he is a futile pedant and a petty tyrant – and also pathetic, for to the reader he is deeply appealing. Lydgate is a doctor who wants to bring the most advanced knowledge and the highest ethical and professional standards to Middlemarch, but is obstructed by local stagnation and irrationality, and his life's ambition is finally wrecked by his marriage to Rosamond Vincy, beautiful embodiment of all the proprieties, who cares only about social success. These and many other convincing characters are shown in their interconnected lives with the skill of a great artist. There is plenty of humour, and the sharp observation of manners that novel-readers like. And in one at least of the subplots (Raffles and Bulstrode) George Eliot shows herself capable of writing a tense thriller: no one has any difficulty about turning pages in this part of the book! But even the reader who reads only for plot and character will soon become aware that he is not reading Trollope. The states of mind and soul into which we must enter if we are to grasp what the book is saying are expressed largely through imagery, i.e. metaphor and extended figurative description. Here George Eliot leads straight on to Henry James and *The Portrait of a Lady*, and to Marcel Proust, who both greatly admired her.

Artistically and morally George Eliot is a transitional figure, between the old novel of personal responsibility and the new, psychological novel where we aren't so sure about that. From the point of view of modern liberationism her position is equivocal. She sees clearly how Dorothea's misfortunes are in part due to the restrictions placed on women in this culture, but the same compassion does not appear to be extended to Rosamond. Many male readers have suspected that (as with Hetty Sorrel in *Adam Bede*) George Eliot here shows her prejudice against a pretty woman – she herself was not one. But pretty Gwendolen Harleth in *Daniel Deronda* – in some ways not unlike Rosamond in character – while being made the object of unflinching moral analysis and condemnation, is allowed to attain tragic status through her appalling punishment.

Daniel Deronda (1876) is in some ways George Eliot's most original and exploratory work, reaching beyond *Middlemarch* in psychological depth and literary experimentation. It is unfortunately marred by the 'Zionist' plot centred on the hero, Deronda. This is much studied by critics to-day, but it is surely far inferior to the 'Gwendolen' plot, with its witty dialogue and credible characterization. George Eliot's great failing as a novelist is the inert material which her novels contain; the historical novel *Romola* (1862–3) consists of almost nothing else, while *Felix Holt* (1866) half-buries a powerful story in conscientious 'period' documentation. Still, she has survived these and other criticisms, and the swing of opinion against her from the 1880's to the 1950s. When all due reservations have been made she remains a great novelist.

Much else in Victorian fiction is current to-day, and not only among students and scholars. One day it may well be seen as a great symphony of motifs and ideas exchanged between this, that and the other writer like the Elizabethan drama. If only one writer, agreed not to be quite of the first rank, is to be mentioned it should be Wilkie Collins (1824–8), author of *The Woman in White* (1860) and *The Moonstone* (1868), the two best of his many novels, in which his unsurpassed mastery of intricate plot makes 'sensationalism' into literary art.

Collins's moral point of view was nearer to present-day ideas than to those of the mainstream Victorians. He was bohemian by temperament, and his domestic life was irregular by Victorian standards. Dickens, who was closely associated with him as a writer, thought he overdid his attacks on the respectable (Dickens's own critique was conducted more cautiously and obliquely).

We have now reached the later part of Victoria's reign, when there was a new turbulence in the spiritual atmosphere. In this time of unrest the confident voices of the earlier years became muted. An age of criticism began, often harsh. Carlyle had become too extreme to be taken very seriously, but Matthew Arnold, the 'elegant Jeremiah', as he was called, made some effective mischief with his urbane gibes, as in *Culture and Anarchy* (1869). The most challenging critic was John Ruskin (1819–1900). Ruskin had won his fame as a writer on visual and plastic art. In some ways he was for the Victorian public what Lord Clark (1903–83) has been for our contemporaries. But Ruskin was the master of a variety of rhetorical styles and an ability for word-painting which no twentieth century art critic has ever approached. The colourful soarings of Ruskin had a practical justification. Where Clark could point to works of art on television, where to-day's expert or journalist can refer to excellent reproductions of them on his own pages, Ruskin had to create a verbal equivalent for the visual experience he wanted his readers to share. The consequence for English literature was valuable. But Ruskin, who was a great man – rather like Tolstoy, another rich man with an agonized social conscience – could not be content to bask in the merited admiration he received as a prose-poet. With bitter, down-to-earth language he assailed the orthodox political economy in the essays collected as *Unto this Last* (1862). They aroused so much indignation when they first appeared in the *Cornhill* magazine that Thackeray, the editor, put a stop to them.

Ruskin's greatness as a writer is of a kind which it is difficult to define. He produced an enormous mass of work, but no single literary masterpiece. If he has to be represented by a single book this probably should be his charming, fragmentary autobiography, written at the end of his active life, *Praeterita* (1885–89) – the title means 'past things'. Students who need to strengthen their sense of the movement of nineteenth-century cultural history would do well to read it along with the *Autobiography* (1873) of John Stuart Mill (1806–73), Newman's history of his religious opinions, *Apologia pro Vita Sua* (1864), and for an epilogue, the autobiography of Beatrice Webb (1858–1943), especially the first volume, *My Apprenticeship* (1926). There is no better way to learn to appreciate the achievement of the great men and women of the Victorian age.

After George Eliot's death in 1880 the leading novelists were George Meredith and Thomas Hardy. Meredith's immense prestige among the intellectuals of the time is a reminder that the highbrow/lowbrow divide had by now become very marked, for while Dickens, Thackeray and George Eliot had all reached a wide public Meredith did not. To-day his bizarre opera-like novels have few readers, partly because of the mannerisms of his style, which resembles Carlyle's, but mainly because he could not tell a story. Yet *The Egoist* (1879) is still well worth reading, especially by anyone comtemplating marriage. Meredith was supposed to stand for optimism, cheerfully accepting the battle of life; Hardy was the opposite, gloomy and pessimistic. To-day Hardy's works, besides being accepted as among the major classics of English literature, continue to be widely popular, especially among younger readers. This is perhaps surprising. Hardy's technique was old-fashioned even in his time, and his English, except when his characters are using dialect, is very stilted. His novels are full of melodramatic scenes which recall the Victorian popular theatre. The dialogue he assigns to educated speakers is impossible. And his philosophy, combining the pessimism of the German thinker Schopenhauer with a mournful 'Social Darwinism', has no followers to-day; it belongs to the museum. Finally, Hardy's novels, especially those from *The Return of the Native* (1878) onwards, now and again indulge a taste for what most people would consider morbidity, and contain lurid episodes, most notoriously in *Jude the Obscure* (1895), e.g. the hanging of the children. The blend of horror-novel with bitter criticism of society is found elsewhere in this period, notably in the memorable Scottish novel *The House with the Green Shutters* (1901) of 'George Douglas' (1869–1902). But Hardy had a special liking for the mixture. His novels, then, have apparently a great many defects. Yet not only does he surmount them in his best work, he actually seems able to turn them into the expression of what can only be called greatness. The famous chapter on 'Egdon Heath' in *The Return of the Native* epitomises the critical problem about Hardy: clumsily written, full of laborious literary allusions, naively obvious in intention, it none the less reaches a plane of thought and feeling far beyond the art of any other novelist: the Heath becomes a symbol of the Universe.

Hardy's greatness had nothing to do with the advanced thought current in his time; it rested upon his view of men and women, from a great height, as products of History and of Nature. Certainly his books were affected by the controversies of the day, and Hardy put himself firmly on the radical side in his attacks on the educational system and the marriage laws. Deep down, however, he had no belief in the efficacy of social reforms to work any fundamental change in the 'blighted star' he thought humanity had to live on, and his masterpieces, *The Mayor of Casterbridge* (1886), *Tess of the D'Urbervilles* (1891), and *Jude the Obscure* (1895) are all hard-luck stories. In the end the overruling emotion in Hardy was pity. He was not primarily a moralist. His tragedies are not rooted in the sins of individuals.

On its more 'period' side Hardy's fiction reflected the tendency that now came to the fore among the intelligentsia: what may be called anti-

Victorianism, the rejection of religious, moral and social attitudes that had been conventionally accepted down to the 1870s. William Winwood Reade (1838–75) in his remarkable *Martyrdom of Man* (1872) gave colourful expression, in a highly readable demotic English, to a historical world-view which frankly rejected Christianity. Samuel Butler (1835–1902) was at the same time teasing Victorian orthodoxies in his *Erewhon* (1872): the title, 'nowhere' backwards (more or less), indicates the genre as that of the Utopia. The 'Musical Banks', a satire on the Victorian Church of England, is one of the few allegories that really work well, because it is short, amusing, and easy to grasp. The personal animus behind Butler's anti-Victorianism – his hatred of his own clergyman father – emerges clearly in his posthumous novel *The Way of All Flesh*, not published till 1903, though it dates from a much earlier time. Butler's point of view – that of the 'High Ydgrunites' in *Erewhon* – anticipates that of Shaw, of Maugham, of E.M. Forster. Another study in generation-revolt, but less savage than the *Way of all Flesh*, mingling sorrow with its satire, is *Father and Son* (1907) by Edmund Gosse (1849–1928). Religious autobiography, in various degrees of fictitiousness, becomes a leading late-Victorian genre. *The Autobiography of Mark Rutherford* (1881) – pen name of William Hale White (1831–1913) – is one of the best known. The nature-mystic Richard Jefferies (1848–87) wrote one in his *Story of my Heart* (1883), once much discussed, but to-day perhaps less read than his boys' story *Bevis* (1882) and his essays and sketches concerned with English country life. The scholar-aesthete Walter Pater (1839–94), successor to Ruskin both in the elaborations of his style and the subtle discrimination of his impressions of visual art, created a new kind of historical novel with *Marius the Epicurean* (1885), alluding obliquely, through the inward narrative of a cultivated young Roman pagan's gradual drift towards Christianity, to his own spiritual progress. A more mannered and exhibitionistic document is the confessional *De Profundis* (first published posthumously in 1905) of Pater's disciple Oscar Wilde (1854–1900). The fuller version of this work, which was originally a long accusatory letter written to Lord Alfred Douglas from prison, can be read in Rupert Hart-Davis's edition of Wilde's letters. In the 'private' part of this letter Wilde abandons his mannerisms and writes with great force, and with some degree of insight, about his relations with Douglas.

The aesthetic religiosity of the Nineties makes a belated, eccentric reappearance in the novel *Hadrian the Seventh* (1904) by Frederick William Rolfe (1860–1913), self-titled 'Baron Corvo', the paranoid homosexual psychopath who was the subject of an enthralling biographical inquiry pursued by Alphonse James Symons (1901–41) in *The Quest for Corvo* (1934). A link between the mockery of the 1920s and the preciosity of the 1890s can be seen in the work of another very strange writer, Ronald Firbank (1886–1926), for example in *Concerning the Eccentricities of Cardinal Pirelli*

(1926). Rolfe's hypnotic grip on the reader does not preclude the uneasy suspicion that he is insane, whereas Firbank's 'camp' manner and his nonchalant aloofness suggest a completely conscious and self-possessed artist – even if one working only in miniature.

Anti-Victorianism in the drama impinged on the theatre-going public, with the usual journalistic chorus of alleged moral outrage, as the work of Henrik Ibsen became known. Ibsen was bracketed with Zola as vicious and filthy because he referred to unpleasant subjects like venereal disease in *Ghosts* (1881). The Scotsman William Archer (1856–1924) was the translator and chief apologist for Ibsen. Archer's own plays are of no great consequence. The Ibsen influence appears in a watered-down form in the plays of Arthur Wing Pinero (1855–1934), who was able to persuade West End audiences that his plays were grappling with serious problems (the woman with a past, etc.). They are in truth only contributions to the history of theatre fashion and convention. The plays of Wilde for the most part bear only that kind of relation to serious drama, but his wit is there, often expressed through the *persona* of the Clever Bad Man, and a plea for greater moral tolerance, ostensibly on behalf of 'fallen women', but more probably (in coded form) on behalf of his fellow homosexuals. Wilde's personality is still vivid and attractive to-day, though the intrinsic value of his writings, and their relative merits, remain matters of dispute. His critical dialogues and essays, and some of his short fiction, especially the stories written for children like 'The Happy Prince' (1888), seem to have lasted better than most of his work outside the drama. *The Picture of Dorian Gray* (1891), a blend of allegorical fable with Gothic novel, has scenes which cry out for performance on the stage. Wilde was essentially and explicitly a fantasist, whose talents were not for the realistic novel. The most popular of his plays is *The Importance of Being Earnest* (1899), an excursion into a self-sufficent world of witty nonsense, like a sort of adult *Alice in Wonderland*.

Before the days of Wilde the Victorian drama had been rather mediocre. The liveliest things in it were the comic operas of William Schwenk Gilbert (1836–1911), set to music by Arthur Sullivan. The phrase 'Gilbert and Sullivan' at once suggests the indescribable mixture of farce, extravaganza and satire, and the use of absurd situations as dramatic postulates, which added the word 'Gilbertian' to the language. The business about the name 'Ernest' in Wilde's *Importance*, or the reason for the enrichment of the dustman Higgins in Shaw's *Pygmalion*, are examples outside Gilbert of Gilbertian motifs. In later twentieth-century comedy they seem to have died out.

The Scottish playwright James Matthew Barrie (1860–1937) employed a different comic method, more connected with real life, in his well-crafted plays that entertained audiences up to the time of the first world war and for some years afterwards. His best known play *Peter Pan* (1904), a fantasia on the tragic theme of the boy who refuses to grow up, has usually been regarded as entertainment for children, but it was given its full adult dimension in a production in 1982 by the Royal Shakespeare Company. The realistic depiction of the British Establishment by Harley Granville-Barker (1877–1946), as in *Waste* (1909), about a scandal involving a politician, has also been revived with success. Plays of John Galsworthy (1867–1933), such as *The Skin Game* (1920), have not become too dated to lose their edge.

The chief dramatist of this period was the long-lived George Bernard Shaw (1856–1950). Shaw did not expect his plays to be remembered, since they were full of topicalities which he knew would become very dated; he intended them as part of his campaign for socialism. But the musical qualities of the plays, the lovely speakability of the dialogue, together with the heightened operatic quality that appears in so many of them, has kept them alive on the stage, and even those who find Shaw's characterization bloodless and the plays lacking in emotional depth can relish the qualities they share with his delightful *Prefaces*: the combination of the forceful with the nimble and elegant. Controversy to-day turns on Shaw's capacity or otherwise to handle serious and tragic material. Was he enough of a poet for this? The debate goes on. The test for Shaw's possible greatness outside comedy must be *St Joan* (1924), in which he rescued the saint from the Shakespearean travesty in *Henry VI* and re-stated in deliberately anachronistic terms what he considered to be the true significance of Joan of Arc's career and her martyrdom.

Shaw had begun as a novelist, but like Wilde his gifts were essentially more suited to the theatre. The tradition of the Victorian novel meanwhile continued, but the livelier spirits were becoming bored with it and were attending to new possibilities, for a novel freed from Victorian moral and artistic conventions, which had been opened up by the great French novelists and later by the Russians. The Irish novelist George Moore (1852–1933) earned notoriety by his battle against the circulating libraries to win authors the right to talk about whatever they wanted to talk about, and in the way seemed appropriate to them. His own *Esther Waters* (1894) was an interesting attempt to introduce the French kind of realistic novel into English, abstaining from melodrama and moralizing in this straightforwardly told story of a servant girl. No fault can be found with Moore's novel, but it seems lifeless beside (say) Hardy's *Tess*, which is full of melodrama and moralizing and improbabilities, but sweeps the reader along by the force of its passion and poetry. George Gissing (1857–1903), author of an excellent study of Dickens, also sought to incorporate the effects of French and Russian realism into the English kind of novel. His most remembered novel, *New Grub Street* (1891), casting a harsh light over the commercializing and corruption of London literary life, has perhaps more interest as a documentary than as a living work of art. Of the new school of novelists, consciously post-Flaubert and post-Turgenev, the one who has lasted best is the American Henry James (1843–1916), who interwove the tradition of 'New England' – the tradition

adorned by Nathaniel Hawthorne, of whom James wrote a penetrating study –
with the English tradition coming down from George Eliot. James's favourite
subject was the 'international theme', the comedy of the relationships between
the visiting wealthy Americans from the 'Gilded Age' that followed the Civil
War (1861–5) and the ladies and gentlemen (sometimes very sinister) of old
Europe. *The Portrait of a Lady* (1881), one of James's most brilliant novels, is
his masterpiece on this subject. James settled in England, but only became a
British subject at the end of his life, as a gesture towards the British cause in
the 1914–18 war, which he vehemently supported. The war destroyed the
special Jamesian world he had created partly out of shrewd observation and
partly from his own singular fantasies. But already, as in *The Golden Bowl*
(1905), it had become very esoteric, 'gold to airy thinness beat', and James's
own public had become a very small and specialized one. James's work must
really be considered as part of the American heritage. But his contribution to
English literature cannot be ignored. He was perhaps the greatest critic of the
novel, the first to take it with the same seriousness as had traditionally been
awarded to tragedy or epic.

Only occasionally, as with his tale 'Daisy Miller' (1879), did James achieve
wide popularity; and throughout his career he chafed much at the immensely
greater commercial success which was being won by writers he considered his
artistic inferiors. Readers without James's special bent may be prepared to
grant more readily than he would that the period was one of excellent popular
writers. Rudyard Kipling as a very young man had soared to instant celebrity
with his early stories about India in *Plain Tales from the Hills* (1888). His
more lasting claim to fame lies in his long story *Kim* (1901), which might be
called the *Huckleberry Finn* of Anglo-India. The political controversies stirred
up by his resolute support of Imperialism, especially during the South African
War (1899–1902), resulted in many baseless legends about Kipling and his
work and his views and attitudes, which have not yet died away. But nowadays
his mastery of the short story, in the volumes from *Plain Tales* to *A Diversity
of Creatures* (1917), is widely recognized.

The Jungle Books (1894–5) and *Just So Stories* (1902) are among the
enduring and uncontroversial works of Kipling. *The Jungle Books* have
acquired something of the immemorial anonymity of folktales. Kipling is one
of the greatest English writers for children, and his example inspired the
many books in which Edith Nesbit (1858–1924) established the genre of
intelligent, uncondescending writing for and about young people which
flourishes to-day. The (literally) tiny books of Beatrix Potter (1866–1943),
with their incisive prose and exquisite draughtsmanship, must also be
mentioned. *The Wind in the Willows* (1908) of Kenneth Grahame (1859–
1932) introduces the youthful reader to the Falstaff kind of character in the
beast-fable guise of Mr Toad. The 'Pooh' books (1926, 1928) of Alexander
Milne (1882–1956), more than any of the others mentioned, are perhaps

those which children and their parents most love to read together.

To this outpouring of 'genre fiction' — fiction which is not committed to the realism, and the claim to omnicompetence, of the mainstream novel — the work of Robert Louis Stevenson (1850–94) contributed greatly, with *Treasure Island* (1882), the best of all stories about pirates, *Dr Jekyll and Mr Hyde* (1886), a moral fable which added a notion to the language, and other stories which still appeal to readers with anything boyish in them, whatever their actual gender and chronology may be. Stevenson was also one of the best of all poets of childhood in the *Child's Garden of Verses* (1885) — the poems being not so much for children as *about* them. Another great entertainer whose work has lasted was Arthur Conan Doyle (1859–1930), creator of Sherlock Holmes, symbol of the great detective, the personification of reason and justice. (Later, alas, he was to yield in world fame to James Bond, the secret policeman.) Doyle also introduced a welcome element of humour into science-fiction with Professor Challenger, an intentionally comic portrait of the Great Scientist. Even more hilarious romance is provided in the exploits of Brigadier Gerard, the stupidest man in Napoleon's army. Henry Rider Haggard (1856–1925) won great fame for *King's Solomon's Mines* (1885) and *She* (1887). Haggard's mythopoeic imagination was more powerful than his gift for literary style, so that while these romances continue to fascinate readers (and unfortunately are mishandled by film-makers) critical controversy can still be easily roused over the question whether they are literature at all. Hence the usefulness of the term 'genre fiction'.

The popular fiction of the 1880s and 90s survives vigorously in individual books, which those who dislike them are apt to describe as 'facetious'. *Three Men in a Boat* (1889) and *The Diary of a Nobody* (1894) are much more famous than their authors — Jerome K. Jerome (1859–1927), and George Grossmith (1847–1912) and his brother Weedon (1852–1919), Ernest William Hornung (1866–1921), Doyle's brother-in-law, is remembered for *Raffles* (1899), gentleman burglar, whose partnership with his friend Bunny provides a criminal (and faintly homosexual) counterpart to the Holmes/Watson relationship which inspired it.

The greatest master of popular fiction to arrive in the Nineties was Herbert George Wells (1866–1946). Wells made his name with his long-short story 'The Time Machine' (1895), and it soon became plain that he was a new kind of writer. The old, classically-based, dignified conception of writerhood, still nostalgically held by Wells's friend Gissing, must now yield to a more modern and democratic one, responsive to the new advances in science and technology. For many years Wells was one of the best known writers of the world. He has been called the Shakespeare of science fiction, but much of his success in Britain was due to the exuberant comedy and cheekiness which he brought into the traditional forms of fiction. But Wells was too restless to confine himself to developing and improving his art as a novelist. He became more and more a prophet, impatiently striving to set the world to rights. His neglect of art for 'message' in his later works brought on the decline of his reputation. Even to-day his genius is largely under-valued.

The Edwardian novel was centred on Wells, Bennett, and Galsworthy, who can be seen readily as corresponding to the Victorian trio of Dickens, Trollope, and Thackeray. Arnold Bennett (1866–1931) in *The Old Wives' Tale* (1908) wrote the acknowledged masterpiece about the people of the Potteries district of Staffordshire. Galsworthy's *The Man of Property* (1906), which owes something to Tolstoy's *Anna Karenina*, gave the world a still surviving image of the English high bourgeoisie of that epoch. To-day the Edwardian novelist most highly rated by academic critics is, however, Joseph Conrad (1857–1924). His reputation in the years after his death was largely due to the advocacy of T.S. Eliot, who quoted 'Mistah Kurtz. He dead' from Conrad's story 'Heart of Darkness', and critics have often seen in this story a sounding of the dark depths of modern nihilism. The story is highly prized to-day all over the world for its insights into the spiritual and moral and material consequences of colonial exploitation. In this mysterious work Conrad introduced into English a new kind of symbolic narrative – without, perhaps, full awareness of what he had done. His achievement was to have many would-be emulators. Some of Conrad's other short narratives, such as *Typhoon* (1903) and the later *The Shadow Line* (1917) deal less ambiguously with the responsibilities that can be placed on a ship's captain (Conrad, a Pole, had served in his early years in the British Merchant Marine). These *nouvelles* make more lively reading than Conrad's longer novels, which, though undoubtedly distinguished, are rather slow in movement. It is difficult to imagine a reader of Conrad eagerly turning his pages to find out what is going to happen next. But Conrad's novels are high in academic favour. They invite, and repay, ample explanation and commentary. Their manner is rather strange: typically they are adventure tales, but presented in a clotted style with much flamboyant description of nature and ponderous introspection: it is as if Thomas Mann had written *The Thirty-nine Steps*. The novels of Conrad most praised by critics begin with *Lord Jim* (1900), often a set book for students; it might have been too confusing to be popular, yet readers have found phrases from it linger in the mind long afterwards. *Nostromo* (1904) has a strong central incident (the stealing of the silver) which is presented with great dramatic force, but the South American setting and characters are not very memorable. In curious contrast is *The Secret Agent* (1907). Here the fictional scaffolding is excellent, but it supports nothing: the act of terrorism, which is the main incident, is not presented. *Under Western Eyes* (1911) suffers a little through being a treatment, from the inside, of a tormented young Russian: Conrad does it well, but we naturally go for this sort of thing to Russian novelists, especially Dostoevsky, and *Under Western Eyes* seems to draw a good deal, for its emotional effects, on *Crime and Punishment*.

Conrad's occasional collaborator Ford Madox Ford, originally F.M. Hueffer (1878–1939), wrote many novels, of which the best are *The Good Soldier* (1915), famous in literary history for its use of 'the unreliable narrator', and the four 'war novels' about 'Tietjens' (1924–28). (*The Good Soldier*, despite its title, has nothing to do with the war.) Ford was a gifted writer and his novels have a faithful following; but they seem extraordinarily unconvincing, which his memoirs, though alleged to be at least as fictional as his novels, are not.

More in the public eye were writers like Hilaire Belloc (1870–1953), Catholic publicist and frequent antagonist of other pundits such as Shaw and (especially) Wells; he is most remembered now for his admirable comic verse. Gilbert Keith Chesterton (1874–1936), his peer as a controversialist, was the kind of all-round man of letters who defies classification. He is most read to-day for his 'Father Brown' stories of the priest detective, which show that the 'Sherlock Holmes' genre can be a means to the expression of great wit and wisdom and of a haunting poetry which puts them in a class apart from all other detective fiction. A few of Chesterton's poems (such as 'Lepanto') still delight readers who do not flinch from bold colours and emphatic rhythm. But Chesterton left no single masterpiece, and his best things have to be looked for amid a great mass of fiction, essays and miscellaneous journalism. *The Man who was Thursday* (1908) is sometimes said to be his best novel, and it is certainly an original work, a 'nightmare' as he himself called it, obscure and terrifying. But in the late chapters farce like the 'Ealing Comedies' films of the 1940s and 1950s co-exists uneasily with a sense of doom and apocalypse. Among fictional forms it was the short story that suited Chesterton best, and the 'Father Brown' stories taken together should be allowed to compensate for his missing masterpiece.

Much more selective, and modest in output, was the caricaturist and essayist Max Beerbohm (1872–1956), who admired Belloc and Chesterton, but never tried to emulate their popular appeal. The parodies in his *Christmas Garland* (1912) and the stories in *Seven Men* (1919) may outlive most of the productions of the 'big' Edwardian writers. Often in English literature the small works, the *bibelots*, have a habit of staying put when the rest of the literary furniture has been changed. Montague Rhodes James (1862–1936) of the *Ghost Stories of an Antiquary* (1904) produced work of timeless appeal in that very special genre. Meade Falkner (1858–1932) wrote the best tale of smuggling ever in *Moonfleet* (1898), and a fine romantic novel in *The Nebuly Coat* (1903). Other 'amateur' writers – Maurice Baring (1874–1945), of *Diminutive Dramas*, Ronald Knox (1888–1957), priest, translator of the Bible, and tireless apologist, with is masterpiece about an Oxford common room over the centuries, *Let Dons Delight* (1939) – belong to a category which again and again graces English literature, and which was especially distinguished in the years before 1914.

The many pleasant lighter works of the period contribute to the common notion of the Edwardian era as a golden afternoon. But the sense of a time of trouble, foreign and domestic, was already growing. Two of the best novels of the pre-1914 time, Beerbohm's Oxford fantasia *Zuleika Dobson* (1911) and *The Unbearable Bassington* (1912) by 'Saki' (Hector Hugh Munro, 1870–1916) seem prophetic in their symbolism; both, in their very different ways, turn on the sacrifice of the young for a thing of beauty whose value is in the end felt as equivocal. These writers, if unconsciously, had perhaps glimpsed what Housman had already revealed in poetry, what was to come for Europe and the world:

> Far and near and low and louder
> On the roads of earth go by,
> Dear to friends and food for powder,
> Soldiers marching, all to die.
> (from *A Shropshire Lad*, no. XXXV)

SEVEN

The twentieth century

The transition from the pre-War to the post-War writers is conveniently illustrated by the poetry of Rupert Brooke (1887–1915). Brooke's most considerable poem before 1914 was 'The Old Vicarage, Grantchester', written in 1912. He was essentially a philosophical poet, a poet of 'the intellectual imagination', endeavouring to evoke a substantial reality for the other-world of Plato. In 'Grantchester' English country life provides the symbolic population for the poet's idea of heaven.

> Stands the church clock at ten to three?
> And is there honey still for tea?

Brooke's feeling for English villages was influenced by A.E. Housman, but his peculiar compound of conscious sentimentality and irony is unmistakably his own. Another interesting feature of this poem is that love of England is heightened by hatred of Germany. Brooke welcomed the war with Germany in 1914. His most famous poem, the last of a short sonnet sequence, is 'The Soldier'. There is no more magnificent example of pure patriotic poetry in existence. After the first line the poet himself, the 'I', vanishes from the poem; if his body is a 'richer dust' in some 'foreign field' it is only because his body is part of the earth of England. Those who are not lovers of England can still enjoy the poem if they mentally substitute for the name of 'England' that of some other country which they prefer.

Brooke was not a 'war poet' in the sense in which this term came to be used. He was in the Navy and did not die in battle; the war poets were soldiers fighting on the Western Front, 'trench poets'. Most of the verse written by soldier poets at this time was patriotic, like Brooke's, but as the massacres in France and Flanders continued a new note came to be heard, above all in the poetry of Siegfried Sassoon (1886–1967) and his friend and disciple Wilfred

Owen (1893–1918). Sassoon's war poetry is rightly famous for its immediate sharpness of impact.

> 'He's a cheery old card', grunted Harry to Jack,
> As they slogged up Arras with rifle and pack . . .
> But he did for them both with his plan of attack.
>   ('The General')

Sassoon, recklessly brave, several times decorated, came to believe that the slaughter was being unnecessarily prolonged, and made the gesture of refusing to serve, but was persuaded by Robert Graves to obtain leave on medical grounds, and eventually to go back to the front. Sassoon's verse might seem in the nature of the case likely to be ephemeral. But in fact his biting phrases, denouncing the smug staff officers at the base, and the indecency of Home Front patriotism, still retain point and colour. His best poem of this period, 'Everyone Sang', is the best poem written on the armistice of 1918. In his later work Sassoon was more technically experimental. He became preoccupied with inward problems, partly the after-effects of the war, partly his own homosexuality, about which he had very mixed and problematic feelings, and partly the appeal of Roman Catholic liturgy (he had become a convert to Catholicism). In the Second World War he acclaimed Churchill and the Allied cause in a very different spirit from that of the fierce satirical outbursts which had made him famous.

Wilfred Owen had begun as a decorative poet in the line of Keats, but the effect of the war, and of Sassoon's work, showed itself in his remarkable trench-poems of 1917–18. Owen invented a technique of half-rhymes and harsh, grating dissonant sound-effects which became part of the repertoire of English poets from the 1930s onwards. Owen's poetry is less emotionally satisfying than Brooke's or Sassoon's. It seems to suffer from a divided aim. On the one hand Owen wanted passionately to bring home to his readers the awful suffering of the men at the front, and the need to replace the Christianity which his war experiences had caused him to reject by a new kind of religious humanism. 'The poetry is in the pity'. On the other hand he was absorbed in technical experiments, like Gerard Hopkins. The two motives do not seem to harmonize. But the most successful and beautiful of his poems, 'Anthem for Doomed Youth', is not open to these objections. And it must be added that Owen's war poetry, taken together, is in irreplaceable historic document. This was life in the twentieth century, this was war as modern man chose to conduct it. But the force of the poetry as a record of experience does not entail the validity of the pacifist and socialist ideas which for Owen and many of his readers of the next generation were bound up with it. It is understandable that Owen's view of the war and the suffering of soldiers was partial. In 'The Parable of the Old Men and the Young' he sees the old as callously sacrificing their sons. But weren't there many of the old who would gladly have made this sacrifice themselves? 'Would God I had died for thee, O Absalom, my son, my son!' Sometimes the anguish expressed in Owen's poetry is the anguish of the nerves and sensibilities, 'shell shock' rather than the laceration of the heart. He is poignant, rather than tragic. But his place as the chief of the war poets cannot be challenged.

Isaac Rosenberg (1890–1918), a London Jewish private soldier, is sometimes judged to have been a more promising poet than Owen, less limited to the immediate subject-matter of the war. Certainly his poems include powerful lines and passages. But too often his language is over-strained.

> The streaming vigours of his blood erupting
> From his halt tongue are like an anger thrust
> Out of a madman's piteous craving for
> A monstrous baulked perfection.
>> (from 'Moses', a play)

His poetry is very uneven, over-ambitious, uncertain in direction, fragmentary. Even his best poem, 'Dead Man's Dump', contains awkward inversions and unsuitable poeticisms, which detract from the stark force of the statements and descriptions evoking a world of horrors.

Edward Thomas (1878–1917) who like Owen and Rosenberg was killed in battle, has proved to be a poet of continuing appeal. Thomas began as a poet during the war years. He had been a prolific prose writer, and wrote only prose till encouraged to write verse by the example of his friend the American poet, Robert Frost (1875–1963). Little of his poetry touches upon the war. Most of it consists of sensitive self-exploration, using the English countryside, and symbolism drawn from nature, to define the elusive melancholy from which he suffered, and expressed in a rhythmically varied, unrhetorical verse-form. Among Thomas's poems, only 'Adlestrop' is widely known, but even by itself this short piece is enough to suggest the characteristic unemphatic tone of this poet.

> And for that minute a blackbird sang,
> Close by, and round him, mistier,
> Farther and farther, all the birds
> Of Oxfordshire and Gloucestershire.

Edmund Blunden (1896–1973) has much in common with Edward Thomas, but he survived the war. Like Thomas he leaves the impression of having been a very distinguished poet without ever quite managing to produce one poem in which he strikes with his whole force (except perhaps 'Report on Experience'). His prose book, *Undertones of War* (1928), has been more widely read than his verse. Robert Graves (1895–1985) is an even more paradoxical figure. For some readers he is a poet who was able to develop after his war poems (which are, in fact, not very good) into one of the leading writers in the modern school of poetry, learning through the influence of the American woman poet Laura Riding (b. 1901) to write in a cryptic, cerebral, oracular manner far remote from the simple pastoralism in which he began. Yet Graves's writings have left no imprint on the language, except for the title of his autobiography, *Good-bye to All That* (1929). It seems likely that he will be remembered for his autobiography rather than his poetry. This may also be the case with the Scottish poet Edwin Muir (1887–1959). But Muir did produce one short magical poem, 'Merlin', while Graves, for all his insistence on inspiration and the Muse and 'poetic unreason', has not done so.

Muir and Graves, unlike Blunden, were affected by the new fashions in verse that appeared in the 1920s and 30s under the influence of American and French 'modernism'. The chief figure in this school was Ezra Pound (1885–1972). The final judgment on Pound's achievement as a poet must rest with Americans, but there can be no doubt of his historical importance as the impresario of the new school on both sides of the Atlantic. He discovered Eliot and lent him support at a crucial time, and there seems no doubt that his excisions did much to extricate the really first-rate parts of *The Waste Land* from inferior matter. Pound also did much to get recognition for Joyce. And (though this is more doubtful) he may have done something by precept, if not by example, to bring about the changes in W.B. Yeats's poetic style. The value of Pound as a poet in his own right is a more controversial question. His recommendation of the 'Imagist' style of writing poetry has been influential on British and American poets. Countless poems have been written, and are still being written, in accordance with Pound's doctrine that poems should be word-pictures, in which the emotional or intellectual or imaginative content is not stated explicitly by the poet but inferred by the reader. And some of Pound's own most taking poems do meet this requirement.

> The apparition of these faces in the crowd:
> Petals on a wet, black bough.
> ('In a Station of the Metro')

The volume called *Cathay* (1915) employs this style to conjure up a make-believe 'China' which has proved very appealing to other poets and lovers of poetry. But to limit poetry to 'images', to the visualizable, seems arbitrary, and quite inadequate to the actual practice of the great poets from Homer onwards. It is not even adequate to Pound's own work. Pound is often hortatory, he wants to persuade and argue. The strongest part of the very problematic and obscure series of poems called 'Hugh Selwyn Mauberley' is the passage summing up the war (it begins 'There died a myriad,/ And of the best, among them') and its force derives from the open indignation and horror with which the poet passes judgment on the tragedy of 1914–18.

Most of Pound's poetic career was devoted to the writing of his long poem, or sequence, called the *Cantos*, and it is on the strength of this work that his admirers (chiefly, but not wholly, Americans) claim for him the rank of one of the supreme poets of the world, the American Dante. But surely the 'imagist' method works well only for short poems, flashes, glimpses, sketches. To extend it to poetry so panoramic and would-be symphonic is self-defeating. And the *Cantos*, like other poems of Pound, suffer from the pull of conflicting forces·which sometimes reduce them to incoherence; on one side Pound's (very American) tendency to cast an idealizing glamour over the past and the exotic, and on the other his obsession with being Modern ('Make It New'). The result is that even his best work, such as his translation of Sophocles's *Women of Trachis* (1954) seems neither ancient nor modern, but simply anomalous, like a Greek statue clothed in a garageman's overalls.

For those who think Pound a great poet the presence in the *Cantos* of obvious craziness and crankiness, brutally reductive and scatological depictions of human life, and outbursts of fascism and anti-semitism, must present a problem. They have to maintain either that these things are not there, or that the *Cantos* is a great work in spite of them. Either position is difficult. Controversy flared up when the Bollingen award was made to Pound in 1949 for his *Pisan Cantos* — one of the most esoteric of his writings — at a time when he was confined in a mental hospital in the United States, not so much because he was really insane (unless holding unorthodox economic views is insanity) but in order to defer his having to stand trial for wartime treason. (He had been the 'Lord Haw-Haw' of Fascist Italy.) The moral, aesthetic and political problems raised by all this are immensely complicated and painful, and perhaps the *Pisan Cantos* may be left here with the simple literary observation that by general agreement one of the best passages occurs when Pound briefly takes up the manner and movement of FitzGerald's quatrains in the *Rubáiyát*: which seems to cast doubt on his own insistence, over a half-century, on the necessity of rupturing the iambic pentameter.

A poet of an older generation, William Butler Yeats (1865–1939) was for a time closely associated with Pound, and acknowledged a debt to the hustling young man from Idaho for getting him out of the 'Celtic Twilight', the wavering rhythms and elusive misty landscapes of his earlier verse. It is possible that the 'obscurity' for which modern verse is notorious began with Yeats. Like Pound's, his work readily lends itself to elaborations of academic commentary, and has, especially in America, become the centre of an industry of 'explication' which must tend to put off non-academic readers. And the exclusively Irish character of Yeats's work makes it often feel remote from English readers, whether the references are ancient and legendary (with unpronounceable names like 'Caoilte') or modern and local ('It's with O'Leary in the grave'): But none of this should obscure the immediate and overwhelming impression of poetic genius which Yeats conveys in his best work. Again and again he finds, not just the 'right' word, but the word that strikes us at once as both surprising and inevitable.

> Was it for this the wild geese spread
> The grey wing upon every tide,
> For this that all that blood was shed,
> For this Edward FitzGerald died,
> And Robert Emmet and Wolfe Tone,
> All that delirium of the brave?
>   (from 'September 1913')

The appearance of that drab word 'delirium' is most effective here. But more typical of Yeats is sudden, breath-taking beauty, rare in modern poetry, but not rare in Yeats.

> O what if gardens where the peacock strays
> With delicate feet upon old terraces,
> Or else all Juno from an urn displays
> Before the indifferent garden deities . . .
> (from 'Meditations in Time of Civil
>   War')

> I would be ignorant as the dawn
> That merely stood, rocking the glittering coach
> Above the cloudy shoulders of the horses;
> I would be – for no knowledge is worth a straw –
> Ignorant and wanton as the dawn.
>   (from 'The Dawn')

If what you value in poetry is above all diction, then among modern poets Yeats has no rival. He is a lord of language, of Shakespearean splendour. And in the disjointed, chromatic world of modern verse he did what no English poet had done since Swinburne: he *sang*, though to a un-Victorian tune.

> 'O cruel Death, give three things back,'
> *Sang a bone upon the shore*;
> 'A child found all a child can lack,
> Whether of pleasure or of rest,
> Upon the abundance of my breast';
> *A bone wave-whitened and dried in the wind*.
>   (from 'Three Things')

Yeats was not only a great poet, but one who consciously acted the part of a great poet (a little uncomfortably for English taste). He has been described as 'a peacocking Irishman', a fellow countryman of Oscar Wilde, Bernard Shaw, and James Joyce, who were all apt to strike poses. But to use words like 'poseur' and 'pretentious' implies that Yeats's grand manner arouses expectations which it does not fulfil. For some of us it may be sufficient rebuttal of that allegation merely to remember or read over the title-poem of *The Wild Swans of Coole* volume, or 'A Dialogue between the Self and Soul.' However, some of Yeats's postures can be tiresome. His gift of utterance was truly regal, but in the modern world kings are not what they once were, and Yeats was all too conscious that the modern world, which he hated, was radically antithetical to poetry, magic, aristocracy, and the traditional Irish landscape. As a result, his tone of voice is too often defiant and consciously arrogant to make continuous reading of his verse enjoyable.

Perhaps Yeats's problem was that he did not have a great deal to *say*. When he made his song 'a coat/Covered with embroideries/Out of old mythologies', he found that his imitators were using it as an opportunity for empty affectation. But he himself was given to that. Apart from the 'embroidery' his early subject is mostly frustrated love, No poet of the world has written better on that subject. But his emotional problems with Maud Gonne cannot be of inexhaustible interest to most readers, and it is something of a relief when Yeats begins to bring wider human relationships into his poetry; the world of politics (as in 'Easter 1916', his searching poem on the Irish nationalist rising of 1916), the fight at the side of Lady Gregory to create an Irish national theatre, the antipathies and smugnesses of middle-class philistinism. As an escape from all this Yeats created his own country of the mind, an eighteenth-century Ireland of his own imagining. The preoccupation with occultism, which he and Maud Gonne and others in his circle had always had, became more and prominent, as another form of rejection and of escape from the uncongenial realities of twentieth-century urban industrialism, rationalist philosophy, commerce and bureaucracy. That strange book *A Vision* (1917) is based on the communications which he believed he had received from 'unknown instructors' speaking through his wife in her mediumistic trances. How much astrology and spiritualism Yeats actually did accept in cold prose it is difficult to say. Cold prose was not Yeats's *métier*. He is a poet-mage. His spells still work for many readers.

The period of Yeats's poetry most admired to-day is the mellow penultimate phase of such poems as 'Sailing to Byzantium' and 'Among School Children'. They are beautiful poems, which invite and repay close study. The last phase of his poetry, when he is the 'wild old wicked man', obsessed with 'lust and rage', is for obvious reasons less popular academically. But it is a reminder that Yeats's poetry came out of the heart and soul of a real human being, irascible, self-questioning and suffering. The great virtue of Louis MacNeice's book on Yeats (1940) is that he sees Yeats as a poet like himself, though greater, with all the problems of a man who is doomed to be a poet in these times. The scholarly studies of Yeats which began in the 1950s tend to lose this sense of a real person. 'Yeats' becomes merely a grammatical fiction, a convenient label for a series of masks. But Yeats prayed to be remembered as 'a foolish, passionate man'.

Yeats's earlier poetry, though distinctive in its genius and its Irish colouring, did not present a radical challenge to late Romantic taste. Though even before 1914 he was clearly a more powerful poet than Walter de la Mare or Robert Bridges, there was no question but that he was the same sort of poet as they were. And by the time he effected the striking change of style and subject-matter which established him as a successful competitor with the moderns his ascendancy was too generally accepted for any open questioning of his ways. The victory of T.S. Eliot (1888–1965) was much more controversial. The literary public was divided into two camps: those (chiefly the younger generation) who acclaimed him as the first great poet of the modern world, and the traditionalists, who declared his verse unmetrical, wantonly obscure, maddeningly esoteric, and a fraud. Controversy was soon abated by his personal urbanity and clubbability, which helped him to succeed in the take-over of the London literary establishment that brash Pound had failed to achieve. In Pound's case there was also the obstacle of anti-Americanism, never long absent from the twentieth-century English literary world. Eliot too was an American, but he paid England the compliment of becoming a British subject and more English than the English in his manner and way of life. His conversion to Anglicanism, together with his growing social and political conservatism, also did much to secure conventional acceptance for this poet who had once been called a 'literary bolshevik' (by Evelyn Waugh's father) and associated with modernist riff-raff, bohemianism, illiteracy, Dadaist hoaxing, atheism, and sexual depravity. Despite the hints of a shady past in Eliot's early poems, as a public figure he was thoroughly respectable. His mysterious relationship with his first wife, which now preoccupies would-be biographers and dramatists, was no part of public knowledge until years after Eliot's death.

In his early criticism, such as *The Sacred Wood* (1920), Eliot laid great stress on the 'impersonality' of poetry. He banished biography from literary criticism, and sometimes spoke of the poet as if he were a kind of scientist, manipulating chemical substances, rather than the sort of person Wordsworth had in mind when he said that a poet is 'a man speaking to men'. It is difficult to-day not to suspect that in assimilating all subjective poetry to exhibitionism Eliot was hoping to divert attention from the deeply personal character and sources of his own poetry. Whether this is so or not, it is now clear that generalizations about 'Modern Poetry' are wide of the mark. Eliot's poetry shows several changes of manner, from the *Prufrock* volume, through the poems of 1920, to *The Hollow Men* and *Ash Wednesday* and *Four Quartets*, but in each phase he is wholly himself and unique. Although his poetry is a mosaic of quotations, sometimes in untranslated foreign verse or prose, it could never be mistaken for anyone else's. But it does have one thing in common with the poetry of his rival Yeats: it abounds in lines and passages which speak with commanding authority, the major note now absent from British and American poetry.

> We have lingered in the chambers of the sea
> By sea-girls wreathed with seaweed red and brown,

Till human voices wake us, and we drown.
(from *The Love Song of J. Alfred Prufrock*)

These fragments I have shored against my ruins.
(from *The Waste Land*)

And the lost heart stiffens and rejoices
In the lost lilac and the lost sea voices . . .
(from *Ash Wednesday*)

Also pray for those who were in ships, and
Ended their voyage on the sand, in the sea's lips
Or in the dark throat which will not reject them
Or wherever cannot reach them the sound of the sea bell's
Perpetual angelus.

(from *The Dry Salvages*)

Lines and passages like these put Eliot's power beyond question. What *is* open to question is whether his greatness is anything more than a greatness of 'fragments'. In *The Waste Land* the attempts by critics to exhibit a definite plan or structure have not issued in any agreement about what it is. There is no single voice in the poem, and the ancient myths and legends, and the symbolism of the Tarot pack which underlie it, glide into each other in the manner of dreams. Whatever Eliot's intentions, the poem came to be read as an evocation of the plight of Western man, an emblem of sexual and spiritual desolation, in a mechanical civilization which had lost touch with the immemorial religious experience of mankind. Christ, the prayed-for saviour of the world of which Eliot had despaired, appears towards the end of the poem, but only as the hooded unrecognized figure of the journey to Emmaus.

In *The Hollow Men* (1925) the sense of the meaninglessness of life produces a haunting music of despair:

Eyes I dare not meet in dreams
In death's dream kingdom
These do not appear;
There, is a tree swinging,
And voices are
In the wind's singing
More distant and more solemn
Than a fading star.

But in Eliot's next major poem, the sequence called *Ash Wednesday* (1930), a religious symbolism drawn in part from Dante (mainly the *Paradiso*) indicates the poet's search to 'construct something', to find a way out of the Waste Land. Some of this poetry is obscure to the point of incomprehensibility, partly through grammatical innovations, as in these lines from *Ash Wednesday*, where 'Who' is used un-interrogatively, yet without antecedent:

Who walked between the violet and the violet
Who walked between

> The various ranks of varied green
> Going in white and blue, in Mary's colour . . .

Yet it seems to reach a region of our minds which no other modern poet has ever entered.

Eliot's masterpiece is to-day usually agreed to be *Four Quartets* (1943), four long poems composed over a period of years. The first, *Burnt Norton*, was written before the Second World War, independently of the others: it is a philosophical meditation on the meaning of such words as 'the past' and 'eternity'. The coming of the war meant that Eliot had to shelve his plans to write more plays. (*Murder in the Cathedral* (1935), a drama on the martyrdom of Archbishop Thomas Becket in 1170, had been turned by Eliot into an occasion for alluding obliquely to the problems of England, Church and State, in the 1930s.) His poetic effort now went into the composition of three more poems on the identical structural model of *Burnt Norton*, alternating rhymed lyrics in strict stanza-form and metre with more relaxed, prosaic passages in unrhymed and freer verse. This repetition of a verse-form is unique in Eliot; his other major poems all have a pattern used once and once only. From the second of the poems (*East Coker*) onwards the sequence was envisaged as a whole, and themes and motifs recur, though in different versions, throughout the sequence. The last of these poems, *Little Gidding*, recalls the atmosphere of the war years in which it was composed; the most admired section, in a blank verse suggesting the effect of Dante's *terza rima*, alludes to Eliot's experience as an air-raid warden in bombed London, and conjures up a hallucinatory vision, as in Dante, of a 'familiar compound ghost' who incorporates more than one 'dead master', but most of all represents the poet's own *alter ego*. *Little Gidding* ends on a note of religious and patriotic affirmation:

> . . . the fire and the rose are one.

The 'fire' is the fire of hell, and of purgatory, and of sexual torment; the 'rose' is the traditional emblem of sexual passion, but also the invocation of Eliot's commitment to the ancient cause of Royalism, and the mystic Rose of Dante's *Paradiso*.

When he is at his best Eliot seems a poet of a higher order than any writing in the twentieth century, with the exception of Yeats; a poet who could without incongruity be compared with Aeschylus or Dante. One sign of his greatness is that though he wrote in many different manners, ranging from the Samuel Beckett-like *Sweeney Agonistes* ('That's all the facts when you come to brass tacks') to the majestic devout choruses of *Murder in the Cathedral* and *The Rock*, we always recognize the same poet. In other words, he has range as well as depth.

Some of the attitudes of Eliot's poetry, and of his prose, are not likely to be acceptable to a great many readers to-day. His rejection of secularism is complete, and it involves a rejection of the possibility for happiness and fulfilment in ordinary life, and of the supreme value of love between human beings. In later life, undoubtedly as a result of his happy second marriage, this austerity is softened, and in his last poem, the drama called *The Elder Statesman*, a different note is sounded, when the young heroine speaks of 'the certainty of love unchanging'. But Eliot's most powerful work is characterized by a chilliness in the spiritual climate.

Most of Eliot's verse takes the form of drama, though he is not usually regarded as a great dramatist. The psychological study of a son/mother and husband/wife relationship in *The Family Reunion* (1939) presents many difficulties to the producer, and to the actor who plays the tormented hero 'Harry', and the attempt to adapt Greek tragic motifs to a play of modern life, though ingenious, is hardly successful. *The Cocktail Party* (1951) was the first of Eliot's plays to have something like a popular success. It employs the convention of the West End play *á la* Noel Coward, to attempt to convey an Eliotic message about sin and redemption. But Eliot has not convinced many of his admirers that his talents included a gift for drawing-room comedy.

Among Eliot's prose works his many essays, lectures and short books on social problems are probably the least read to-day, and *Notes towards the Definition of Culture* (1948), for example, tends to be dismissed as élitist. His literary criticism, which occupies by far the largest area of his work, is of great historical importance. Eliot, together with his frequently disapproving disciple F.R. Leavis (1895–1978), is the founder of modern academic criticism, and many of the phrases he coined ('objective correlative', 'dissociation of sensibility' etc.) represent hares which he started and which were caught and stuffed and became the fetishes of critical orthodoxy long after Eliot himself had lost interest in them. Eliot is one of the few critics who have changed taste. Milton was disparaged, ostensibly for his bizarre treatment of the language in *Paradise Lost*, and Eliot for a time lent his support to the 1920s cult of Donne and Marvell, read as forerunners of the early, witty Eliot. Minor Elizabethan and Jacobean dramatists were revived; the Romantics and Victorians (with one or two exceptions, such as Tennyson and Kipling) were played down. Baudelaire and his French Symbolist successors were co-opted into the central line of English poetry. Eliot spoke much, in a very classical-sounding way, about the supreme importance of tradition and orthodoxy, but tradition and orthodoxy turned out to correspond suspiciosly closely to T.S. Eliot's personal taste. Eliot was the Dryden of his day. His personality and example were so strong that for many years he dominated the literary world as no writer has done since.

In one respect the influence of Eliot on English poetry, reinforced by the influence of Hopkins and Yeats, was unfortunate: it led to the alienation of the common reader. Eliot's predecessors, the 'Georgian' poets who followed the lead of Rupert Brooke, had been read by the general literary public; the

Imagists and Symbolists, the poets deriving from American-French Modernism, were not. If they became academically acceptable they were read by teachers and students, but this is apt to be a captive audience, not the best kind for a poet. The left-wing poets of the 1930s, consciously opposing the reactionary views of Eliot (though they continued to revere him as the founder of modern poetry) did what they could to bring poetry back to 'the people', but not with much success. There was a contradiction in their position. They were committed to writing obscurely, because Eliot had laid down that 'poetry must be difficult', yet they considered themselves to be heralds of an ideal democratic society, in which social and educational divisions would be healed. At any rate Eliot, through his publishing firm Faber and Faber, sponsored these poets and got them into print, and from the literary point of view they must be regarded as part of the school of Eliot. They can still be read with enjoyment to-day by a relaxed and undemanding reader, if he is content with a certain amount of lively, though superficial, social observation from a communist point of view.

The dominating figure in this group of 'left' poets was W.H. Auden (1907–73). His early poetry, consciously aware of the years of the Depression and the Europe of the Dictators, has dated so heavily that it is difficult to know by what standards it should be judged, since Auden was obviously aiming at topicality. This dating is not merely due to its being more than 50 years old: Eliot's 'Marina' was written at the same time, and 'Marina' has not dated. Auden made his first real impact on the minority public which followed the experimenting poets of the time with *The Orators* (1932), influenced by *The Waste Land* in its bleak picture of an England in decay and decline, but with a kind of poster-coloured surrealistic incoherence and an atmosphere of schoolboy conspiracy which were entirely Auden's own. This conspiratorial, semi-private allusiveness of Auden's early poetry was criticized for its cliquishness and its obscurity. The poems seemed to be alluding to the social and political upheavals of the post-war years, and at some times hailing the dawn of the Communist Revolution; but at other times the feeling about these changes was one of nameless dread. It was never very clear whether Auden was talking about his own neuroses or about the state of the world. Another difficulty is that Auden's poetry is full of coded references to male homosexuality, a subject then tabooed for open discussion.

When Auden made his home in the United States in 1939 it was generally agreed that his poetry lost its lively feeling for the contemporary English scene and the nuances of English social life which had been a source of his poetic strength. His later poetry was clever and erudite, but his inspiration seemed to have gone. The poems of Auden which are most liked now, at any rate in Britain, belong mostly to the transitional period when Auden was giving up Marx and Freud as his medicine-men and moving towards Christianity. Poems like '1 September 1939' and 'In Memory of W.B. Yeats' are among his most quoted. Auden's later work, especially when he is at his most solemn, echoes the Eliot of *Four Quartets*. The great defect of his poetry is his smart, knowing manner. It seems to impede the possibility of the genuine imaginative and emotional growth we can sense here and there in the later poetry of .Auden's disciple Cecil Day Lewis (1904–72), the Irish poet, Masefield's successor as poet laureate. Day Lewis turned from Auden's influence to Hardy's, and his graceful variations on Hardy have a distinctive personal quality. At his best he has the tenderness of a mature person. In contrast, there was always something of the Peter Pan about Auden. Some of his most successful poetry draws on the longing to return to the world of childhood.

Auden's career is the great disappointment of twentieth century poetry. That he was a poet of rare gifts is clear. In every phase of his work his accent is unmistakable.

> Unshaven horsemen swill
> The great wines of the châteaux
> Where you danced long ago. (from 'Song – "Deftly, admiral . . ." ')

His poetry is without verbal inhibitions; he was able to use a wide range of contemporary language, suggesting traditional poetry in his verse-forms and rhythms, but employing the diction of the modern city without self-consciousness or awkwardness. But few of his poems seem to be able to sustain a consistent level of conviction all the way through. 'The Shield of Achilles' may be mentioned as an exception. For once there is no tittering, no false note, as the poet contemplates the fate of the helpless individual in the grip of unrestricted state power, a society in which

> . . . a voice
> Proved by statistics that some cause was just.

In some ways the poetry of Louis MacNeice (1907–63), the Ulster poet, has worn the best of that Thirties group. MacNeice's work shows him as unusually candid about the problems of a classically-trained Oxford intellectual half-fearing, half-fascinated by, the prospect of revolutionary social change. Some of his most attractive writing is in the form of light verse. The tune of 'Bagpipe Music' runs through many heads. Very different from its reckless jollity, but unmistakably from the same poet, is another lyric on an immemorial theme.

> The sunlight on the garden
> Hardens and grows cold;
> We cannot cage the minute
> Within its nets of gold;
> When all is told
> We cannot ask for pardon.
> (from 'The Sunlight on the Garden')

Of MacNeice's longer poems 'Autumn Journal' can still be returned to with pleasure. Its unpretentious, offhand manner does not conceal a deep sense of foreboding. And simply as a record of the way many intelligent adults felt at the time of the Munich Agreement (1938) it cannot be surpassed. It is a tribute to the liveliness of MacNeice's best verse – rhythmically active, and flowering easily into sensuous imagery – that it can still be read for its intrinsic interest, even at a moment when Western Europe, at least, is free from war-threatening dictators, and the British Revolution has apparently been postponed for a while. The explanation is that MacNeice is at his best with the great simplicities for which lyrical poetry is best suited. His gift as a poet was essentially lyrical.

The coming of the Second World War put an end to 'Thirties' poetry, and for a time there was a reaction against political, argumentative, rationalistic verse. A more romantic conception of poetry, as a matter for the emotions and the imagination rather than the intellect, reasserted itself, and the attraction of the irrational, already marked in the art and literature and general high culture of the Thirties, was unequivocally acknowledged. There was talk of neo-Romanticism, of a New Apocalypse. Two poets of this time stand out as more than period figures: Dylan Thomas (1914–53), the Anglo-Welsh poet, and Edith Sitwell (1887–1964). Thomas's early poetry reinforced the tradition of obscurity descending from Yeats and Eliot (in poems like 'Gerontion'). The singing line (without which it is hard to imagine poetry existing at all) does appear, but Thomas's verse is clogged and cluttered in movement, and his cosmic/sexual imagery carries the mind away from any sense of recognizably human life or intelligible thought. But that Thomas had the common touch is clear in his *Portrait of the Artist as a Young Dog* (1940), a collection of sketches and anecdotes about his native Wales, and in *Under Milk Wood* (published posthumously in 1954), the only work written specially for the then still quite new medium of radio which has outstanding merit (MacNeice's plays for radio lack dramatic sense and make little positive use of the possibilities of that medium). And in some of Thomas's later poems the language does sing: lilting 'Fern Hill' has become almost as popular as Yeats's 'Lake Isle of Innisfree'. The poem of Thomas most quoted now is 'Do not go gentle into that good night'. Addressed to the poet's dying father, it is adaptable as a secular hymn, which can be read as an appeal to us, the human race, to fight for survival in the nuclear age. This beautiful poem has some curious features. It uses the villanelle form which had been revived by Thomas's friend William Empson, but fills it with Yeatsian rhetoric: it echoes the many protests against old age and death to be found in Yeats's poetry. But the music of this poem is not in keeping with the emotional effect appropriate to the sense. The first line

    Do not go gentle into that good night

is a cry of defiance, but the placing of 'gentle' and 'good night' turns it into something quiet, valedictory, elegiac. In

Rage, rage against the dying of the light.

what comes over is less the 'rage' than the 'dying of the light'.

Edith Sitwell is the opposite of Dylan Thomas in that her early work was better than her later work. Her pretty, half-nonsensical verbal tunes of the 1920s were not the work of a charlatan, as some of her ways of getting publicity for them suggested, but the utterances of a genuine poet, taking refuge from a world of private and public suffering which became more and more impossible to bear. Her later work, impassioned and oracular, represents an attempt on Edith Sitwell's part to confront the tragic horror of the nuclear age directly, without wit, prettiness, or nonsense. The sincerity of these later poems is unquestioned, but it seems doubtful whether they are really successful. The theme was too much for the poet, as with Blake (Edith Sitwell's later poetry is very like his *Prophetic Books*). The lyric, 'Still Falls the Rain', inspired by the air-raids of 1940, achieves everthing she could do in this vein; and even here it seems doubtful whether poetry can accommodate such naked anguish. There is much wisdom in Wordsworth's reference to poetry as taking its origin from 'emotion recollected in tranquillity'. But the world Edith Sitwell knew did not give her much tranquillity to recollect in.

The imperfect, uncertain works of Dylan Thomas and Edith Sitwell are explicable by the fact that their poetic maturity coincided with a time of world war and disruption. Neither has left an *oeuvre*, as Eliot and Yeats did. We could hardly expect one to be possible in such a period. Typical 1939–45 literature, like the films and other products of that time, may have a nostalgic appeal to the older generation which can remember the war, but younger generations probably find it absurd. At any rate, there were no war poets of the 1914–18 sort, and few poems directly to do with the war are much quoted now. The best poem of World War II is often said to be the rueful 'Naming of Parts', by Henry Reed (b.1914). The note of much British war poetry at this time, as in Reed's poem, is uneasy boredom rather than lurid horror. It has been said that World War I produced good poems but not good novels, and World War II good novels but not good poems. (Was this something to do with the difference between the two wars, as far as Britain was concerned?) The World War II poet about whom there is real critical controversy is the war-casualty Keith Douglas (1920–44). The present poet laureate, Ted Hughes, has seen in him a potentially major poet who could handle distinctively twentieth-century language with uninhibited energy and freedom. Those not convinced may at least agree that Douglas is very much a poet of this century, anti-heroic, self-preoccupied and self-conscious, and characteristically irregular in versification.

The controversy over Douglas is a reminder that even the 1940s are too near for historical appraisal. As for living authors, they are our foes or friends, said Hazlitt. It is (in more than one sense of the word) impertinent to offer to sum up the qualities of poets who are still writing. But it may at least be in order to express an opinion about the general direction taken by English poetry from the 1950s onwards. This is sometimes described as a reaction against 'Modernism', the achievement of American and Irish poets, in favour of the native tradition represented by Hardy, Edward Thomas and others. This could be illustrated by the difference between *The North Ship*, the first book of poems published by the chief poet of the new school, Philip Larkin (1922–85), and Larkin's later volumes. In *The North Ship* (1947) Larkin is under the spell of Yeats, but in the later volumes he is not. It seems that Hardy's poetry was the agency through which this change was effected. But this does not mean that Larkin imitates Hardy. It is rather that he learned from Hardy that it was possible to make poetry out of things that were of genuine first-hand interest to him. And this may turn out to be the real service rendered by Larkin to English poetry: he brought it into touch with the world in which most people in Britain actually live, the familiar urban world, the surface of everyday life that other twentieth-century poets, brilliant and spectacular as they often were, seemed largely to have ignored. So, appropriately, Larkin had a particular admiration for the poetry of John Betjeman (1906–84), who succeeded Day Lewis as poet laureate. In Betjeman's case there was no question of escaping from the spell of Yeats, or Eliot, or Pound, since he had never been influenced by them. He was as purely English a poet as Cowper or Hood. Betjeman's genius for topographical poetry, and his nostalgia, intense but discriminating, for the English past (he was the fiercest battler against architectual vandalism since Ruskin) has made him the most loved and admired of recent poets.

It is likely that if English literature of this century survives at all it will be in selections from poetry, for the theatre and the novel are even more ephemeral than the art which depends on the *mot juste*. English drama revived after a very mediocre period during the Victorian age, though it is notable that the leading figures in the revival were Irishmen – Wilde and Shaw in comedy, Synge in tragedy (*Riders to the Sea*). In the 1920s the Irishman Sean O'Casey (1880–1964) was the leading dramatist in English, apart from Shaw. *Juno and the Paycock* (1925) juxtaposed the farcical with the tragic while remaining within the convention of naturalist drama. Ordinary Irish speech is given eloquence and dignity:

Where were ye, Mother of God, when me darlin' son was riddled with bullets, when me darlin' son was riddled with bullets? Sacred Heart of Jesus! take away our hearts of stone and give us hearts of flesh.

(Compare 'Where were ye, nymphs, when the remorseless deep/Closed o'er the head of your loved Lycidas?') O'Casey was able to turn naturalism into poetry. *Juno* is as much comedy as tragedy, and scathing about certain features often thought typical of one sort of Irishman. *The Plough and the Stars* (1926) throws an equally sardonic light on the heroics of the period known as the Troubles. There was the usual storm about 'insulting Ireland' which seems to be almost a historic necessity when an Irish writer (Yeats, Synge, Joyce, O'Casey) writes anything of real distinction. After these two great achievements O'Casey continued to write plays and to work towards a less naturalistic type of drama, but with little success. He became more and more bitter in his antagonism to authors whom he regarded as rivals, or cheating the public. In his autobiography he shows violent anti-English feeling and espouses Communism. He describes his boredom at listening to the weeping widow of one of Stalin's victims (what happened to that 'heart of flesh'?).

In the commercial theatre of the 1920s and 30s much the same range of entertainment was available as we have now, but the best playrights working there, Noël Coward (1899–1976) and Terence Rattigan (1911–77) were surely better than any now writing. Coward's work represents the precise borderline between entertaining literature and entertainment that is not literature. His *Blithe Spirit* (1941) is unsurpassed among twentieth-century stage comedies. It does not lessen the depth beneath the light surface of this piece that the relation to the supernatural is established through the extraordinarily incongruous character of 'Madame Arcati'. Often Coward wrote with the deliberate intention of creating a period piece, crystallizing contemporary manners, and what he has left us is a kind of stylized social history. His songs are the most notable things of their kind before the advent of the Beatles and their successors. Rattigan, like Coward, was once very popular, then went out of favour, but may now be coming back again. His plays, such as *The Browning Version* (1948), are *théâtre de papa*, even in their time old-fashioned in their craftsmanship, and are careful to avoid anything unacceptable to 'Aunt Edna', the symbol of conventional propriety. But they probe deeply into the bitter sufferings and hang-ups of the emotionally repressed and frustrated in a context of English respectability. The theme of homosexuality had a special personal interest for Rattigan, as for Coward, but both of them deferred to 'Aunt Edna' to the extent of transposing problematic homosexual situations into a heterosexual setting. This makes some of their plays at times sound strangely unreal.

It is now customary to say that after 1956 and the production of John Osborne's *Look Back in Anger* the English theatre was revolutionized. This may be an over-statement, especially as the theatre is now such a minor feature of English life. But certainly Osborne's play discredited the Rattigan stereotypes and ensured the new drama some years of success as an opportunity for railing. His 'Jimmy Porter' may be compared to Byron's 'Corsair', as a period figure with an appeal to his time that will need a good deal of historical interpretation. It is sometimes said that the new drama was important because it gave the 'lower orders' a voice, but anyone who thinks that the 'lower orders' had not appeared before must be very ignorant of the history of English literature (Defoe? Richardson? Dickens? Wells? D.H. Lawrence?). It may be nearer the truth to say that the theatre, as in Shaw's time, was out-of-date and intellectually backward, and usually is. At the moment, for example, a raucous rhetoric, saluted as political drama, appears to be the only alternative to Shaftesbury Avenue vulgarity or sentimentality. It is depressing to remember the brilliance of Shaw's comedies. Shaw was identified with the Left in his day, but he knew that the enemy ought to be given good lines, too.

Many names are mentioned in books on contemporary British drama, and until a few years ago it was usual to say that this was a part of English literature that was really flourishing. But *is* it literature? Will these plays be read in a few years' time? Discussions of them seem to turn on 'theme' or 'ideology' in the most obvious sense. The important thing is political opinions of the correct brand. How wise Friedrich Engels was to say that in a work of art the author should conceal his opinions. Meanwhile the 'kitchen sink' type of play has become as lifeless as the poetic drama, briefly fashionable before the middle 1950s, of Eliot and Christopher Fry.

It may be that at the present time there are signs of a reaction against the ingenious pattern-making and theatrical tricks which for a time won acclamation in the drama of the Englishman Harold Pinter (b.1930), the Americans Sam Shepard and Edward Albee, and the Irish-Parisian Samuel Beckett. This reaction has been detected in the work of Tom Stoppard, who in plays like *Jumpers* (1972) and *Travesties* (1974) seemed very much to belong to the school of stunts and ingenuity. His later work may signalize a return to stories about flesh-and-blood people, characters in whom it is possible to take a sympathetic interest. Tom Stoppard (i.e. Tomas Straussler, b.1937, of Czech parents) was perhaps shocked into greater seriousness by the brutal Soviet take-over of Czechoslovakia, which he has passionately condemned.

The twentieth century appears to have produced fewer good novels than the nineteenth, but this is a matter of controversy. The point of issue is the standing of the 'serious novel'. The serious novel, or art novel, is something of an anomaly. This category seems to exist only for the purpose of awarding prestigious prizes, since what the fiction readers really enjoy is either satire or what used to be called 'light reading' but is now, more usefully, described as 'genre fiction'. Now the standards for judging these are intelligible. Satire can be judged according to how pointedly it mocks the conditions of human life, either at a particular time and place, or universally. Genre fiction is judged by whether or not it entertains the reader. But with the serious novel it is impossible to discover what the standard of judgment purports to be. It presumably claims to be 'true' in some sense in which other forms of fiction are not true, yet it is concerned with the doings of imaginary characters. In theoretically innocent days, before the advent of Henry James, none of this bothered novelists. They simply mingled fact and fiction, regardless of the aesthetic consequences. So with a few exceptions the novel of the eighteenth and nineteenth centuries was a pedestrian genre, conveying little artistic impression. The great exception is Jane Austen, one of the few novelists to be successfully, and completely, an artist. Otherwise the English novelists taught, entertained or preached, shifted their point of view at will, neglected form, and produced a cheerful confusion. But the best of them managed, however they may have shocked the artistic conscience of Henry James, to tell stories well and introduce their readers to credible characters. In the twentieth-century this seems to happen more often in genre fiction than in the self-conscious art novel.

So much fuss was made by and about the leading novelists of the 1920s that it is difficult to get them into clear perspective. Were they, as is sometimes said, the last major English novelists? Or is it rather that the category of 'major novelist' is now useless? There is no doubt that these novelists, D.H. Lawrence (1885–1930), James Joyce (1882–1941), and Virginia Woolf (1882–1941) devoted a large amount of attention to their own artistic status. 'A man of genius makes no mistakes', said Joyce. 'I tell you I have written a great book,' declared Lawrence, speaking of his novel *Sons and Lovers*. As for Virginia Woolf, her preoccupation with the barometer of her own reputation makes her journals painful reading.

D.H. Lawrence's reputation has varied greatly since his death in 1930. His work undoubtedly had a great deal of influence on the writers of the 1930s, both in prose and verse, but there was at the same time a widespread feeling that he had been over-rated because of the personal appeal he exercised and the prophetic preaching about sex which he expounded in his novels and 'think-books'. The usual critical opinion was that, while undoubtedly gifted, he was an artist *manqué*. But in the 1950s, due largely to the campaign of F.R. Leavis, Lawrence was acclaimed as a great novelist. His curious ideology was played down, and credence (surely rather naively) was given to his assertion that his novels came 'unwatched out of his pen'. They could be seen as self-sufficient works of art, without reference to Lawrence's ideas. This view is implausible, in face of the very obvious evidence for the deliberate structuring of Lawrence's novels and the correspondence of much in them to what he says in non-fictional works, in his own person, about the relations between men and women. Leavis conceded that Lawrence's later novels were propagandist, and at the time when 'the *Chatterley* ban' was lifted he dissociated himself from the pro-*Chatterley* liberal enlightenment, pointing out that *Lady Chatterley's Lover* is a mixture of novel and tract, and declared it to be a bad novel. But he never withdrew his judgment that *The Rainbow* and *Women in Love* were great novels. His claims for them now seem to belong to another era. Yet the achievement of *The Rainbow* (1915) should not be under-rated. The *serious* treatment of sexual relationships – in contrast to the sentimental or pornographic – is so rare in English fiction that even if

Lawrence is not always successful in this novel the degree of his success remains remarkable. In the sequel, *Women in Love* (1920), there is so much that is unintentionally ludicrous that it is hard to see it as a masterpiece. But any novelist could be proud of the subtly drawn character of 'Gudrun' (played so crudely in the Ken Russell film). It is a pity that as an expression of Lawrence's doctrines about love the novel is marred by the constant effect of hard, rasping reiteration – surely contrary to Lawrence's own proclaimed principles as an artist?

The best thing Lawrence wrote in novel form may be the early part of his semi-autobiographical *Sons and Lovers* (1913). It has a freshness and candour he never achieved again. At one time it was alleged that Lawrence could not create character, and Lawrence's defenders resorted to special pleading on the ground that he had developed a wonderfully profound method which enabled him to get beyond or beneath character. But the best answer to the allegation is that Lawrence *could* create character – in *Sons and Lovers*. Are there any better drawn characters in English fiction that Mr and Mrs Morel?

How far will it be possible in the future to establish a positive, but non-Leavisian, claim for Lawrence? The best chapter in Leavis's otherwise rather unbalanced and over-stated book on Lawrence (1955) is the one on the Tales. It is possible to read these without bothering about Lawrence's doctrines (though these can of course be brought in). Surely it is here, rather than in the novels, that a sound claim can be made for Lawrence's artistry. Even a short one like 'Samson and Delilah' can have depth beyond depth. Yet the critics of Lawrence ignore the Tales and go on and on about the novels, which are full of dead wood, and (apart from *Sons and Lovers*) only good in occasional episodes. Another attractive area of Lawrence's work is the travel-book, to which he gave a distinctive form. Verse, apart from a few striking poems, was something Lawrence wrote a lot of but did not do well: the most poetically effective passages in his work occur in the novels and tales. But in the *Birds, Beasts and Flowers* volume he created a new kind of poem. Even here Lawrence's unpoetic looseness with words, his failure to concentrate his effects, has to be noticed. The contemporary poet Ted Hughes (b. 1930), who in his early work clearly owed something to *Birds, Beasts and Flowers*, does this kind of poem (anthropomorphic fancy about nature) more strongly and decisively. Lawrence is unsurpassed in another new genre created by him, *Studies in Classic American Literature*. Completely original in method, and challenging in judgment, these *Studies* have won applause from American critics, and have influenced the way they see the history of their own literature (just as Lawrence's American contemporary, T.S. Eliot, influenced the way English readers see the history of theirs).

Lawrence died in 1930, but he remains a living writer, not only studied as a literary classic, but avidly read. He divides opinion, as he always did. Some readers cannot stand the sultriness of his work; whether because of his diseased lungs or not, the atmosphere of Lawrence's writing is febrile and his manner rapt and intense. Others are put off him because they resent the way in which (to use John Sparrow's phrases) the doctrinaire of sex usurps the place of the poet of love. And an all too convincing picture can be drawn of Lawrence as the sinister prophet of irrationalism, hankering for dictatorship. But there is quite a different side to Lawrence's work. A miner's son from the English Midlands, he knew in a way few great English writers have done the life of the men and women who do the practical work of the world. Though like many writers of the twentieth century he was a restless traveller, and some of his best work evokes the impact on an English temperament of the exotic, of peoples and cultures remote in time or space, again and again the tone of the sardonic, sharp-tongued English Midlander returns. Whatever their defects, Lawrence's books always suggest things that are living and moving and growing. It seems probable that he is one of the leading writers of the world; yet his place among them is uncertain, and judgment on his significance and interest must remain tentative.

Lawrence's contemporary James Joyce represents a different conception of art, and his later work, unlike Lawrence's, is wholly esoteric and of interest only to specialized scholars. But his earlier work contains much that is in the main current of English literature and can be appreciated by the common reader. Joyce's idol, when he was a young man, was the Norwegian dramatist Henrik Ibsen (1828–1906), and it was on Ibsen that he modelled his conception of the great artist, sternly aloof from the crowd, technically innovatory, and shocking conventional moral opinion. Joyce left his native Ireland for ever after some early rebuffs, in the mood of Coriolanus: 'I banish you!' But Ireland, and Dublin in particular, dominated everything he wrote. His book of stories, *Dubliners* (1914), which he managed finally to get published after many rejections from publishers afraid of the laws of libel – nothing would make proud Joyce compromise his unflinching realism – is a study of the moral and political paralysis which he saw in his fellow-citizens. Joyce added himself, as 'Gabriel Conroy', to the cripples of *Dubliners* in his magnificent story 'The Dead', the greatest short story ever to come out of Ireland. 'The Dead' has an emotional outgoingness rare in Joyce's work, and usually found only here and there in his poems (such as 'Tilly' in *Pomes Penyeach*). The story touches many notes: humour, pathos, naturalism. It shows the deep influence on Joyce of the Irish Catholic piety and morbidity which he had consciously rejected, but could not escape. The other stories in *Dubliners* have been so influential that it is difficult now to see how original they were. They introduced into English the story which is not an anecdote or yarn, which has no clear 'point'; as it were, a chapter from a novel the rest of which is lost. Katherine Mansfield (1888–1923), a New Zealand writer who came to England, also wrote some very fine sketches of this kind, though she was influenced not by Joyce but by Anton Chekhov. Afterwards the genre was standardized and commercialized by American writers as the 'New Yorker story', and eventually became a deterrent to readers.

Meanwhile Joyce turned to the longer forms of literature and reworked an attempt at an autobiographical novel into A Portrait of the Artist as a Young Man. Critics, following the lead of Joyce's brother Stanislaus, insist with good reason that this novel is art, fiction not autobiography. But a writer who calls a book Portrait of the Artist must expect to be taken at his word. This book has been one of the most widely read of twentieth-century novels. It employs new techniques to render from inside the story of how Stephen Dedalus grew up (the book is an example of what German critics call the Bildungsroman), arrived at awareness – as in Sons and Lovers – of the conflicts and exigencies and angers and affections in his immediate family, and after fancying that he had a vocation to become a Jesuit comes to realize that he is called to the priesthood of art. Stephen's story is continued in Ulysses (1922), which made Joyce one of the most famous writers of his time. Here at last was the great work, and the scandal, inseparable from the triumph of the great artist on the Ibsen model. Ulysses seems to have grown out of an idea for a Dubliners-type short story about one day in the life of an ordinary Dubliner. This became the famous 'Bloomsday', the story of 'Leopold Bloom', an incongruous Odysseus (if we assume that the 'Ulysses' of the title refers to him). To his epic of the common man Joyce added the figure of the artist, Stephen Dedalus, in whom – though this is not altogether clear – Bloom on Bloomsday recognizes his Telemachus or spiritual son. Joyce's intentions in Ulysses, the most famous twentieth-century novel, were communicated through various commentators, of various degrees of authority. Since his time the volume of commentary and exposition has greatly multiplied. To the London-Irish interest in Ulysses, concerned with identifying the people and places in the book, has now been added the American-academic interest, discovering sources, breaking codes, and revealing hidden patterns. And so it has now become difficult to judge Ulysses as a work of art, made to face the audience. To some extent Joyce himself encouraged this kind of interest; he deliberately made mysteries, in addition to those that are inevitably generated by art and poetry. All the same, the non-specialist lover of literature who enjoys Ulysses probably reads it as a report, largely humorous, on some very believable people in the Dublin of 1904. Joyce took great trouble to get as many as possible of the factual details right, and there can be no doubt that he had something of the talent of a reporter. But his reporting is marred by a lack of proportion. Few British readers can have shared his addiction to the details of Dublin.

Ulysses caused scandal because Joyce insisted on showing life as it is. Bloom excretes and masturbates in full view of the reader, Mrs Bloom perhaps menstruates. This was once literary pioneering, but is now yawn-provoking. The objection to it is purely aesthetic, not moral as the 'censor-morons' pretended. The emancipation from censorship represented by the free circulation of *Ulysses* and *Lady Chatterley's Lover* has not been followed by an outburst of great literature. The mention of pubic hair, though frequent in modern fiction, is neither a necessary, still less a sufficient, condition for literary genius.

Ulysses is of considerable historical importance. Other writers before and contemporary with Joyce can lay claim to having originated the misnamed 'stream of consciousness' method, but no one has done it more amusingly than Joyce, in Bloom's artless meditations. However, as usual Joyce overdoes it. Molly Bloom's famous interior monologue in bed, at the end of *Ulysses*, goes on much too long in proportion to the chief fact about human nature it has to reveal, viz. that women can't punctuate (Joyce was thinking of his wife Nora's letters). As for the chapter which, we are told, parodies all the main styles of English prose in historical order, it was surely an artistic mistake. Joyce was not a good parodist. When Max Beerbohm parodies Edmund Gosse we think of Edmund Gosse; when Joyce parodies any other writer we can only think of Joyce. *Ulysses* familiarized the concept of the 'experimental novel' now a frequent signal of charlatanism and bad work, though for Zola, who invented it, and for Joyce, the description is honorific. Even so, most of these 'experiments' fail. Novels are not laboratory-work.

The deeper reasons for Joyce's strange development, shown in the later parts of *Ulysses*, and in *Finnegans Wake* (1939), which is written in a language invented by him, no doubt lie in his personal psychology. There can be no question of condemning dogmatically the writer who creates new words out of old ones and writes in a prose suggestive of music, or of the River Liffey babbling to herself. In small doses the *Wake* can be very charming, as in Joyce's well-known gramophone recording of one passage. (The poem by Lewis Carroll, 'Jabberwocky', which introduced the *Wake* type of language into English poetry, is the best of his poems.) But to write a 'Jabberwocky' at such colossal length seems a misjudgment. However, for some distinguished critics *Finnegans Wake* is the great modern masterpiece, the literature of the future, which we haven't caught up with yet. To say (stating the obvious) that it represents in an extreme form the rejection of the common reader and of English literature and the English language would, for these critics, not be an adverse judgment. In any case, it is beyond dispute that *Finnegans Wake* is obscure. There is no equivalent here of the official or semi-official commentaries on *Ulysses*, only the meagre hints which Joyce for financial reasons was compelled reluctantly to impart to Harriet Shaw Weaver and other puzzled patronesses. Since 1939 there has been a flourishing Joyce industry. Are they frustrating the Master's purposes? It seems ludicrous to try to turn *Ulysses* and the *Wake* into the straightforwardly intelligible narratives which Joyce himself did his utmost to obfuscate.

It is interesting to learn that Pound, an early admirer of Joyce, disliked the *Wake* (then known as *Work in Progress*) which surpasses his *Cantos* in obscurity, despite their being written in many languages, including Chinese. Joyce similarly ridiculed the *Cantos*. Readers other than Joyce or Pound may be more impartial in regarding *both* these famous works as artistic monstrosities.

On English writers *Ulysses* has had little influence. Joyce influenced fellow-Irishmen 'Flann O'Brien' and Samuel Beckett, the French writer Jean-Paul Sartre, the American William Faulkner, but no-one in England of comparable eminence. The possible exception is Virginia Woolf. There was once a controversy about whether in *Mrs Dalloway* (1925) she had been influenced by *Ulysses* – the controversy being sharpened by the fact that she and her husband had refused to publish Joyce's book for their Hogarth Press. However that may be, there is something to be said for the view that *Mrs Dalloway* is the better novel. Virginia Woolf does without filth and pedantry. She suggests the 'feel' of a day in a great modern city quite as well as Joyce does, and without his tedious detail. And she handles the 'stream of consciousness' method with more tact and skill. All the same, quite apart from the question of originality, *Ulysses* is surely the greater work. It suggests an openness to human life which makes Virginia Woolf seem precious and limited.

Virginia Woolf, like Joyce, and unlike Lawrence, was an aesthete. She has no 'message'. She does not seek to judge life, only to depict it. Objections have been raised – trenchantly by a critic like Leavis – that depiction without judgment is impossible, because human life cannot exist without moral decisions (even if the decision is like Oblomov's, to do nothing and just go to sleep). But this is only to say that the *characters* must be shown as judging, not that the *author* has to be. Mrs Woolf's coolness and detachment are her legitimate prerogatives as an original writer.

At the moment Virginia Woolf is attracting more attention and commentary than any other writer of her time. There is a constant stream of publications devoted to the doings of her literary circle. Her name immediately suggests 'Bloomsbury', lesbianism, feminism, madness, and suicide. Heiress of the aestheticism of the 1880s and '90s, she is now seen as a contemporary of Sylvia Plath and Harold Pinter. Those excited by the prospect of neurotic violence and flaunted abnormality will be disappointed to discover that Virginia Woolf's novels are rather tame. There is no plot or suspense. She depicts character well, but within very narrow limits, and she is blinkered by snobbery. *To the Lighthouse* (1930) is agreed to be her best novel because of the effective depiction of 'Mr and Mrs Ramsay', no doubt based on her own parents. 'Mr Ramsay' has been criticized as a caricature of her distinguished father Sir Leslie Stephen (1832–1904), but there is no reason to think that he represents everything Virginia Woolf felt about her father, and much reason to think otherwise. And anyway 'Mr Ramsay' is not merely, or mainly, ridiculous, but a figure of deep pathos. *To the Lighthouse* comes the nearest of her novels to justifying her characteristic mood of confronting some vague, tremendous question to which she is not quite sure that she knows the answer. *The Waves* (1931), the most experimental of her novels, is more effective in quotation than as a whole; the best things in it are short prose-poems, Virginia Woolf's songs of solitude. She was a poet *manqué*. Novelists have no wings; they have to make their way up Parnassus on foot. The novel was too pedestrian a genre for a writer who was essentially a singer and fantasist.

The familiar essay was a form in which Mrs Woolf was most at home. She has no superior among the English essayists, Addison, Lamb, Hazlitt, or Max Beerbohm, all of whom she admired. Where fiction is concerned she is the best English critic of the twentieth century, because she is both sensitive and sensible. The characters we meet in her essays are better drawn than those in her novels. Two of her most enjoyable books, *Flush* (1933), purportedly a biography of Mrs Browning's spaniel, and the fantasy *Orlando* (1928), combine what is best in her 'straight' novels with what is best in her lighter essays.

The critics who admire Mrs Woolf's work are divided about her rank among writers. It seems best to regard her as occasionally great but very uneven. She was obsessed by the artistic problem of how to convey the passage of time. Time was the characteristic preoccupation of typically twentieth-century writers, as Wyndham Lewis (1884–1957) argued in his *Time and Western Man* (1927), and their attempts to deal with it led to many disappointing results, as with D.H. Lawrence in *The Rainbow*, Bennett in *The Old Wives' Tale*, or the masterpiece of the Dutch novelist Couperus, *Old People and the Things that Pass*. It would be tempting to conclude that it is simply impossible to convey the passing of time in fiction, were it not for the success of Tolstoy in *War and Peace*, with his 'Pierre' and 'Natasha'.

Of the other writers associated with Bloomsbury Lytton Strachey (1880–1932) became famous and notorious for his debunking of leading nineteenth-century personalities in *Eminent Victorians* (1918). For a time Strachey was regarded as the most important and most typical writer of the years between the wars. It was held that he had invented a new form of biography, making it part of imaginative literature, and the successor of the novel. At present, however, the novel seems to have survived, while the imaginative biography has fallen out of favour. Biography in general continues to attract a large number of readers, but after the years of Strachey's vogue there has been a tendency to go back to the very long and shapeless kind of *Life* which Strachey scorned as inartistic. (Ironically, the standard biography of Strachey himself belongs to this category.) A middle way between Strachey's ironic brevity and the later twentieth-century blockbusters is found in Rupert Hart-Davis's *Hugh Walpole* (1952), which has claims to be the third best English biography (after Boswell's *Johnson* and Smith's *Nollekens*).

Strachey's reputation has fluctuated. It is a story of inflation, followed by a prolonged slump. He is now sometimes mentioned in literary histories as a worthless writer, who owed his success solely to social and personal influence. This is very unfair. Strachey's views on biography and history may be open to question, but the reaction against him had led some critics to overlook the truth and wisdom which they contain. His *Queen Victoria* (1921) by no means lacks depth of insight. And here, as in *Eminent Victorians*, Strachey shows his mastery of comedy. It was understandable that with the war of 1914–18 in the immediate background there should have been a mood of disillusionment with the eloquence and 'spirit of seriousness' of the Victorian age. Strachey was applauded, or denounced, for showing great men and women as figures of fun. To this the answer might be, first, that it is difficult to see some historical characters as anything other than figures of fun. Pope Pius IX is an example (he makes several entertaining appearances, always speaking in Italian, in Strachey's essay on Cardinal Manning). Secondly, it is healthier to regard celebrities as figures of fun rather than as supermen. But finally, when he is at his best Strachey does not deal in figures of fun or in supermen, but in real men and women, off their pedestals.

As far as lasting historical influence is concerned the most important member of the Bloomsbury set is without doubt John Maynard Keynes (1883–1946). And it may well be that, apart from his importance as an economist, he was also the greatest writer of the circle. His *Economic Consequences of the Peace* (1919) owes something to Strachey in its method of literary portraiture, but here as elsewhere Keynes has more versatility and power of style than anyone else in Bloomsbury. His *Essays in Biography* (1933, 1951) rank among the best non-fictional prose in English. *Two Memoirs* (1949) shows emotional depth, as well as penetrating intelligence.

From the 1920s to the 1960s another writer of the Cambridge-Bloomsbury connexion was widely regarded as the greatest living English novelist, though his fame in his later years was largely based on a series of novels which came to an end in 1924. Strangely, the reputation of E.M. Forster (1879–1970) steadily grew while his silence as a novelist continued. Forster's novels before *Howards End* (1910) seem to be more of an age – the Edwardian period – than for all time, but *Howards End*, despite some improbabilities and even absurdities, is a striking late addition to the 'condition-of-England' type of novel that began in the 1840s. Forster had other claims to a high place in literature, in his short stories, his essays and critiques, and the memoirs of friends and relatives which he did so elegantly. His studiedly quiet, unassuming liberal individualism had an immense influence. For many writers of a younger generation, such as Christopher Isherwood, he became the living personification of the England they loved.

There has now been a reaction against the values Forster was thought to stand for – or rather, against his claim to stand for them. The late Oliver

Stallybrass, editing the scholarly 'Abinger Edition' of Forster's works, summed it up when he said he could no longer bear Forster because he was 'so wet'. In many ways, indeed, Forster might be called the super-wet. His liberalism has come to seem timid. While he displeases one kind of reader because of the homosexual themes in his novels, he displeases another by refusing to acknowledge that there were any. (His avowedly homosexual short novel *Maurice*, not one of his best, was not published till 1971, after his death.)

The pendulum of literary opinion has swung against E.M. Forster at present. No doubt he was over-rated during the inter-war years, and more recently the treason of people belonging to that Cambridge artistic-homosexual culture has brought on him a kind of guilt by association. Time will sort all that out. Meanwhile Forster's masterpiece, *A Passage to India* (1924), has not been seriously discredited, though as a record of British rule in India it is – to put it mildly – somewhat one-sided. But it is a mistake to see *A Passage to India* as primarily a historical document, a predecessor of Paul Scott's *Raj Quartet*. Arguments about whether Forster is 'fair to' Hindus and Muslims – not to speak of Anglo-Indians, to whom it is now agreed that he is grossly unfair – are largely beside the point. *A Passage to India* neither is, nor implicitly claims to be, an authoritative treatment of India. Nor is it, as some of its admirers have claimed, an inclusive study of the whole human situation. It is a work of art: the result of the impact of certain quite particular experiences on the memory and imagination of a highly gifted English individual. As a story, it centres on an experience of which Forster is the supreme delineator in literature: panic. One of his shorter fictions is called 'The Story of a Panic'. That is what Miss Quested's story is. But the setting and occasion of the story create the opportunity for a profound sifting of a question that for long had interested Forster: the relevance, or otherwise, of religion to Western man. To Forster's liberal-humanist friends, like Leonard Woolf (Virginia's husband), religion was merely an evil and an obstruction to human progress: Woolf very much disliked the last section of *A Passage to India*. Forster's own attitude was more complex.

After *A Passage to India* the religious preoccupation seems to be less prominent in Forster's work. Like his Mrs Moore after her traumatic experience in the Marabar Caves, he had come to reject the religious view that life has intrinsic meaning. In his later thought he moves towards an un-metaphysical form of existentialism. 'Significance' is conferred on what happens merely by the arbitrary personal decisions of individuals.

Religious preoccupations figured largely in the more ambitious kinds of fiction in the first half of the twentieth-century. Since then, strangely, they seem to have disappeared. Questions about ultimates have always traditionally been central in philosophy and literature, and it is difficult to see how these can survive the indefinite extension of that unreflective secularism which seems to be taken for granted in recent and contemporary novels. At present such books as Aldous Huxley's *Time Must Have a Stop* (1944), Somerset Maugham's *The Razor's Edge* (1944), or Evelyn Waugh's *Brideshead Revisited* (1945) seem to have dated less because of inevitable changes in social manners and literary modes than because of their attempts to evoke a religious dimension.

Of course, some of the religious interest of early twentieth-century novels may have been merely a matter of fashion. But it is notable that it also appears in the work of less popular but still read novelists who in quite different ways pursued the study of human nature in the light of their preoccupation with the mystery of God: T.F. Powys (1875–1953) of *Mr Weston's Good Wine* (1928), and L.H. Myers (1881–1944) of *The Root and the Flower* (1935), the first set in a stylized rural Dorset, the second against a backdrop of an imaginary sixteenth-century India.

Aldous Huxley (1894–1963) was a greater influence on the thinking young than any other of these novelists. He won his first fame as the lively smart satirist of the brittle 1920s, but even then there was an underlying 'Victorian' seriousness in his work, which became more and more evident later on. With family origins in the Arnolds as well as the Huxleys he seemed well qualified to close the gap between the Two Cultures later to be deplored by C.P. Snow. After his wide-ranging and ambitious novel *Point Counter Point* (1925), and *Brave New World* (1932), a brief, trenchant satire on the misuse of science to instal a society of tranquillized insipidity (the predictions about genetic engineering are now coming true) Huxley's fiction in his middle period became rather dull. The essay was a better form for what he had to say, and taken together Huxley's essays show the remarkable range of his interests and the liveliness of his style. He had never been greatly interested in the minutiae of personal relationships and manners to which the genre of the domestic novel had committed him.

Like his younger contemporary Christopher Isherwood (1904–86), Huxley became primarily a writer with a message. Their messages, however, changed from time to time. Huxley's rejection of modern civilization, and his puritanical disgust with sex and the whole physical aspect of life, drove him towards an inhuman mysticism, an austere search for moments of transcendent significance. In his later years he made the tragic and terrible mistake of supposing that these could be artificially induced by drugs. The mystics in whom Huxley was interested always insist that such ecstasies are something *given*, a grace, not something to be compelled in some mechanical manner. Not only does mescalin, it would seem, not have the enlightening effects on consciousness claimed by Huxley, but it is actually deleterious. And other substances, for which the same claim is made, are even worse. There can be few cases of a good man doing so much harm. In comparison Isherwood's conversion to Vedantism was harmless. In recent years his message has become that of homosexual liberation. But in every phase of his work a certain kind of wilful silliness intervenes, rather like that of his friend Auden, which makes it hard to take this gifted writer as seriously as he deserves. Of all his books the short novel *Mr Norris Changes Trains* (1935), a study in the fascinations of a con-man/double agent, best deserves its status as a minor classic.

The fading of the Joyce/Lawrence/Woolf period was followed by a renewal of contacts between 'highbrow' and 'popular' forms of fiction, which may be typified by the rise to fame of Graham Greene (b.1904). Greene's first master was Conrad, whose *Secret Agent* (1907) anticipates Greene's mature work in its sophisticated use of the thriller. He owed something to Joyce later on, making a modest use of interior monologue, but more to American novelists of the 1920s, such as Ernest Hemingway (the staccato, breathless style, rather than Hemingway's 'white hunter' point of view) and to films, which fascinated the new generation of authors in the 1920s and '30s. That Graham Greene still had one foot in the Joyce/Lawrence/Woolf camp is evident from his practice, abandoned in later years, of distinguishing some of his novels as 'entertainments' (the others weren't described as anything). To-day, for good or ill, or for good *and* ill, it is taken for granted that all novels should be entertainments – except when they are interminable 'protests', long, sincere, and intermittently intelligible, by Latin-Americans.

Greene first came to the notice of the literary world with his novels of the 1930s, such as *Brighton Rock* (1938). With such books he introduced his characteristic genre, the thriller with theological and moral significance. The 1930s flavour of conspiracies, sinister capitalists, lurking revolutionary forces – the landscape of Auden's early poetry – is very apparent in Greene's work, and at this period his attention was focused on English life and English types, as in *England Made Me* (1935), one of his best novels, though now rather neglected by critics. But after *The Power and the Glory* (1940), set in Mexico, which many think his best novel, Greene rarely returns to the English scene. His stories are usually set in some foreign political storm-centre. It is interesting to speculate whether his manifest concern with up-to-date problems – the catastrophes most of us merely read about in the newspapers and which Greene often foresees before they reach the newspapers – is likely to mean that many of the books he has written during his long and still continuing career as a writer will come to seem ephemeral. At the moment this does not seem to be the case. *The Quiet American* (1956), for example, was written before what Americans think of as 'the Vietnam war' but still retains point and interest (the problem with this book is not that it has dated but that the narrator-hero is vile). Graham Greene is the most famous living British novelist. He has a huge international readership, and has been taken seriously as a moralist and theologian, as well as a romancer and a sort of super-reporter. That he has not been awarded the Nobel Prize for Literature can only be due to political reasons.

Greene's fiction in his later phase shows the influence of Somerset Maugham (1874–1965), a writer of an older generation. Maugham's career as a writer goes back to the days of late-Victorian naturalism. In his second phase he was for a time a highly successful playwright, capturing West End audiences with his tone of mordant cynicism, especially attractive after the orgies of patriotism and the false hopes of 1914–18. Maugham's most popular work belongs to his third phase, when he returned to prose fiction and perfected the urbane story-telling which won him world fame and great wealth. Maugham's standing in literature, or his lack of it, remains a puzzle. He was hated and despised by academic critics, perhaps because he achieved great commercial success without their approval, and his works require no explication. The ostensible objection to Maugham was that he was sub-literary, that he wrote badly, in a commonplace style. Whether these critics have some *a priori* notion of good style, which Maugham did not live up to, is not clear, but in any case such notions are based on a mistake. A good style is one which is perfectly adapted for its purpose, and Maugham's style was designed to do what was essential for him, to create the device his stories turn on: in other words, to establish the narrating personality, 'Somerset Maugham', through which we grasp the persons and events of his stories. But it must be admitted that Maugham can be rather banal. His best known story, 'Rain', suffers like Conrad's 'Heart of Darkness' from being too predictable: it is obvious from the start that the missionary is going to fall for the call-girl. Yet even when too obvious Maugham is a wonderfully good story-teller. Many of his stories take place in exotic settings, and it is delightful to see how quickly Maugham can take the reader to Java, or wherever, in a few commonplace sentences, without the souvenir-shop elaboration and too poetic cadences of Conrad, or the mannerisms of Kipling (to mention his chief rivals in this field).

Maugham's most influential book was *Ashenden* (1928), which established him as the founder of a new and sophisticated kind of treatment of the story of espionage and international intrigue. In contrasts interestingly with the work of an earlier master of this genre, John Buchan (1875–1940), who was by no means so naive in his thrillers as it is usual to suggest. The more metaphysical significance of the plots and the symbolism in Buchan were to be perceived by Graham Greene, another 'entertainer' with ideas.

Maugham's chief contribution to English literature is *Cakes and Ale* (1930), still unsurpassed as a satire on the literary life. Its *roman à clef* interest, as a novel about novelists, is not important – and it is malicious, since Maugham himself had stooped to all the means to career-advancement he ascribes to 'Alroy Kear', an amusing caricature of Hugh Walpole (1884–1941). Its superiority to his other novels may be that here and there he gives us glimpses of deep and impassioned feeling beneath the superficial cynicism. Maugham's perhaps excessive concern with ridiculing and exposing shams of all kinds, and his dread of sentimentality, may have originated in the problems of his personal life: he was himself a case 'of human bondage'. At present he is still out of favour with the critics, though now not on account of his bad prose, but because of biographical information – some of it made known by his former protégés – which is supposed to reveal the horribleness of his personality. The personality that can sometimes be detected in the work is different: one that could be moved by a concern for justice and an admiration for genuine self-sacrifice, and that could recognize one important function which art can perform for the artist – the relief from suffering.

Maugham is in many ways not a typical English writer; the debt to the French language, and to French literature, which he knew well from his early years, is obvious in his work. But an even more influential import to international literature appears to be wholly British: the classical detective story, which came to its best period in the years before 1939. Of the innumerable practitioners of the genre at that time only two are now widely read, Dorothy L. Sayers (1893–1957) and Agatha Christie (1891–1976). Sayers's detective fiction commands a British and American rather than world public. It has been attacked, on the ground that her detective, 'Lord Peter Wimsey', is a rather sickly wish-fulfilment fantasy, whom the novelist embarrassingly falls in love with. It would be fairer to say that when this happens 'Wimsey' ceases to be a fantasy-figure and becomes a real man, with a real man's imperfections, tirednesses, and problems. Sayers, like Maugham, was never forgiven for her popularity. Because of the success of her 'Wimsey' novels her efforts as playwright, Christian apologist and theologian, and translator of Dante, were brushed aside or ignored. She is a very gifted, though faulty, writer whose work as a whole would repay the kind of critical sifting it has never received. Agatha Christie has conquered the world, and the critics are puzzled. Part of her charm for her readers is the setting of many of her mysteries in a context of English village life, but her stories appeal to people in countries remote from England who know nothing about England and have no interest in the English. It will be said, of course, that her appeal is merely that of the puzzle, but there were plenty of other ingenious puzzlers in this period, and they are forgotten. Why has she succeeded, with her flat style (even her warmest admirers concede this) and her cardboard characters? Perhaps the answer is that the characters (in the books, rather than the dramatization of them) are not cardboard – or not all of them. There is something deeply appealing about Christie's stories which has not yet been adequately analysed. Conan Doyle created the genre with 'Sherlock Holmes', establishing it on a basis of English comedy, as unclassifiable as the 'Alice' books, or the 'Pooh' books of A.A.Milne (1882–1956). But strange and terrible things in the 'Holmes' stories remain strange and terrible, whereas Agatha Christie assimilates everything to what would seem on the face of it a self-stultifying literary form: the reassuring tragedy. It is no wonder that her books are indispensable reading for hospital patients.

Agatha Christie thrilled the world: P.G. Wodehouse (1881–1975) made it laugh. A quotation from one of his books convulsed Goering and Ribbentrop with laughter when they were on trial for their lives at Nuremberg – quite a tribute to so quintessentially English a writer. It is pleasant to see the young of to-day enjoying Wodehouse's stories as their great-grandfathers did, and in the same way. There have also always been people who do not find Wodehouse funny, and nothing can be done about that. But before pronouncing the cult of him to be inexplicable they might pause to wonder why so many readers of high character and intelligence, over several generations, have enjoyed his work so much. It is usual to say that Wodehouse's virtuosity with the English language is the source of his charm, and there is some truth in this. His use of different layers of style, his timing, his apparent effortlessness (in fact his work went through many drafts) – all these can be analytically appreciated. But there are many other things in Wodehouse for those who like his books: story-telling, and with all the farcicality and the manifest and cheerful non-realism, some shrewd observation of life. Wodehouse accepted absolutely the distinction between 'serious writing' and 'entertainment'. He wrote only to entertain, and never allowed his work to touch anything in the least disturbing or tragic. His forms of comedy, however, are various, and sometimes (as in his Hollywood stories) he allows a certain hardness of edge and satire into his work. But his most loved creations are predominantly farcical – the sponger 'Ukridge', 'Jeeves' and 'Bertie Wooster', and 'Lord Emsworth'. Wodehouse's artistic conscience is shown, not in loud proclamations about his inspiration and genius, but in an unobtrusive but always vigilant concern with stylistic appropriateness, and in his meticulous craftsmanship. He is the most complex plotter in English literature since Congreve; and Congreve's plots are too hard to follow. Wodehouse did not care for the greatest English comic writer, Dickens (can this have something to do with the inextricability of Dickens's plots?). But one reason why many readers like both authors is that their books can be picked up and opened anywhere, and at once you are in Wodehouse-land, or Dickens-land.

Wodehouse and Evelyn Waugh (1903–66) admired each other's work, and there is a close relationship between them as artists, but they are very different. Waugh in praise of Wodehouse depicted him as the creator of an unfallen world, with 'Blandings Castle' as a Garden of Eden. Waugh's own world is the confused, terrible, absurd world of modern man: the recognition of pain and cruelty, so far from being excluded from his comedy as it is from Wodehouse's, lies at the heart of it. Waugh came to attention as the even more brilliant and smarter successor of the young Aldous Huxley. His early books belong to the same genre as Huxley's *Antic Hay* (1923). If *Decline and Fall* (1928) seems to have less 'period' flavour than Huxley's book this may be because in the book Waugh is so astonishingly prescient, e.g. about the significance of ultra-modern trends in architecture, or proposals for penal reform. But the charm of this youthful masterpiece is that it can be enjoyed for its extravagant humour without a thought of such matters. The more sombre aspects of *Vile Bodies* (1930), and the introduction of Roman Catholicism as a theme, prepare the way for the bleak picture of modern godlessness in *A Handful of Dust* (1934), where the title, a quotation from Eliot's *The Waste Land*, suggests the underlying similarity of vision between the poet and the novelist. But Waugh's gift for broad farcical comedy was still evident in such novels as *Black Mischief* (1932) and *Scoop* (1938). The division of opinion among Waugh's critics (apart from those who rejected his work altogether) turned on the question whether his powers as an artist were limited to deft economical satire, or were of sufficient imaginative range and emotional depth to give substance to the religious and moral absolutes to which he was explicitly committed. Is *Brideshead Revisited* (1945) merely the expression of social snobbery and idealizing sentimentality? Or is it a profoundly serious novel in which a considerable artist convincingly renders his sense of ultimates? Even those who incline to the former view will usually agree that at any rate Waugh offers the readers the company of lively characters and a well told and interesting story. Waugh's comic gift showed no signs of enfeeblement in the hilarious tableaux of the 'Home Front' in *Put Out More Flags* (1942). But the series of novels making up *Sword of Honour* (1952–61), where the serious 'straight' novelist predominates, while showing a warmth of feeling and a gentleness new in his work, also shows increasing uncertainty in his comic touch: compare 'Apthorpe' with 'Colonel Blount' in *Vile Bodies*. Of Waugh's later novels the remarkable *Ordeal of Gilbert Pinfold* (1957) comes the nearest to autobiography, indeed to confession.

Evelyn Waugh's work arouses strong feelings. He has been hated as few modern English writers have been. He seems to have no moderate admirers. Though he was too much of an artist to disclose his opinions directly in his fiction, the sense of a strong unflinching personality comes through, and it is not an amiable one. Yet in his best work the power seems to derive from, and not merely arouse, a storm in the soul. Waugh's writing cannot be fully understood without an awareness of his deep interest in the visual arts and his sense of a moral obligation to do the best he could as a stylist and craftsman.

George Orwell, i.e. Eric Blair (1903–50), Waugh's contemporary, differed from him over many political and social issues, but shared with him an overpowering preoccupation with English prose style. They may have been poles apart, Waugh a maverick of the Right, Orwell a maverick of the Left, but the poles were connected by an axis: their intense Englishness. Orwell had less of a novelist's gifts than Waugh, though he wrote a number of novels: the best of them is probably *Coming up for Air* (1939). There is much less free invention in Orwell than in Waugh, or any other of the leading novelists of the period. Orwell is remorselessly, narrowly political in much of his fiction.

His great contribution to English literature was the 'Orwellian essay'. He created the character of 'George Orwell', and the seemingly transparent, hard-hitting prose style that went with it. To the social observation characteristic of many 1930s writers he gave his own inimitable personal quality and literary distinction. Orwell's power as a stylist is to make the reader feel as if he were in the presence of bare facts, which make their testimony irresistibly evident. But of course the appearance of objectivity is an illusion, and Orwell's stark 'realism' belongs to the art of persuasion, as his opponents on the Left have not been slow to point out. Orwell's chief fictional achievements are the political beast-fable *Animal Farm* (1949), a satire on the Russian revolution and the consolidation of Stalin's power, and the horror novel about betrayal, the 'anti-utopia' *Nineteen Eighty-Four* (1945). As with Arthur Koestler (1905–83) in his one important contribution to English literature, *Darkness at Noon*, (1940), the events and passions that inspire these works are too close to us for impartial literary judgment. Only when the Soviet Union is as remote as the Guelfs and Ghibellines can it be seen, as in Dante, whether great art can co-exist with fierce partisanship and ideological hatred.

Orwell and Waugh have added phrases to the language, and their work is now widely known in the English-speaking world. Other notable novelists of that time, Ivy Compton-Burnett (1884–1969), Joyce Cary (1888–1957), Elizabeth Bowen (1899–1973), and 'Henry Green', i.e. Henry Vincent Yorke (1905–73), have attracted continuing and devoted admirers, but are little known outside England. Something their otherwise very different books have in common is a large number of extraordinary mannerisms of technique, which could no doubt be defended as relevant to their special purposes, but which mark their work out sharply from that of Waugh or Orwell, who are easily accessible to the ordinary fiction-reading public. To these names should be added that of Angus Wilson (b. 1913), who began as a short story writer but won fame as a novelist with *Hemlock and After* (1952), in part a psychological study of a writer, 'Bernard Sands', similar to E.M. Forster, in part a nightmarish caricature of the homosexual culture in which 'Sands' becomes involved.

The new generation of novelists who made their names in the 1950s were sometimes grouped together under various labels – the 'Angry Young Men', 'the Movement', etc. – but this attempt at instant literary history appears to have proved premature, since they do not really have a great deal in common as writers. Philip Larkin had published two novels, *Jill* (1946) and *A Girl in Winter* (1947), before he arrived as a poet with *The Less Deceived* (1955). He himself has spoken disparagingly of them, and it is true that they belong to the art-novel tradition which the 1950s novelists repudiated; but they contain fine things and may in fact be actually better than any of the other 1940s art-novels. Larkin's college friends John Wain (b. 1925) and Kingsley Amis

(b. 1922) are still in full vigour as writers and it would be out of place to attempt to predict how their achievement will eventually be judged. Wain began as a novelist with *Hurry On Down* (1953), which has something in common with Amis's even better known *Lucky Jim*, published a year later in 1954. *Lucky Jim* has had an extraordinarily large number of imitators. It could even be said to have brought into existence a whole subgenre, the British university novel, practised more recently by David Lodge and Malcolm Bradbury and others. Perhaps none of them offers so broadly-based and searching a comedy as the American Randall Jarrell's *Pictures from an Institution* (1954), with its college 'President Baxter' so perfectly adjusted to his environment that it was impossible to tell which was environment and which was 'President Baxter'. But *Lucky Jim* may one day be discussed in other than topical and social-historical terms. Readers should take the cue from its title, as an invitation to reflect on the nature of *luck* in human life.

As we approach the recent and contemporary it is only possible to mention some of the books which are still widely current among people who enjoy ambitious novels. Iris Murdoch (b. 1919) first became known as a novelist with *Under the Net* (1953), and though she has written many other novels it still remains a good introduction to her 'philosophy-fiction', a species of 'magic realism' which has won her a large and loyal readership. William Golding (b. 1911) had his biggest success with *Lord of the Flies* (1954), using the desert-island type of story as the setting for a study of evil (here among boys). In some ways his work recalls H.G. Wells, but his dark view of sinful humanity is nearer to the earlier work of Graham Greene. Golding was awarded the Nobel Prize for Literature in 1984. Muriel Spark (b. 1918) may be best known for her study of a sinister Edinburgh schoolmistress, *The Prime of Miss Jean Brodie* (1962), in which she introduces one of the few memorable characters in recent fiction. Spark has been technically experimental, like John Fowles in *The French Lieutenant's Woman* (1969), and like him she has run the risk of alienating readers who like to feel that the novelist behind the page is fully participating in a shared fantasy. Other trends in fiction are of interest to the cultural historian rather than to the literary critic, such as the prominence given to non-genteel characters, outside London/Home Counties milieux, in *This Sporting Life* (1960) by David Storey (b. 1933), or *The Loneliness of the Long Distance Runner* (1959) by Alan Sillitoe (b. 1928). The emergence of these and similar novels coincides with the change from a period when 'hat' was pronounced 'het' in Received Pronunciation to the present time, when it is pronounced 'hat'. The shift away from accents and idioms associated with the South-Eastern genteel seems to have accelerated in the 1960s. To-day British films of the 1950s, even good ones, have come to sound absurdly affected.

The most obvious fictional development at the moment is the hunger for length shown by writers and readers. C.P. Snow (1905–80), though now out of critical favour, came early into this trend with his revival of the *roman fleuve* in his *Strangers and Brothers* sequence of novels; and Anthony Powell (b. 1905) with his *A Dance to the Music of Time* sequence, Paul Scott (1920–78) with his *Raj Quartet*, and Lawrence Durrell (b. 1912) with his *Alexandria Quartet* and more recently *Avignon Quintet*, bear witness to its continuing popularity. This longing for series must reflect a wish to be able to take as extended a journey as possible through an alternative world. It may have a bearing on the astonishing commercial success of J.R.R. Tolkien's sequence *The Lord of the Rings* (1954–6), which must have been one of the least predictable of all bestsellers. It owes nothing whatever to the literary tradition in which D.H. Lawrence and James Joyce are acclaimed, but seems rather to belong to the same genre as medieval histories (it even includes long genealogies). Various opinions have been expressed about Tolkien's achievement. It has affinities with the success of Ossian, and the more posthumous Tolkien material is published the more it looks like Ossian.

Whatever else *The Lord of the Rings* may or may not be, it has a strong appeal to the reader who loves a 'yarn'. Successful genre fiction has to cater for this taste. To-day children's books, science fiction, the thriller (from Oppenheim to Le Carré) – all have their schools and phases. Taking over F.W. Bateson's labels for schools of poetry we can detect in each the Experimental Initiators, the Protagonists of the New Style, the Assured Masters, the Polished Craftsmen, and the Decadents. It may be that literary historians of the future will see the really live literature of the period here rather than in the art-novel. No one knows. It is quite possible that the quiet domestic novels of Barbara Pym (1913–80), which have recently come back into favour, may outrank them all. Such things have happened before.

The general reader in this period consumed also much entertaining non-fiction, the work of popular historians, readable philosophers, and eminent scientists who either communicated well with the layman, or pleasantly mystified him. The turn away from philosophic idealism had its greatest literary exponent in Bertrand Russell (1872–1970). At one time Russell's position as the leading philosopher of the century was obscured by the spell cast by his ex-pupil Ludwig Wittgenstein, but it is now usual in philosophical circles to acknowledge his originality and genius. To use words of the Cambridge philosopher John Wisdom, Russell's work ranges from the icy regions of logical space to the tropical jungles of marriage and morality and 'the conquest of happiness'. Everywhere he has been the pioneer, the explorer. Russell as historian and essayist, wit and publicist, cannot be excluded from a leading place in English literature. He is the finest philosophical writer in English since David Hume, and he is wittier than Hume. Unfortunately Russell has left no one volume which can be called a literary masterpiece. The nearest perhaps is the book of essays called *Mysticism and Logic* (1918) – despite its catchpenny title. His view of logic can only be judged by experts; his ethical views, profoundly influenced by Spinoza, must command the attention of every thinking person. Russell always stirred things up, and continued to do so till the very end of his long life, with his passionate campaign against the Bomb. Twice, at widely separated periods of his life, he was imprisoned for his opposition to official conduct which he thought wrong. As a writer he can be constantly amusing, or annoying, or both together. D.H. Lawrence denounced his 'inexperience'. Yeats thought him 'a featherhead'. By a wider public he has been long revered as a super-intellectual and a sage. His *History of Western Philosophy* (1946) was called a pot-boiler by experts, but the common reader has taken it home.

In his publications (though not in his letters and private writings) Russell was scornful of religion, at any rate in an organized form (the mysticism of Plotinus, or of Spinoza, which deeply appealed to him, is another matter). There seems to be no religious writer in our time of very great literary or intellectual standing. As far as contemporary ecclesiastics are concerned the title of a play by James Bridie sums it up: *A Sleeping Clergyman*. Some people would urge the candidature of Charles Williams (1886–1945), idiosyncratic in his theological thrillers – another example of upgraded genre fiction – and even more so in his highly esoteric 'Arthurian' quasi-epic. But thousands of English-speaking readers, especially in the United States, would give the highest place here to C.S. Lewis (1898–1963). The first impression Lewis's work makes is its versatility. For one reader Lewis is pre-eminently the scholar of *The Allegory of Love* (1936), or *English Literature in the Sixteenth Century (Excluding Drama)* (1954). For another, he is the Christian apologist of *The Problem of Pain* (1940) or the mordant ironist of *The Screwtape Letters* (1942). For yet another kind of reader, particularly children and young students, he is the author of the 'Narnia' books. Lewis had much to do, both in his precept and his practice, with the rise to respectability of genre fiction. He himself wrote science fiction, introducing the serious religious and moral motifs which pervade the whole of his work. He never wrote a 'straight' novel, maintaining that he had little interest in modern life and manners. But the college scenes in *That Hideous Strength* (1945) are pungent. The most striking characteristic of Lewis's work in general is his pellucid prose style. (To his regret, he did not establish himself as a poet.) He has much in common with Samuel Johnson, if you can imagine a Johnson who lets himself go in romance and fantasy more than Johnson did. His mind was as prompt as Johnson's, as those who knew him personally can testify. Lewis was a leading figure in the war-time revival of Christianity and was much in demand as a speaker and popular apologist. Triumphant though he so often was, either in person or on paper, he did not escape some of the difficulties, and some of the temptations, of this rôle. It is not hard to find crudities and sophistries in his propagandist writings, a show of knock-down argument, a misuse of his sharp lawyer-like mind in areas where the forensic has no place. Lewis was aware of these faults and asked for God's forgiveness in a touching poem: forgiveness for his victories much more than his defeats. The cocksure manner disappears from his later work. In *A Grief Observed* (1956) the occasional coarseness of grain and the zest for polemic have gone. His writing, still marvellously lucid, became deeper and gentler. No one should suppose that he has taken the measure of Lewis without reading his profound story, *Till We Have Faces* (1956). In both the old and the modern senses of the word he was truly a magnanimous man.

Russell, though active publicly, was only on the fringe of great affairs; Lewis (who was for a time under the impression that Tito was the King of Greece) totally ignored them. At the vortex of them was Winston Churchill (1877–1965). What to make of Churchill is a key test for a historian. Does greatness exist? – and if so, did Churchill have it? Whatever the answer to these questions, which are for the historian and for the thinker about history, it is clear that Churchill committed many errors and perhaps crimes. Perhaps more are yet to be disclosed. It would be rash to say of him what Tennyson said of Wellington in his ode on the Duke's death: 'Whatever record leap to light/He never shall be shamed'. How does Churchill look from the literary point of view? His life of his ancestor Marlborough and his wartime oratory seem to belong to a remote epoch: despite his feud as a historian with Macaulay he was steeped in Macaulay's style. In his purple passages he can even go back to Burke. 'But not in vain her valiant deeds'. What other writer in the twentieth century could have written (or more probably dictated) such a sentence? Literary history cannot pronounce on many aspects of the Churchill problem. He may be compared with Caesar or Clarendon, as a distinguished writer on great events who himself took part in them. Or it may be that his war memoirs may come to rank no higher in literature than those of other politicians, such as Lloyd George. And parts of his World War II memoirs may not even have been written by him. Churchill's place in literature is secure with his autobiography, *My Early Life* (1930). It is full of charm, not least because of its unexpectedness. Who would have predicted that page or two in which Churchill (in the opinion of one who has a right to judge, Sir Karl Popper) shows himself a philosophic thinker of great insight and originality?

Whatever the verdict of the future on Churchill it is hard for a lover of English literature and the English language (which Churchill also loved) not to feel that he was great in 1940, when these were the chief weapons he had to fight with. Martin Gilbert in his biography of Churchill quotes the following unpublished minute of May 1940:

By all these processes, and by the confidence, indulgence, and loyalty by which I was upborne, I was soon able to give an integral direction to almost every aspect of the war. This was really necessary because times were so very bad. It was accepted because everyone realized how near death and ruin we stood. Not only individual death, which is the universal experience, stood near, but, incomparably more commanding, the life of Britain, her message and her glory.

E I G H T

Postscript: English Literature – national heritage or disputed concept?

Winston Churchill died in 1965, in the same year as T.S. Eliot. It is natural to take these deaths as marking the end of an epoch, as the Victorians saw the death of Sir Walter Scott in 1832. The new period, in which we still live, brings many questions for the literary student. Has English literature come to an end? When we ask this question we may be wondering how much, if any, of what has appeared since 1965 is likely to be added to the canon. But there is no way of knowing that, and what the asker of the question is more likely to mean is not whether this or that book should or should not be added to the canon, but who or what decides whether *any* book should be added. In short, we have turned from English literature to 'English Literature', not a series of texts, but a concept. This whole set of assumptions on which an essay like the present one is based – 'English', 'literature', 'literary value', 'work of art', 'the common reader' – has been questioned, and even in so brief an essay it is not possible to draw to a conclusion without recognizing that the enterprise of literary history has become uncertain.

The installation of English literature as a school and university subject, and as a national heritage, has recently attracted some historical inquiry, most notably from authors writing from a radical point of view, such as Chris Baldick in *The Social Mission of English Criticism 1848–1932* (1983), and Terry Eagleton in *Literary Theory (1982)* and *The Function of Criticism* (1984). Many of the statements in these books can be disputed on historical grounds. For example, much stress is laid by these authors on the comparatively late date (the end of the nineteenth century) at which 'English' (in the literary sense) was invented as an academic subject. Perhaps they are merely following the usual English convention of ignoring Scotland, where Hugh Blair at the University of Edinburgh was giving professional lectures on English literature as early as 1762. But in any case the part played by London and Manchester Universities in the establishment of 'English' goes back much earlier than the Late Victorian/Edwardian period. The insistence on assigning the rise of 'English' to that period, of course, makes it easier for Baldick and Eagleton to affirm the intimate connexion of the new subject with Victorian imperialism.

Well, perhaps it had such a connexion. And there certainly was a 'social mission', from Arnold to Leavis, and there certainly was a paternalistic element in it, expecially in its post-1918 phase. But we should not be too sarcastic about this. Surely it was a good thing to discredit Parnassian notions of 'literature' and 'the Classics' in favour of an educational policy which brought them within the reach of previously excluded groups of people? The founders of 'Eng.Lit.' wanted to modernize and democratize Johnson's common reader. From the radical point of view there is no doubt an objection to this use of Shakespeare (and the rest). They could be manipulated to induce a false feeling of social harmony and unity, instead of intensifying that sense of division and conflict without which Karl Marx's dream of creating a revolutionary proletariat cannot be realized. This is a political argument which cannot be pursued here. The older British socialists, such as Robert Blatchford (1851–1943), were in no doubt about the value of the great things in English. They wanted to bring to an end the domination of literature by the socially and educationally privileged, not to decry it as a reactionary fetish. Weren't they right? Why should the Devil have all the best tunes?

At any rate there is no doubt about the historical fact that during this century English Literature became a major school and college subject. This greatly changed British culture, as can be seen by contrasting the modern scene with the conditions shown in George Gissing's *New Grub Street* (1891). Previously literary criticism had been associated with 'men of letters', i.e. creative writers and their entourage of literary journalists. Now it was taken over by the universities. As usual, there were both good and bad consequences. The bad consequence was the systematization of the insights of original minds into a bleak pedestrianism. Too often the conversion of an academic to criticism is the conversion of criticism to academicism. The good consequence was (at least in aspiration) a higher intellectual standard than in the old, lax days. If something was lost when easy-going *belles lettres* and boudoir scholarship were discredited, something was gained also. Sharper and stronger minds were attracted to literary study.

The founders of twentieth-century Anglo-American academic criticism were T.S. Eliot – the best known and most powerful force among them – and I.A. Richards (1893–1979), F.R. Leavis, and William Empson. The last three were all associated with the University of Cambridge (England). Oxford and London and other homes of learning continued the honoured and indispensable tradition of scholarship, without which literary culture withers.

But it was the Cambridge Three who were to prove the most influential in giving form to English studies as we now know them. Richards must be given due credit as a pioneer. His critical ideas came from Eliot. But he had had a philosophical training at a time when philosophy in Cambrige was iconoclastic and exciting – these were the great days of G.E. Moore, Russell and Wittgenstein – and he brought a new liveliness, an air of twentieth-century briskness, to what was then the stagnant region of Literary Theory. Richards got the problems of the study and teaching of literature sharply into focus in *Practical Criticism* (1929). This was the record of a (somewhat amateurishly conducted) scientific experiment. From his lecture-audiences Richards obtained comments (described by him, mysteriously, as 'protocols') on a number of English poems, a very mixed lot, distributed by him without disclosing the poets' names. The sometimes ludicrous results showed beyond question that the innocent eye was not enough for the intelligent reading of poetry. Doggerel by 'Woodbine Willie' was much applauded; a great sonnet of Donne was much scorned. Clearly teaching was necessary, and Richards's expression 'practical criticism' has passed into the professional idiom of higher education as the accepted description of an indispensable teaching routine. But this is now done differently; the selected texts are no longer analysed in the void but are related to their historical context.

In the 1930s F.R. Leavis supplanted Richards as the leading Cambridge critic. Down to the 1970s he campaigned for the causes he had at heart with characteristic intensity, and his treatment of opponents was ruthless. Concepts such as 'literary criticism', 'English Literature', 'the University', 'Downing College' (where he taught at Cambridge), or '*Scrutiny*' (the quarterly journal he dominated for twenty years), became quasi-religious symbols, though Leavis always insisted on their literal reality. Leavis's critical insights in his earlier work were derived from Eliot. But he systematized and corrected Eliot's ideas and developed them into weapons for his war against what he saw as a rapidly growing degeneration in both élite and popular culture. 'The Line of Wit', 'the Dissociation of Sensibility', 'the Great Tradition', 'the Common Pursuit', 'the Organic Community' – these phrases, some of them his own, some Eliot's, became credal formulations. A tendentious view of English social history underlay his literary judgements. By the 1950s, influenced by the work of his wife Q.D. Leavis (1906–1981), whose field of interest was the novel, he turned more to prose fiction than to poetry for the documentation of his imaginary history. But in his later years he came back again to poetry, especially that of Blake, and of his earlier master Eliot, as if tacitly recognizing the largely ideal nature of his view of the past. Even so, he seemed still inclined to judge a work of literature according to how far it could be mobilized for the campaign against 'technologico-Benthamism', his general term for what he saw as the ever-accelerating dehumanization of modern mechanical civilization. Bitterly as he attacked Utilitarianism, there was perhaps something of a utilitarian element in his own approach to literature.

Whether the very dark picture of modern life drawn in Leavis's later work is correct or not, Leavis had much influence, and his affirmations and rejections are still live issues. But much in his criticism that had seemed startlingly radical when it was opposing the genteel tradition has now come to seem old-fashioned and conservative to the younger generation of critics.

The criticism of William Empson may at the moment be read with more pleasure and interest than Leavis's (or Eliot's or Richards's), although – or because – he founded no critical school. Empson has his niche in literary history because he familiarized the concept of 'ambiguity' in a book written while he was still an undergraduate. But in his later work he went far beyond the extravagant interpretative ingenuity, applied to short poems or passages of verse, which had made him notorious. His most challenging book is *Milton's God* (1961), defending *Paradise Lost* from the censures of Eliot and Leavis, and offering a highly unconventional account of Milton's purpose which does not shirk a hostile confrontation with the central doctrines of Christianity. Yet Empson was always more of a poet than an academic, even after he had long ceased to write glowing poems such as 'Legal Fiction' and 'To an Old Lady'.

The period from the 1920s to the 1950s was one of critical controversy. Many skirmishes were fought over the interpretation of famous poems. By the 1950s the new ideas had settled down with older ones, even if not always with strict consistency. While no-one in the new generation of British critics achieved the fame and influence of the pioneers, literary criticism continued to enjoy much prestige and was felt to have attained a reasonable degree of equilibrium and intellectual respectability.

Since the 1970s all this has changed. A controversial tornado has blown up, after the relative calm of the post-Eliot consensus. There is room only to mention a few of the reasons for this. An obvious change of perspective came with the political and cultural ascendancy of the United States. Since the early nineteenth century American literature had circulated widely in Britain. American classics were read alongside the British ones. By the time of Mark Twain and Walt Whitman it was clear that (despite the objections of a custodian of tradition like Matthew Arnold) American literature must be recognized as a major literature in its own right. By the early twentieth century the American component in 'Modernism' was obviously important. Eliot, the chief figure in twentieth-century criticism in the English-speaking world, was himself an American. The 'New Criticism' deriving from him in the United States followed a similar course to what was then called 'Cambridge Criticism' in Britain. First it was a minority movement, tilting at the academic Old Guard of 'scholarship' and 'history of ideas'. Then it became itself an academic orthodoxy. Finally in its turn it was challenged by new schools of criticism, and anti-criticism. In the process a great deal of traditional English literature simply dropped from view.

Meanwhile the position of Britain in the world had greatly changed. 'Britain has lost an empire and has not gained a rôle', said the US Secretary of State Dean Acheson, in an epigram which continues to annoy the British. The empire had been not so much lost as given away, but it was not given away with a good grace. The 'American Century' was an idea that writers and critics, like many other people in the world, have not found it easy to come to terms with. Not that the ascendancy of the United States overthrew the cultural prestige of English Literature. On the contrary, American criticism (not to speak of American scholarship) devoted much attention to it. But the texts were often treated so differently from the ways the British were used to that the British were alienated. The repercussions can be seen in 'Morris Zapp', in David Lodge's novel *Small World* (1984), and in 'Jake Balokowski', Philip Larkin's caustic sketch of his imaginary American biographer.

American dealings with the literary canon were influenced by new developments in France and Germany. In recent years there has been the greatest expansion of Literary Theory in Continental Europe since the time of the Italian Renaissance. Magisterial pronouncements by masterful 'men of letters' have now less authority. At the same time the study of Comparative Literature, already well established in Continental Europe and the United States, was growing in Britain. This also tended to put in question the primacy and uniqueness of 'English', so much dwelt on in the pioneer and the Leavis periods. English is now seen as one literature among many. Even when 'English' was in its prime there were awkward questions about the place of the Scots and the Welsh and the Irish. It was possible, with an effort, to see the Scots and Welsh as queer kinds of Englishmen, but what about the Irish? Now the situation is further complicated by the large and growing amount of poetry and fiction in English written in the former British dominions and colonies. Should these be assigned their own traditions? – or judged as part of 'English Literature'? Again the problem of standards and criteria becomes acute.

This is a time of new sciences, or would-be sciences: linguistics, psychology, anthropology, sociology of literature. None has yielded assured results on the scale their supporters hope for. But they are unignorable influences in unsettling notions about writing and reading which had until the quite recent past been held unreflectively. The French writer Roland Barthes (1915–80) for a time dazzled the fashionable literary world with the prospect of a new science of 'semiotics'. Literature was seen only as one of many alternative 'sign-systems'. The imprecision of the concept of 'sign' deprived Barthes's programme of any scientific value, but his formidable jargon angered and discomfited traditionalists. Another *chef d'école*, Jacques Derrida (b.1930) teased Anglo-American philosophy and critical theory with his 'deconstruction', a revival of ancient philosophical sophistries. The unquestioned axiom in all these studies was that 'things are not what they seem'. The innumerable varieties of Western Marxism, sometimes in shifting collaboration with or opposition to other radical trends, offered to 'demystify' literature by uncovering hidden class-biases. Feminism, long dormant after the 1920s, became again a force to be reckoned with, so that 'gender' was now seen alongside other forms of social bondage. There was talk of an alternative canon of literature, though it was not always clear whether this meant the disinterment of forgotten or neglected works, or merely a change in the relative valuations of established ones. Those more interested in literature than in politics (and prepared to beg a question by distinguishing the two) were apt to urge the claims for the historical study of literature. But 'history' itself is a problematic concept. Genre study, stressing formal aspects of literature, was also much to the fore; but once again the notion of 'genre' is far from being simple and ideologically uncontaminated.

There can be no pretence of listing, let alone discussing, all the present-day proposals to recast the study of literature and the practice of criticism. Not even the most extreme radicals want to discard these altogether. They are firmly entrenched in universities, and (despite 'the cuts') are likely to remain so. Never was there a time when more reading was demanded. Yet this is also the age of the electronic media. These, unlike books, can capture a public on the huge scale typical of the modern world. But the devices of the media are still saturated in literature. The underlying forms are those of poetry and drama, however crass the uses to which they may at times be put.

There is no need to end on a pessimistic note. More of the English classics are in circulation at the present time than at any previous period of history. The young write poetry and prose, and are encouraged to do so, even if few of them gain celebrity, and still fewer money. Misguided, irrelevant or even pernicious as much academic activity around literature may be, it does at least ensure that great poetry and fiction are constantly frequented and in full view. English Literature can now no longer be taken for granted as a national heritage. It has become a disputed concept. But clearly there are a large number of people who find it well worth disputing.

Suggestions for further reading

Most of the major works of English Literature are readily available in various paperback editions and in popular series like *The Penguin English Library*, *The World's Classics* (Oxford University Press) and *Everyman's Library* (Dent), and in *Oxford Books* and other anthologies. Those wishing to make a thorough study of English Literature of any period will need to consult *The New Cambridge Bibliography of English Literature*, ed. George Watson (4 volumes, 1969–74), but Oxford's *Select Bibliographical Guides* (ed. Dyson and Wells), though less comprehensive, are easier to use. There is in addition a *Concise Cambridge Bibliography* (2nd edn. 1965), also edited by George Watson. *A Guide to English and American Literature*, ed. Bateson and Maserole (3rd edn. 1976), and the Pelican *Reader's Guide* (1984), ed. Boris Ford, do even more to temper the wind for the inexperienced student.

The British Council's *Writers and their Work* series (since 1950) is useful, especially for twentieth-century authors.

The largest of the large-scale histories of English Literature is *The Cambridge History of English Literature* (14 volumes, 1907–16), which contains valuable information but is now very out of date; and much of it is unattractively written. The *Oxford History of English Literature* (from 1945) is still incomplete, and apart from C.S. Lewis's sparkling volume (1954) much of it is pedestrian, though it is useful on minor authors. The best modern one-volume history remains *A Literary History of English* (ed. A.C. Baugh, 2nd edn. 1967). *The Pelican Guide to English Literature*, ed. Boris Ford, was accused, fairly or unfairly, of being too 'Leavisist' (i.e. influenced by F.R. Leavis's ideas) in its first edition (in seven volumes, 1954–61), but the new edition (1982–3) is more representative of general academic opinion as it is at present.

The Oxford Companion to English Literature (5th edn. 1985, ed. Margaret Drabble), is invaluable, though the 4th edition (1967), not just edited but wholly written by Sir Paul Harvey, should be retained because it gives so much assistance with classical allusions.

A few recent critical works have already been mentioned in the text of this essay. These may be supplemented by the following (extremely selective) list, a half dozen of so per chapter, of books for background reading. Since these greatly differ in subject-matter, point of view, and level of difficulty, they should give the reader some idea of the variety of literary-historical discussion in the twentieth century.

Chapter 1

F.M. Stenton, *Anglo-Saxon English* (3rd edn. 1971) is the fundamental textbook.
S.B. Greenfield, *A Critical History of Old English Literature* (1965)
M. Alexander, *Old English Literature* (1983)
J. Burrow, *Medieval Writers and their Work* (1982)
D.W. Robertson, Jr, *A Preface to Chaucer* (1962)
D. Brewer, *English Gothic Literature* (1983)
B. Cottle, *The Triumph of English* (1969)

Chapter 2

F.P. Wilson, *Elizabethan and Jacobean* (1945)
F. Yates, *Astraea: the Imperial Theme in the Sixteenth Century* (1971)
M. Evans, *English Poetry in the Sixteenth Century* (1967)
C.S. Lewis, *Spenser's Images of Life*, ed. A. Fowler (1967)
M.C. Bradbrook, *Dramatic Forms in the Age of Shakespeare* (1983)
E. Jones, *Scenic Form in Shakespeare* (1971)
N. Frye, *A Natural Perspective: the Development of Shakespearean Comedy and Romance* (1965)

Chapter 3

G. Parfitt, *English Poetry in the Seventeenth Century* (1985)
J. Carey, *John Donne* (1981)
H. Vendler, *Poetry of George Herbert* (1975)
J.B. Leishman, *The Art of Marvell's Poetry* (1966)
C. Ricks, *Milton's Grand Style* (1963)
M. Van Doren, *John Dryden* (1946 edn. repr. 1960)
R.D. Hume, *The Development of English Drama in the Late Seventeenth Century* (1976)
F.P. Wilson, *Seventeenth Century Prose* (1960)

Chapter 4

P. Rogers, *The Augustan Vision* (1974)
M. Mack, *Alexander Pope* (1985), the first full-scale biography of Pope since 1900.
M. Doody, *The Daring Muse* (1985), on eighteenth-century poetry.
I. Watt, *The Rise of the Novel* (1963), the most influential modern essay on this subject.
R. Brissenden, *Virtue in Distress: Studies in the Novel of Sentiment from Richardson to Sade* (1974)
J. Wain, *Samuel Johnson* (1974), the best modern biography of Johnson.

Chapter 5

M. Butler, *Romantics, Rebels and Reactionaries* (1981)

M.H. Abrams, *The Mirror and the Lamp* (1953), on the critical ideas of the Romantics.

H. Bloom, *The Visionary Company* (1962)

N. Frye, *Fearful Symmetry* (1947), a bold attempt to demonstrate the structure of Blake's *Prophetic Books*.

S. Prickett, *Coleridge and Wordsworth: the Poetry of Growth* (1970)

A. Grant, *A Preface to Coleridge* (1972), useful documentary material.

J. Wordsworth, *The Music of Humanity* (1969), an interesting modern critique of Wordsworth, by a collateral descendant.

P. Quennell, ed., *Byron, A Self-Portrait* (2 vols., 1950), based on Byron's letters and journals.

J.D. Jump, *Byron* (1972)

R. Holmes, *Shelley: the Pursuit* (1974), the best recent biography.

W.J. Bate, *Keats* (revised 1969)

D. Cecil, *Portrait of Jane Austen* (1978), an interesting contrast with Q.D Leavis's view in her *Collected Essays*, volume 1 (1983) – half the latter book is about Jane Austen. Nearly all the known facts are in R.W. Chapman's *Jane Austen: Facts and Problems* (1941).

Chapter 6

W.E. Houghton, *The Victorian Frame of Mind* (1957)

G.K. Chesterton, *The Victorian Age in Literature* (new edn. 1966)

H. House, *All in Due Time* (1955)

C. Ricks, *Tennyson* (1972)

I. Jack, *Browning's Major Poetry* (1973)

E.D.H. Johnson, *The Alien Vision of Victorian Poetry* (repr. 1968)

K.J. Fielding, *Charles Dickens: a Critical Introduction* (rev. 1966)

D. Cecil, *Early Victorian Novelists* (rev. 1964)

T. Hilton, *John Ruskin: the Early Years* (1985)

J. Batchelor, *The Edwardian Novelists* (1984)

Chapter 7

W.W. Robson, *Modern English Literature* (repr. 1984)

M. Bradbury, *The Social Context of Modern English Literature* (1971)

C.H. Sisson, *Modern Poetry 1900–50* (1971)

R. Ellmann, *Eminent Domain* (1967)

R. Hayman, *The Novel To-day* (1971)

J.R. Taylor, *Anger and After* (rev. 1964), and *The Second Wave: British Drama for the Seventies* (1971)

Chapter 8

D.J. Palmer, *The Rise of English Studies* (1965)

R. Wellek and A. Warren, *Theory of Literature* (3rd edn. 1963)

F.R. Leavis, *English Literature in our Time and the University* (1969)

F.W. Bateson, *Essays in Critical Dissent* (1972)

F. Lentricchia, *After the New Criticism* (1980)

A. Jefferson and D. Robey, *Modern Literary Theory* (1982)

Index